THE PEACEMAKERS

THE PEACEMAKERS

Peaceful Settlement of Disputes since 1945

Hugh Miall
Oxford Research Group

Foreword by Sydney D. Bailey

MACMILLAN   in association with the
OXFORD RESEARCH GROUP

First published 1992 by
THE MACMILLAN PRESS LTD
Houndmills, Basingstoke, Hampshire RG21 2XS
and London
Companies and representatives
throughout the world

ISBN 0-333-54708-X

A catalogue record for this book is available
from the British Library.

Printed in Great Britain by
Antony Rowe Ltd
Chippenham, Wiltshire

Reprinted 1994

To my parents

Contents

List of Tables

List of Figures

List of Abbreviations

ACAS	Advisory, Conciliation and Arbitration Service
ANC	African National Congress
AZAPO	Azanian People's Organization
CDE	Conseil de l'Entente
CSCE	Conference on Security and Co-operation in Europe
FLN	Front de Liberation Nationale (Algeria)
FLNA	Frente Nacional de Libertacão de Angola
FLOSY	Front for the Liberation of South Yemen
FRELIMO	Frente Libertacão de Moçambique
IRA	Irish Republican Army
MNR	Mozambique National Resistance Organization (Renamo)
MPLA	Movimento Popular de Libertacão de Angola
NATO	North Atlantic Treaty Organization
OAU	Organization of African Unity
OPEC	Organization of Petroleum Exporting Countries
PAC	Pan Africanist Congress
PDYR	People's Democratic Republic of Yemen
PFLO	Popular Front for the Liberation of Oman
PKK	Kurdish Workers' Party
PLO	Palestine Liberation Organization
SVP	South Tyrol People's Party
SWAPO	South West African People's Organization
UAM	Union Africaine et Malgache
UDF	United Democratic Front
UNC	National Union of Cameroon
UNITA	União Nacional para a Independencia Total de Angola
UPC	People's Union of Cameroon
WTO	Warsaw Treaty Organization
YAR	Yemen Arab Republic
ZANU	Zimbabwean African National Union
ZAPU	Zimbabwean African People's Union

Foreword

Peace and conflict research is a relatively new discipline. The first conference of British professionals concerned with these issues was held at Windsor in 1963, and the International Peace Research Association was founded at a conference held in Switzerland under Quaker auspices later the same year.

Initially, peace researchers drew mainly on the expertise of social psychologists and those with theoretical or practical experience of bargaining techniques. During the past three decades, however, the field of study has been substantially widened, though much work remains to be done. In any case, the challenge has always been to make the conclusions of scholars intelligible and useful to practitioners.

Many academic disciplines raise ethical issues, and peace research is no exception. Is peace always an absolute goal, to be pursued at all costs, or is peace fragile if it is based on injustice? Does a responsible mediator seek to reconcile an aggressor and the victim? Are some wars just, or do wars always cause more injustices than they remove? Indeed, are we not all victims of past mistakes and in that sense have inherited the inevitability of conflict, or can the conflict we have inherited be managed without violence? Some social evils like slavery have been virtually eliminated. Is it utopian to believe that we can eventually abolish war if only we exert enough moral and intellectual effort?

Hugh Miall has made a notable contribution towards that distant goal by studying more than 80 actual conflicts, some resolved, some partially resolved, and some still active and dangerous. He is meticulous about facts, astute in judgement, and clear in his conclusions.

Mediation is not simply a matter of technique, for the intermediary must understand the cultural norms of the parties and what lies behind words and deeds. This book was finished in the spring of 1991, as the war between Iraq and the UN coalition was taking place. One could not but be struck by the cultural abyss separating the parties. President Saddam Hussein seemed not to understand words like *unconditional, ultimatum, deadline*; we in the West were baffled when he threatened 'the mother of all battles'.

When James Whistler made a witty remark, Oscar Wilde commented, 'I wish I had said that', to which Whistler replied, 'You will, Oscar, you will.'

Nobody need repeat this book. Reading it in draft has taught me a great deal.

SYDNEY D. BAILEY

Preface

Conflicts are normal and endemic in human life. There will always be conflict as long as there is difference and change. But how we deal with conflicts is a matter of learning and choice: we can settle them through violence, or in ways which foster peaceful change. In the twentieth century people have experienced destructive conflict on an unprecedented scale, but there have also been significant advances in peacemaking in institutions, in procedures, and in practice. The question is, how can we institutionalize peaceful settlements and eliminate war?

This book explores the conditions which favour peaceful settlement of conflicts. It draws on theories of conflict resolution, the experience of mediators and conciliators, and the historical experience of peacefully settled conflicts. The main part of the book is a study of how 81 interstate and civil conflicts were resolved in the period 1945–1985.

The book also includes case studies of peacefully settled conflicts. Perhaps recklessly, I have touched on conflicts that are recent and even still in progress. The danger of referring to such cases is that future events may alter and date the present picture. It is possible that situations which now seem to be on a peaceful trajectory may turn violent again in the future. Moreover, the full facts about recent conflicts are not yet known. Some of the mediation efforts in recent disputes remain unpublicized, and the inner records of the decision-makers have yet to see the light of day. My justification is that the years since 1985 have seen dramatic developments in conflict settlement. The progress in South Africa, for example, and the end of the Cold War itself, seemed too important to leave out. The Gulf crisis will be in readers' minds as an example of a dispute where many considered a peaceful settlement was impossible. I judged that the importance of these cases merited their inclusion, but I hope readers will bear these caveats in mind.

I would like to thank those who shared their wisdom and experience through interviews: Sydney Bailey, Adam Curle, Peter Jarman (Society of Friends), Kate Gardner (Swindon Family Conciliation Centre), John Hamwee (Open University), Chris Mitchell, Tony de Reuck (Centre for the Analysis of Conflict), Tony Shepherd (Advisory, Conciliation and Arbitration Service (ACAS)), Jill Townsend (Foundation for International Conciliation) and Martin Ennals (International Alert).

I thank Hayward Alker, Jr, Sydney Bailey, Scilla Elworthy, John Hamwee, Anatol Rapoport and Paul Smoker for their comments and criticisms on parts of earlier drafts. I am grateful as ever to my friends and colleagues in the Oxford Research Group for their help and support.

This book grew out of a research report written for the United States Institute of Peace and I am grateful for its financial assistance. I also thank the Woodstock Trust whose support enabled me to complete this book.

The opinions, findings, conclusions or recommendations expressed in this book are those of the author and do not necessarily reflect the views of the United States Institute of Peace. Likewise, I alone am responsible for whatever shortcomings and errors remain.

HUGH MIALL

Part 1
Introduction

1 Introduction: Conflict Resolution after the Cold War

We were teetering on the bridge of a precipice. In my view the other camp had already made its decision. The map showing the dispersal of armed forces over the whole country was explanation enough . . . In the north, the Warsaw Pact were manoeuvering their forces. We were warned that martial law might be declared at any moment. We also knew that lists had been drawn up of activists who were under surveillance . . . It seemed absolutely incredible that those with whom I had been sitting at the negotiating table should have concealed such a scenario from me. Perhaps, within the government, there were other influential groups who thought they would settle accounts clandestinely, in their own way and fast – by force, even with a bloodbath if necessary.

We were not in a position to fight. I trusted in the wisdom of our people. We weren't armed and we didn't want to fight. We would simply continue along the path we had chosen.

Lech Walesa, *A Path of Hope*, pp. 186–7

March 1981 was a turning point in the struggle between the Polish free trade union movement, Solidarity, and Poland's Communist government. Solidarity's supporters were about to declare a general strike. An armed clampdown was imminent. In a crucial strategy meeting of the union's National Commission, Lech Walesa argued for a token warning strike instead of a general strike. Failing to win the argument, he slammed the door and walked out of the room. After hours of further debate, the union swung round to Walesa's position,

3

and decided on a warning strike. A violent outcome was narrowly avoided.

Eight years later the unpopular Communist government, under popular pressure, conceded political reforms and free elections. A government representing Solidarity supporters came to power. Martial law, which had seemed to be a death blow for Solidarity, in fact turned into a trap for the regime. In 1989, the government was forced by economic breakdown and popular unrest to concede reforms. Solidarity's policy of nonviolent struggle had succeeded. The Polish struggle was the first crack in the bastion of the old Stalinist regimes of Eastern Europe, and the beginning of the end of the Cold War.

The Polish revolution was not without violence, yet it succeeded in avoiding a civil war and the intervention of Soviet troops. Moreover, the party without military power had emerged the victor.

There have been other cases since 1945 of disputes resolved without war, but on the whole they receive less attention than armed conflicts. Violence attracts media coverage; peacemaking, and peaceful prosecution of conflicts, attracts less. The negotiations and discussions which lead to the settlement of conflicts tend to be protracted, and the details often pass unreported. Consequently more is known about how to make war than how to make peace. There are academies and textbooks in military strategy, but there is no equivalent corpus of knowledge about how to conduct conflicts peacefully and how to achieve peaceful settlements.

How are peaceful settlements of conflict actually brought about? What lessons can be drawn from the historical experience of conflicts that have been settled peacefully? Is it possible it apply methods of peacemaking that have been successful in past conflicts to contemporary situations where violence threatens? These are the questions this book aims to address.

The great majority of disputes between people are settled by peaceful means. The human family numbered some five billion people in 1990. We relate to one another as individuals, in small and large groups, and through nations. The scope for disputes among all these relationships is immense, but most of them are regulated by social conventions and social institutions so that they never come to blows. Considering the number of potential and actual disputes, it seems striking that relatively few are settled through fighting.

Yet the disputes which are prosecuted through armed conflict are dramatic and tragic events. Twice this century world wars have engulfed mankind. With 50 000 nuclear weapons deployed, and control of weapons of mass destruction spreading to more powers, continued armed conflict has come to threaten human survival. For this reason, the quest for peaceful settlements of disputes has become a theme of twentieth-century history, gathering urgency with the increasing destructiveness of wars.

THE QUEST FOR PEACEFUL MEANS TO SETTLE DISPUTES

In April to June 1945, after Germany's defeat but before the first use of nuclear weapons, the wartime allies decided to establish a new framework for the post-war world order. Meeting in San Francisco, they established the United Nations (UN). Its first purpose was to 'save succeeding generations from the scourge of war', and to this end the Charter called upon member states to 'settle their international disputes by peaceful means in such a manner that international peace and security, and justice, are not endangered' (Article 2.3). The Charter created a Security Council capable of enforcing UN decisions as well as the General Assembly and the Secretariat. Disputes were to be resolved in the first instance by negotiation between the parties, or by enquiry, mediation, conciliation, arbitration, judicial settlement, resort to regional agencies or other peaceful means of their own choice. If they failed to settle the dispute, the Security Council was empowered to recommend procedures or terms for settling the conflict. Failing that, the Security Council could use nonmilitary measures and, if necessary, military force to respond to threats to the peace and acts of aggresssion.

The hopes for establishing a new world order did not last long. No sooner had the war ended than the divisions between the former Allies began to deepen. By 1947 the Cold War was under way. Western and Eastern Europe were organized into rival economic systems, NATO and the Warsaw Pact were set up, and the victorious armies began to deploy nuclear weapons against one another. The long political and military confrontation between East and West had begun. In these conditions, the UN could not work as its framers had intended. It could hardly uphold the principles of international peace and security while the greatest threats to them arose from the conflict between its most powerful members. The East–West conflict permeated other disputes, limiting the extent to which the Security Council could settle international conflicts. Vetoes undermined its capacity to act.

BOX 1.1   DECLARATIONS FOR THE PEACEFUL
SETTLEMENT OF DISPUTES

The participating States . . . will use such means as negotiation, enquiry, mediation, conciliation, arbitration, judicial
settlement or other peaceful means of their own choice
including any settlement procedure agreed to in advance of
disputes to which they are parties.

In the event of failure to reach a solution by any of the
above peaceful means, the parties to a dispute will continue to
seek a mutually agreed way to settle the dispute peacefully.

Participating states, parties to a dispute among them, as
well as other participating states, will refrain from any action
which might aggravate the situation to such a degree as to
endanger the maintenance of international peace and security
and thereby make a peaceful settlement of the dispute more
difficult. (Final Act of the Conference on Security and Co-
operation in Europe, or CSCE)

The Member States . . . solemnly affirm and declare their
adherence to the following principles: . . .

4. [Peaceful] settlement of disputes by negotiation, mediation,
conciliation or arbitration.

Member States pledge to settle all disputes among them-
selves by peaceful means and, to this end, to establish a
Commission of Mediation, Conciliation and Arbitration.
(Organization of African Unity Charter, Articles III and
XIX)

States Parties shall settle any dispute between them concerning the interpretation of this Convention by peaceful means.
(Law of the Sea Convention, 1982)

All parties to a dispute will implement meaningfully and in
good faith the CSCE Dispute Settlement Procedure. (CSCE,
Valetta meeting, 1991)

The UN was not without significant successes, but its record in managing conflicts in these years was disappointing. The graph in Figure 1.1 shows how effective the UN and the regional organizations were, first in terms of referrals, and second in abating, isolating and settling disputes, according to a study by Ernst Haas (1983). The study examined 282 disputes between 1945 and 1981, of which 123 were referred to the UN, 28 to the Organization of American States, 25 to the Organization of African Unity (OAU), 22 to the Arab League and 5 to the Council of Europe. The other 79 were not referred to an international organization.

While the effectiveness of the Security Council in settling disputes was limited, other ways were found to develop the UN's peacemaking role. The Secretary-General was empowered to use his 'good offices' in situations where peace and international security were endangered, and

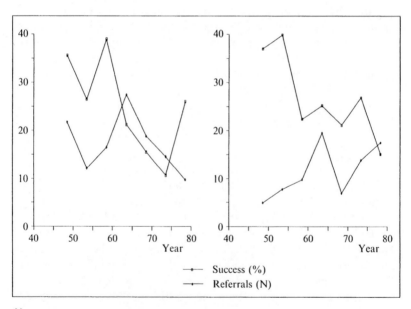

Note
The graphs show referrals to the UN on the left (N = 123) and to regional organizations on the right (N = 80), and the percentage of referred disputes abated, isolated or settled.

Source: E. B. Haas (1983)

FIGURE 1.1 *The effectiveness of the UN and regional organizations in managing disputes: referrals and success rates*

his office became a valuable focus for diplomatic activity. UN peacekeeping forces served a useful function in preserving cease-fires.

The General Assembly also played an important role, especially over decolonization conflicts, and it provided a valuable forum for states to express their grievances. The UN Organization played an increasingly important role in international co-operation, especially in the spheres of economic development, education and culture, refugees, minority protection and human rights.

Moreover, despite the Cold War, the post-war period saw some notable instances of peacemaking and co-operation outside the UN framework. France and Germany achieved a historic reconciliation after 80 years of hostility and wars. The German people turned emphatically away from their nationalistic traditions, following the crushing defeat of German militarism in the Second World War. France, which ended the war in control of Germany's coal and steel resources in the Saar, proposed the economic integration of the two countries' steelmaking industries (see Case 62 in the case studies section). The European Coal and Steel Community then became the basis for the EC. This is one model of peacemaking: the integration of formerly warring nations.

On a smaller scale, a number of longstanding European disputes were settled peacefully. One such case was the territorial and ethnic dispute over Trieste. Both Italy and Yugoslavia claimed Trieste and the surrounding countryside, where ethnic groups from both countries lived. An armed conflict seemed likely in the years from 1945 to 1953, but this was narrowly averted. Another case was the ethnic conflict between German speakers and Italian speakers in South Tyrol. Although similar in some respects to the situations in Northern Ireland and Cyprus, the ethnic communities and states involved reached a negotiated settlement and avoided serious civil conflict. The old dispute between Sweden and Finland over the Åland Islands was finally laid to rest (these cases are dealt with in Chapter 6). The status of Austria, occupied by both Soviet and Western troops, was resolved (Case 9). Other minor disputes over territory and resources among Western European states were settled by agreed procedures.

The post-war period also saw the dismantling of the former European colonial empires which, despite bloody exceptions, saw many peaceful transitions. The taking of independence by the British Cameroons (Case 14) was such a case. In other situations where a political struggle took place over decolonization, there were instances of small-scale violence, in which major armed conflicts were nevertheless averted: see, for example, Tunisia (Case 71) and Malawi (Case 45). Where the white settlers were numerous and formed a well-established elite, as in Algeria (Case 7) and Rhodesia (Case 81), armed conflicts took place.

In the Third World as a whole, the UN was unable to prevent the outbreak of an increasing number of armed conflicts. Some of these were wars of national independence; some were civil wars; some were wars between regional powers; some were ethnic conflicts (for example, those which sprang up along the fault-line between Islamic and Bantu peoples in North Africa). The superpowers and European powers were often involved, either directly or indirectly. In the years since 1945, over 150 armed conflicts are estimated to have taken place, claiming an estimated 25–30 million lives. This excludes the indirect effects of famine and disease. Altogether, since 1945, humanity has experienced only 26 days without war (Kende, 1986).

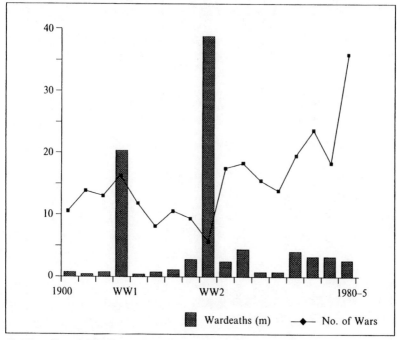

Source: Sivard (1987).

FIGURE 1.2 *Wars and wardeaths since 1945*

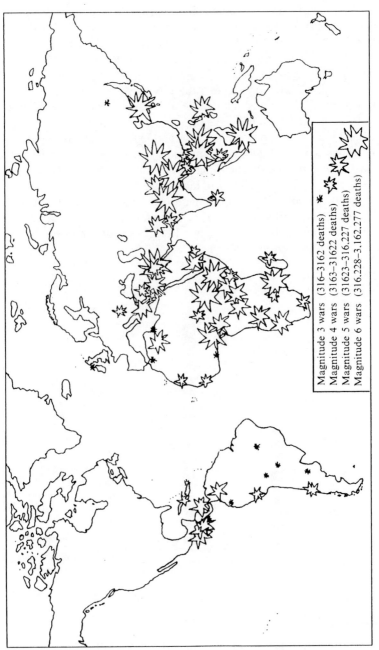

Magnitude 3 wars (316–3162 deaths)
Magnitude 4 wars (3163–31622 deaths)
Magnitude 5 wars (31623–316.227 deaths)
Magnitude 6 wars (316.228–3.162.277 deaths)

FIGURE 1.3 *Wars since 1945*

BOX 1.2   THE HUMAN SUFFERING

Two brief true stories illustrate the human suffering that results.
Both concern people who have been caught up in the civil war in
Southern Sudan in 1988–9.
    Magot is a Sudanese southerner, aged 50, from Gogrial
district.

I and about 30 others walked from our district to Abiye [a
town] – a distance of about 200 miles. We ate leaves off trees,
we cut them and boiled them . . . My mother died on the way,
my wife died in Abiye . . . when we reached the town we were
starving . . . my daughter died of dehydration . . . Now I am
too ill to work.

Sabina is a displaced woman in a camp on the edge of Juba, a
town in the midst of the fighting in the south. She had to flee her
village because it was too dangerous to remain. The journey
took eight days. Two of Sabina's five children died on the way.
Another child is ill, and she has no milk to feed her baby. Now
that she is in the camp, she still cannot obtain food because she
has no money (United Nations Association, 1989).

The Cold War intensified Third World conflicts in several ways.
Each superpower saw the world through its own particular ideological
blinkers and was prepared to support client regimes or guerrilla
movements with financial and military aid; consequently many local
conflicts became proxy wars for the superpowers.
    On several occasions there seemed a risk that one of these 'regional
conflicts' could trigger a direct war between the superpowers. The
Cuban crisis of 1962 was the most dangerous of these occasions, but
threats to use nuclear weapons were made in at least 16 other crises. In
1973 Kissinger and Nixon ordered a worldwide US nuclear alert over
fears that the Soviet Union might intervene in the Middle East. At
times of crisis, the sensors and computer systems of the command and
control systems on both sides could trigger each other into successively
higher states of alert, raising the probability of an unintended war
(Bracken, 1983). As President Mikhail Gorbachev said, 'The fact is
that a fuse smouldering in one part of the globe might cause an
explosion that would tear our planet apart' (Gorbachev, 1986).

THE END OF THE COLD WAR AND THE NEW CLIMATE FOR CONFLICT RESOLUTION

In 1989, however, one fuse stopped smouldering. The Cold War came to an end, offering the best opportunity since 1945 for a new approach to conflict resolution. The easing of East–West tensions reinvigorated the UN and removed a contributory source of Third World conflicts. For the first time since 1945 there seemed to be a possibility that the UN could play the role that the Charter intended.

The international climate for resolving regional conflicts was already beginning to improve in 1987–8. The war between Iran and Iraq was ended on the basis of a UN resolution. A settlement was negotiated to the conflict in Angola and Namibia (Cases 8 and 53). The Soviet Union withdrew from Afghanistan. A negotiated settlement to the Western Sahara dispute (Case 76) seemed possible, and steps were taken towards settlement of the Cambodian conflict. There were promising developments in Cyprus (Case 16), in the Palestinian–Israeli conflict (Case 39), in the Sino–Indian and Sino–Soviet border disputes, and elsewhere.

In 1989, for the first time in 26 years, no new wars were started. Eight wars under way in 1988 came to an end.

It became possible to strip away the outer layer of many Third World conflicts: the rivalry between the superpowers. The withdrawal of the Soviet Union from Afghanistan transformed an international conflict into an internal one. Similiarly the plan for Angola and Namibia put forward by the US Assistant Secretary of State, Chester Crocker, which called for the joint withdrawal of South African troops from Namibia and Cuban troops from Angola, removed the element of East–West confrontation, even if it did not immediately settle the conflicts inside the two countries. The Soviet Union cut back its military and financial aid to liberation movements and client regimes in Africa, the Middle East and South Asia. This stopped or scaled down a number of disputes.

'Regional conflicts' had first become a topic for direct discussion at the superpower summits in 1985. President Reagan put the issue high on the agenda for the Geneva summit and, to the surprise of the Americans, the Soviets welcomed a joint approach.

The development of 'new thinking' in Soviet foreign policy had altered the previously confrontational Soviet stance. Now, according to an official, 'new attitudes about the nature of regional conflict and new approaches to their settlement have become an integral part of the foreign policy of the Soviet Union' (Valenta, 1989). The Soviets saw their interests in regional conflicts as being not in automatic support for 'progressive' against reactionary forces, but in limiting damage to Soviet–US relations and avoiding a drain on Soviet financial resources. This meant avoiding the costs and risks of wars by achieving peaceful settlements.

The first and most important test of the new policy was in Afghanistan. By extricating the Soviet forces, Gorbachev drew out a thorn in East–West relations. Although he failed to bring about an internal settlement, he publicly backed the idea that national reconciliation was preferable to support for a pro-Soviet faction.

The Soviet Union began to co-operate with other members of the Security Council to a greater extent than before. Javier Perez de Cuellar, the Secretary-General, said, 'In matters of international peace and security, the principal organs of the United Nations have increasingly functioned in the manner envisaged by the Charter. The recent improvement in international relations at the global level has opened new possibilities for successful action by the world body.' (Urquhart, 1989).

The climate was also changed by the new consensus about global problems, and the realization that states need to take a common approach to their security in a more and more interdependent world (Palme, 1982). It has become widely accepted that there are shared common and human interests (for example, in the protection of the planetary habitat and the avoidance of nuclear war) that override sectional, class and national interests. This has laid a basis for international co-operation which did not exist before.

BOX 1.3   THE END OF THE COLD WAR

The end of the Cold War was itself a remarkable example of a peacefully settled conflict. For 40 years, the Cold War had frozen Europe and the world into a pattern of military and political confrontation. Yet by 1990 it was suddenly over.

The way in which it ended surprised everyone, including the parties to the conflict. The event which was expected to be the final stage of a reconciliation process – the fall of the Berlin Wall – in fact came first, and paved the way for the unification of Germany and the collapse of the Warsaw Pact.

Several strands of history intertwined to bring about this upheaval. The first was the development of relations between the superpowers. The 1970s had seen the beginning of détente, the launching of the Helsinki process and significant arms control agreements. The 'second cold war' in the early 1980s seemed to threaten this progress and created a heightened risk of war. But then relations eased again, especially following the remarkable sequence of unilateral arms reduction initiatives taken by President Mikhail Gorbachev. The decision of the Warsaw Pact to reduce its forces and adopt a defensive posture convinced Western states that there was no longer an imminent threat.

The second strand was the programme of reform in the Soviet Union. This began with *glasnost* (openness), and led to the ending of the Communist Party's monopoly of power and the holding of free elections. This removed a large part of the ideological element of the conflict.

The third strand was the gradual improvement of relations between East and West Germany. This had been under way since Chancellor Willi Brandt introduced his policy of *Ostpolitik*, and meant growing contacts between citizens, trade unions, cities, factories, churches and people in the two states.

The fourth strand was the development of demands for reform in Eastern Europe. The Solidarity movement in Poland foreshadowed a wave of popular demands for reform; it was followed by movements in Hungary and East Germany. One of the key demands was for freedom of travel. Once this had been granted in Hungary, an exodus began in East Germany which threatened the stability of the regime. Under pressure, a reforming East German government opened the Berlin Wall, and one by one the old Communist regimes fell. Moscow did not lift a finger to intervene.

A volcano had erupted on the fault-line dividing Europe. Free elections in Germany followed and led to unification on 3 October 1990. Suddenly the military confrontation in Europe, which ran down the middle of Germany, was obsolete and absurd. The Warsaw Pact effectively disintegrated. Although the future of the Soviet Union was uncertain, and a return to power by hard-liners was possible, the old division of Europe between two rival ideologies had become a thing of the past. (The ending of this conflict is dealt with in more detail in Chapter 6.)

In Europe the CSCE has been important as a vehicle for co-operation in Europe. Its significance is that it is the only body addressing European security issues which comprises all the members of NATO and the Warsaw Pact, as well as other neutral and nonaligned European states. At the Paris summit of the CSCE in November 1990, the 22 member states of the North Atlantic Treaty Organization (NATO) and the Warsaw Pact declared that they were 'no longer adversaries', and committed themselves to a treaty limiting conventional forces and to European unity.

Among the clauses of the Final Act of the CSCE signed at Helsinki in 1975 was a commitment to refrain from any use of force against other participating states and to 'make every effort to settle exclusively by peaceful means any dispute between them'. The participants resolved to 'pursue the examination and elaboration of a generally acceptable method for the peaceful settlement of disputes aimed at complementing existing methods'. The Paris summit reaffirmed this commitment and extended it:

An essential complement to the duty of States to refrain from the threat or use of force is the peaceful settlement of disputes, both being essential factors for the maintenance and consolidation of international peace and security. We will not only seek effective ways of preventing, through political means, conflicts which may yet emerge, but also define, in conformity with international law, appropriate mechanisms for the peaceful resolution of any disputes which may arise. Accordingly, we undertake to seek new forms of co-operation in this area, in particular a range of methods for the peaceful settlement of disputes, including mandatory third-party involvement. (Charter of Paris, CSCE, 1990)

BOX 1.4   THE VALETTA MEETING ON THE
PEACEFUL SETTLEMENT OF DISPUTES

The meeting of CSCE representatives at Valetta in February 1991 discussed CSCE procedures for peaceful settlement of disputes. This led to a report which listed agreed principles for managing disputes and also to the establishment of a new CSCE dispute settlement mechanism.

The agreed principles stated that parties would:

- abide by international law and CSCE provisions;
- refrain from the threat or use of force;
- recognize that having recourse to an agreed settlement procedure was not incompatible with the sovereign equality of States;
- act to prevent disputes (for example, through prior notification and consultation);
- address disputes at an early stage and consult one another as soon as possible;
- refrain from actions which may aggravate the dispute or impede peaceful settlement;
- seek good relations (for example, through interim measures without prejudice to their legal positions);
- seek to agree on a settlement procedure;
- accept mandatory involvement of a third party through the CSCE Dispute Settlement Mechanism where a dispute cannot be settled by peaceful means.

The Dispute Settlement Mechanism is a panel of conciliators, called 'dispute counsellors', whom CSCE member states in dispute can call upon. The panel will be drawn from a register of names, four nominated by each state. The panel can then seek information from the parties, and comment to the parties on either the procedures to follow or the substance of the dispute. The comments of the dispute counsellors would have no binding force, but parties would agree to consider them in good faith. The Council of CSCE Foreign Ministers in Berlin is expected formally to establish this procedure.

This is an interesting development which could be the first step towards a stronger role for the CSCE in settling political disputes in Europe. It is, however, subject to important exclusions. First, no internal disputes are subject to the mechanism. Second, even of the international disputes, disputes concerning 'territorial integrity, national defence, title to land territory, or competing claims with regard to the jurisdiction over other areas' are excluded, as are disputes which have already been dealt with or are being addressed under other procedures. Unfortunately these provisions exclude many of the vital current conflicts in Europe.

NEW PROBLEMS AND NEW SOURCES OF CONFLICT

There is certainly a need for a co-operative approach to the conflicts of the continent. The end of the Cold War has been an enormous relief in terms of East–West tensions, but it has opened up a Pandora's box of ethnic and territorial conflicts which had previously been suppressed. Figure 1.4 shows a map of the sources of tension in Central and Eastern Europe. Moreover, the serious political divisions in the Soviet Union leave open the possibility that East–West conflicts might re-emerge, probably in a new form. This would put the new declarations and procedures of the CSCE to a severe test.

Outside Europe, the problems are even more critical. The Third World, which has experienced by far the most direct warfare since 1945, remains riven by deep conflicts and stresses. Regional conflicts such as those between Israel and the Arabs and between India and Pakistan threaten to flare. Internal armed conflicts continue in many states. The sources of conflict are, if anything, multiplying, as rapid population growth and social and economic change put new stresses on Third World countries. The trends towards increasing food insecurity, migration into the swelling cities, growing unemployment and refugee flows, soil loss and environmental degradation, store up the seeds of future internal and international conflict.

At a global level the latent North–South conflict is getting sharper. Growing income discrepancies, discriminatory trade practices, debt, low commodity prices and high interest rates are among the forces which are damaging development prospects in the Third World. To these must be added the newer global environmental problems of climate change, deforestation, and desertification.

The proliferation of new weapons adds to the danger of these conflicts. Increasingly sophisticated conventional weapons have spread to most Third World countries. Six newly-emergent nuclear powers now have or will soon acquire nuclear weapons in addition to the five existing nuclear powers. Some 20 countries either possess or are seeking to acquire chemical weapons. Long-range missile technology is also spreading rapidly. The prospects for peaceful resolution of Third World and North–South conflicts seem perhaps even more intractable than those of European disputes, but events in Europe and the rest of the world are closely intertwined.

- - - - Frontiers after the First World War

1	Finnish border	15	Romanian border dispute with Soviet Union
2	Finnish minority in Soviet Union	16	Soviet Moldavians want union with Romania
3	Estonian independence movement	17	Hungarian minority in Romania
4	Latvian independence movement	18	Slovene minority in Austria
5	Lithuanian independence movement	19	Slovenian independence movement
6	Polish minority in Lithuania	20	Hungarian minority in Yugoslavia
7	German minority in Soviet Union	21	Albanian–Serb conflict: Kosovo
8	German minority in Poland	22	Romania–Bulgaria border dispute
9	Belorussian independence movement	23	Turkish minority in Greece
10	Polish minority in Ukraine	24	Macedonia claimed by Bulgaria, Greece, Yugoslavia
11	Belorussian independence movement	25	Turkish minority in Bulgaria
12	Polish minority in Ukraine	26	Aegean Islands: Graeco–Turkish dispute
13	Ukrainian independence movement	27	Cyprus: Graeco–Turkish dispute
14	Hungarian minority in Yugoslavia		

FIGURE 1.4 *Ethnic and national conflicts in Central and Eastern Europe*

TWO CRISES: LITHUANIA AND THE GULF

Two particular crises – one in Europe, the other in the Middle East – brought the issue of peaceful settlement of conflicts to the forefront of world attention in 1990. The first, which was particularly a crisis for the Soviet Union, was the attempt by Lithuania and the other Baltic republics to break free of the Soviet Union and win immediate independence. The second, which became a crisis for the West, was the occupation of Kuwait by Iraq. Both events raised broad questions about the future regime for settling conflicts following the end of the Cold War.

Lithuania was an acid test for the Soviet Union, and for Gorbachev himself. Would the 'new thinking' on peaceful settlement of conflicts be applied to an issue which threatened to precipitate the very break-up of the Sovet Union? If the conflict was to be settled by force not only would these ideas have been discarded, but the improved climate of East–West relations could be destroyed.

BOX 1.5   THE LITHUANIA CONFLICT

The conflict between Lithuanian nationalists and the Soviet government was an important test for Mikhail Gorbachev's policy of *perestroika* (reconstruction) in the Soviet Union, and especially for his policy of 'new thinking'. He had repeatedly called for settlement of conflicts by peaceful political means, but suddenly he was forced to find a way of applying these principles in a conflict which touched his own position directly. If the nationalists won their demand for immediate independence, the Soviet Union faced the prospect of rapid break-up. On the other hand, if the Soviet Union used force to suppress the Soviet Union, not only would *perestroika* be dead, but East–West relations would take a sharp turn for the worse. Gorbachev's own political position was at stake, for he could not be sure of support from the Communist Party's central committee or the hard-liners or the army on this issue.

The course Gorbachev took did not lead to an immediate resolution of the issue but, in the period up to October 1990, it was successful in averting any serious violence. Gorbachev visited Lithuania and declared that he intended to achieve a peaceful outcome. He was slow to negotiate with the Sajudis (the Popular Front for Perestroika), whose actions he regarded as illegal, but he did eventually negotiate with them. The only escape from his dilemma lay in pursuing a new constitution offering looser relations with the republics, and offering republics the chance to secede after a suitable time period. This was the avenue he pursued. When Lithuania declared itself independent he used economic sanctions, a much more restrained step than his predecessors would have chosen. The other Baltic republics showed the way out of this immediate crisis by declaring themselves independent, but suspending the application of the declaration until after negotiations with Moscow. Eventually Lithuania followed the same route. This led to movement of positions on both sides, and the Baltic issue eventually became submerged in the larger issue of the new Union for the whole country. (The conflict is described in more detail in Chapter 6.)

The Gulf Crisis became a matter mainly for the West because of the Western interests in the region, the large numbers of Westerners taken hostage, and the strong support for the Gulf states among Western nations. The crisis dramatically raises the difficulties of seeking a peaceful settlement in the same way that the Lithuanian crisis had for the Soviet Union. Did the failure to find a peaceful settlement have any lessons to teach, or did the crisis show that peaceful settlements are not always available?

BOX 1.6   THE GULF CRISIS

Iraq's invasion of Kuwait on 2 August 1990 precipitated one of the most extraordinary post-war crises. There was a long period, from 2 August to 15 January, in which time was available for diplomatic efforts to solve the conflict. This focused world attention on the feasibility of achieving a settlement.

It is important to stress that the crisis began with a massive use of force by Iraq on 2 August, and therefore after this the dispute was already past the stage of a peaceful settlement (that is, one avoiding the use of armed force). It was in the period before 2 August that the real failure came. The dispute between Iraq and Kuwait had a long history, and there had been several previous occasions when Iraq had threatened Kuwait, and even occupied the disputed territory. Such crises had occurred in 1938, 1963, 1965, 1973, 1975 and 1978. After several of these occasions negotiations were held between the two sides, but the issue was never resolved. A pattern was set up in which Iraq relied on the use of force to attempt to seize the territory it wanted, and Kuwait relied on alliances to defend itself. Neither side seriously took account of the concerns of the other, and consequently opportunities to reach a mutually acceptable settlement were missed. Third-party efforts (by the UN and the Arab League) took place when the dispute reached crisis dimensions but failed to be sustained in the noncrisis periods.

During the long period of stand-off which followed the invasion, US and British policy was to build up reinforcements and threaten the use of force in an effort to secure Iraqi withdrawal. President Bush later said that 'extraordinary diplomatic efforts have been exhausted', but the crisis period was notable for the absence of diplomatic efforts on the Allied side to find a way out. The USA and Britain both stated that they were not prepared to negotiate with Iraq unless and until its forces were unconditionally withdrawn. They dismissed Iraqi moves which one State Department source described as a 'serious pre-negotiating offer', indicating an intention to withdraw.

At a conference in Washington in October 1990, a former US Assistant Secretary of State, Hal Saunders, who had been involved in the Camp David negotiations, was asked how he would advise a US president to seek a negotiated settlement. He said that, having set a cordon sanitaire in place around Iraq, he would advocate the use of intermediaries to explore the conditions under which Iraq might consider withdrawing. He expected that the exploratory talks and the practical steps which would follow to defuse the crisis would be protracted, and that therefore it was necessary to allow time for a process through which the settlement could be explored. The intermediaries would seek undertakings from each side that would allow reciprocal withdrawal of forces to take place. Until a satisfactory settlement had been made, the sanctions would stay in place.

However, this was not the course that the international
coalition took. It gave no support to those making third-party
attempts to find a political solution and, when negotiations were
eventually held, their purpose was only to offer a final
ultimatum. The Iraqi side, which of course created the crisis
in the first place, consistently sabotaged prospects of peace by
its acts in breach of international law. Few conditions conducive
to a peaceful settlement were present, and little effort had been
made by either side to put them in place. (Chapter 6 gives an
account of the history of the dispute and the failure of attempts
to settle it.)

THE STUDY OF CONFLICT SETTLEMENT

These current disputes and the pressing issues likely to lead to disputes
in the future urgently raise the question of how can disputes be settled
effectively by peaceful means, in such a way that justice and peace are
upheld? We are clearly some way from an adequate answer. Nevertheless, there are various sources which can contribute to our understanding of these questions.

First, there is a growing practice of the difficult art of conflict
resolution by governments, intergovernmental organizations, non-
governmental organizations and individuals. From this experience,
what is known about how to tackle conflicts in practice? To what
extent do the different techniques of conflict resolution share common
features?

Second, there is a theoretical understanding of conflict and conflict
resolution in the literature of peace and conflict research. Peace and
conflict researchers are seeking a general theoretical framework for
analysing conflict. They have developed promising theoretical approaches to the study of conflict and conflict resolution.

Third, there is the actual historical experience of peacefully settled
conflicts. Although not so well known as armed conflicts, there have
been many disputes which have been successfully settled without
fighting. Are there lessons which can be drawn from these disputes
for future practice, and to what extent do they substantiate theories
about successful dispute settlement?

Historians since Thucydides have studied war, but peacemaking has
not been such a well-studied topic. The same applies in the disciplines

of international relations and peace research. Peace research emerged as a new field in the 1940s and 1950s, with systematic empirical and statistical studies of armed conflicts, such as those of Quincy Wright (1942) and Lewis Richardson (1960). There is now a large literature in this field. Singer and others have prepared statistics of wars (Singer and Small, 1984) and militarized interstate disputes (Gochman and Maoz, 1984). In the international relations tradition, Luard's magisterial works (1986; 1988) survey wars both in the present international society and in the past.

The aim of this field of studies is to identify the causes and conditions which lead to war. If such knowledge is found, it could then be used, it is hoped, to prevent wars in the future.

Less attention has been given to how wars are brought to an end, but Sydney Bailey (1982) and others (*Annals of the American Academy of Political and Social Science*, 1970; Taylor, 1985) have contributed excellent studies.

The emphasis on wars gives a sharp focus, but wars are only one means of prosecuting conflict. Ending a war does not necessarily end a conflict, and beginning a conflict does not necessarily begin a war. Studies on the settlement of conflicts in general are more rare than studies of war endings. Mitchell (1981), de Reuck (1984), Pruitt and Rubin (1986) and Patchen (1988) are among those who have contributed studies which address this question from a general and theoretical point of view.

Northedge and Donelan (1971) carried out a valuable analysis of international disputes, based on case studies of 50 conflicts (Donelan and Grieve, 1973). They examined the origins, development, limitation and solution of conflicts, the role of international agencies in their settlement, and the role of various methods for peacefully settling disputes, including negotiation, mediation, arbitration and adjudication.

There has recently been a growth of interest in mediation, and scholars have examined the role of states (Touval and Zartman, 1985; Mitchell and Webb, 1988) and private mediators (Yarrow, 1978; Azar and Burton, 1986; Sandole and Sandole-Staroste, 1987). Studies of negotiation (Fisher and Ury, 1983; Gulliver, 1987; Ury, Brett and Goldberg, 1988) are also relevant.

In addition, there have been studies of the effectiveness of international organizations, especially the UN and the regional organizations such as the OAU and the Organization of American States (Butterworth, 1976; 1978; Alker and Sherman, 1982; E. B. Haas, 1983;

Sherman, 1987). Some of these studies cover international disputes which did not become violent.

Previous studies have created lists of armed conflicts and data banks of information about them. Much less has been done on 'peaceful conflicts'. There are no complete lists of peaceful conflicts or resolved conflicts; perhaps it would be impossible to compile a complete list. The fullest to date is that of Sherman (1987).

The present study is focused particularly on conflicts which have been peacefully resolved but, in order to identify factors which are conducive to peaceful settlements, it is necessary to examine failures as well as successes. For this reason, peacefully resolved conflicts are compared with conflicts resolved after violence, and a number of unresolved conflicts, both peaceful and violent, are examined too.

The study rests on several major assumptions. The first is that conflicts are comparable. Each conflict is unique, but conflicts are not so unique as to make any generalization and comparison impossible. The second is that the past is relevant to the future, and that useful lessons can be drawn from past experience. This would not hold if the international system were to experience radical change, but the changes of recent years have not been so radical or discontinuous as to make previous experience irrelevant. Fuller arguments for these propositions can be found elsewhere (Nicholson, 1971; Rapoport, 1974; Luard, 1988).

A more fundamental assumption is that the peaceful resolution of conflict is in itself a desirable aim. This is by no means a self-evident proposition, and the next chapter is devoted to examining it.

2 Conflict, Justice and Power

Remember the last time you were involved in a serious conflict with another person or group. Did you try to settle the conflict amicably, or did you do everything you could to win? Was justice on your side? Who was in the wrong?

Our perspective on conflict varies depending on our point of view. If you are a protagonist, you will have a very clear idea of what is right. Your opponent will also have a clear idea, although it will be different from yours. You will each be prepared to struggle for your objectives and do what is in your power to achieve them.

Those who stand outside the conflict and see the costs each is imposing on the other may seek to find a peaceful settlement. But as both of you are committed to protecting your own interests and upholding the justice of your own causes, you prefer to win than to settle.

Those who frame declarations in the name of the international community would clearly like disputes to be settled by peaceful means. Those who are engaged in armed conflicts evidently do not find this such a compelling value. They usually prefer disputes to be settled by peaceful means if they are settled on their own terms. If not, other aspirations override the value of peaceful settlement. The consequence is that armed conflict continues to be prevalent despite apparently unanimous support for peaceful settlements.

The international community appears to hold inconsistent norms. On the one hand it calls for peaceful settlement of disputes and deplores aggression; on the other, it endorses just wars and just revolutions (Howard, 1981). If justice is threatened and alternative means of action appear to be unavailable, many prefer the use of force to peaceful resolution of disputes.

This is one source of objection to peaceful settlement of conflicts. Another comes from those who believe that 'in the real world', conflicts will always be settled by armed force in the last resort. According to this school of thought, societies can only be secure if they are able to resist the military force of their rivals. Since rivalry is endemic in the international system, and power rests ultimately on the willingness to use armed force, the quest for peaceful means to resolve conflicts must remain a quixotic enterprise.

These are important objections to the value of settling conflicts peacefully. Is the effort to find peaceful settlements of conflicts really a misguided enterprise?

CONFLICTS AND JUSTICE

Let us consider first whether peaceful settlements are desirable in disputes over justice. One important category is conflicts where one or both parties have a just cause. Another is conflicts where the relationship between the parties is unjust, and is itself the cause of the conflict. Let us consider this second type first.

In the 1930s rural China had a society dominated by landowners, who owned most of the land and wealth. The peasants had to give a large portion of the food they produced to the landlord, and if they were in debt they were forced to sell their own children. At times of scarcity, the peasants and their families starved. At times of plenty, the landlords took most of the benefit. This structure was clearly unjust, but it had existed in China for hundreds of years, and both peasants and landlords accepted it as part of the natural order.

In the course of the Chinese revolution, the Communists persuaded the peasants to overthrow the landlords, and redistribute their holdings. In this way, they achieved what they considered to be a more just distribution of land, at the cost of a good deal of violence towards the landlords. The Communists justified this violence as a necessary means of overcoming the injustice in the distribution of land.

According to the Communists, the landlords and the peasants had an irreconcilable conflict of interest. Any efforts to settle disputes between the two groups by peaceful means could not succeed. So long as the system of landholding was 'semi-feudal', there could be no common interest between landlords and peasants; the former were bound to exploit the latter.

The contemporary 'North–South' conflict is another instance of this type of conflict. People in the advanced industrialized countries enjoy incomes many times higher than those in poorer countries. Their expectation of life is higher, they are better fed, and in general their life-opportunities are better. This is so because the rich countries control most of the world's capital assets, manufacturing systems, financial centres and sources of technological progress. The majority of the world's population are shut out by trading and financial relations between the 'metropolis' and the 'periphery' which give a permanent advantage to the metropolis.

Another example of this kind of conflict is the situation in South Africa. The whites own almost all the land and control the country's economic assets. They have forced the blacks to live in townships and homelands where opportunities are poor and life is bleak. For years apartheid maintained this racial domination, and now the distribution of land and wealth continues to preserve it.

In cases such as these, it is impossible to settle conflicts without a fundamental change in the relationship between the parties. 'Structural conflict' can be resolved only by structural social change.

Structural change does not always or necessarily come about through violent means. The ending of apartheid, in fact, owed little to direct violent pressure (see Box 2.1). Other examples of mainly peaceful structural change include the change in the status of women, brought about by the suffragettes and their successors, and the change in the status of industrial working classes, achieved by trade unions.

Developing an awareness that there is a conflict of interest is itself an important part of the process of change. Steve Biko emphasized 'black consciousness' in South Africa. In China Mao and his cadres taught the peasants to 'stand up'. Out of this awareness develops a desire to change relationships and roles. Once people question the roles, they already lose part of their power in a traditional structure. As social movements for change develop, they empower their members. With this empowerment comes a possibility of confronting the defenders of the status quo with a political movement of equivalent power. Then the way may be open to a negotiated resolution, or the use of non-violent sanctions.

When armed force is used, even to challenge injustice, there is no way to avoid imposing injustice on others. Violence is always unjust to its victims and it is a rare war which does not bring unjust acts in its wake. In seeking to move from unjust social structures towards peaceful relationships, the challenge is to find ways to pursue both

BOX 2.1   TOWARDS THE ENDING OF APARTHEID:
THE TRANSITION TO NEGOTIATIONS IN SOUTH
AFRICA, 1987–90

In 1989 and 1990 remarkable changes took place in South
Africa. After 300 years of minority white rule, the Nationalist
government abruptly turned away from apartheid, and sought
negotiations with the black opposition. The government lifted
the State of Emergency, unbanned the African National
Congress (ANC) and released Nelson Mandela from prison.
Later the ANC formally abandoned its policy of armed struggle.

How did these remarkable changes come about?

Pressure had been steadily building for many years. The end
of the Portuguese colonies, and the downfall of the Rhodesian
government, suggested to many that the writing was on the wall
for white minority rule in South Africa. Yet the apartheid
regime had created a uniquely repressive state. Separate homelands for the blacks and enforced transfers of population had
created a society of ghettos. Draconian laws and policing
maintained it. With its rich economy and powerful armed
forces, South Africa seemed able to ignore international
protests and crush domestic opposition.

The fundamental factor that was the undoing of white
minority rule was the structural contradiction between the
policy of apartheid and the demands of a modern industrial
state. As the economy grew more diversified, it became more
important that the labour force should be educated and skilled.
It was less and less feasible for blacks to be kept separate from
their jobs. While gold mines could be run using a black
proletariat, it was harder and harder to do this with modern
cities and industries. The demands of the cities for labour
created huge townships, such as Soweto, which became a focus
for black opposition. No matter how much repression the
whites used, the logic of this structural change was gradually
overwhelming them.

The more the government relied on brutality to control the
situation, the more exposed it became, both internationally and
internally. The suppression of the riots in Soweto in 1976–8
horrified the international community, as did the South African
attack on Angola in 1975. In response, when P.W. Botha
became prime minister, he decided on a policy of limited

reforms. The government permitted the integration of sports, allowed blacks to enter universities, and created mixed business districts in cities. The laws banning mixed marriages were repealed, and some of the most notorious parts of apartheid (including the pass laws and the Influx Control Act) were abolished. New laws permitted the desegregation of public transport, hotels and restaurants. At the same time, Botha's government continued to suppress opposition in the townships, using bulldozers, secret police and tear gas.

Around its borders the South African Defence Forces adopted an aggressive policy of 'forward defence', engaging in wars and raids in neighbouring countries. This policy led to increased isolation for South Africa, the adoption of partial sanctions by the UN, and a trend towards disinvestment which put a tightening squeeze on the South African economy.

In 1984 Botha extended reform to the constitution, dissolving the old whites-only Parliament. In its place he created a new tricameral body, representing whites, coloured people and Indians. But these changes excluded the blacks, prompting a further wave of rioting in the townships in 1985 and 1986. These riots were more dangerous for the government than those of 1976–8.

In response, Botha introduced the State of Emergency, and suspended reforms. This caused the pressure on the government to be increased again. The violence in the townships convinced many whites that South Africa faced a bloodbath unless fundamental reforms were made. As disinvestment increased, many businessmen were becoming convinced that repression offered no long-term future for the South African economy.

During this period third parties made a number of efforts to facilitate discussions between the major parties. The Commonwealth Eminent Persons Group held talks with the ANC, the government and other parties in 1986 (see Commonwealth Group of Eminent Persons, 1986). Organizations within South Africa, such as Hendrik van der Merwe's Centre for Intergroup Studies at the University of Cape Town, the Wiehann Commission on labour legislation, the South African Council of Churches, the Quakers and others, facilitated communications, not always directly, between the parties. Two former MPs, Fredrik van Zyl Slabbert and Alex Borraine, set up the Institute for a Democratic Alternative to encourage this process. This led to a number of white and Afrikaners calling

for dialogue, and actual dialogue between Afrikaners and ANC
leaders. It also resulted in the ANC publishing a statement
about preconditions for negotiations, and a set of proposals for
constitutional reform. At about the same time the Cabinet held
discussions with Nelson Mandela over his possible release from
prison.

In 1989 P.W. Botha suffered a stroke and resigned as leader
of the National Party. F.W. de Klerk succeeded as President
and returned to the path of reforms. He limited the powers that
the security forces had acquired, and abandoned the policies of
destabilizing neighbouring countries. At the same time the
Soviet Union cut back its financial and military help to the
ANC so that the 'armed struggle' appeared increasingly forlorn
as a route to change.

In 1989 the Mass Democratic Movement, a coalition of trade
unions and opposition groups, organized large nonviolent
campaigns to defy the apartheid laws. After an initially violent
police response, de Klerk decided to overrule the police and
allow protest marches. He removed many remaining petty
apartheid laws and, in an important gesture, released Walter
Sisulu and seven other long-serving political prisoners. Nelson
Mandela, still in prison, now became the focal point of
communications between the government and the ANC.
Although he still refused to renounce the armed struggle and
thus meet the government's publicly stated condition for
releasing him, Mandela said that he wanted to 'contribute to a
climate that would promote peace in South Africa'. De Klerk
responded by calling for negotiations between all sides who
wanted a peaceful solution. The government thus abandoned its
refusal to negotiate with the ANC. The ANC now agreed to
suspend hostilities, provided that the State of Emergency was
lifted, political prisoners were released and banned organizations were allowed to take part in political activity. In a speech
to Parliament, De Klerk met most of these conditions. Nelson
Mandela walked out of prison a free man.

The subsequent 'talks-about-talks' have been difficult, and
the process of negotiations on a future constitution still lie
ahead. De Klerk has accepted the principle of a universal
franchise, and the Nationalist leaders have moved from seeking
minority rule to seeking protection and security for the white
minority in the future of South Africa. There are clearly many

difficult hurdles ahead, and the progress that has been made towards a peaceful settlement could yet be lost. The negotiations over a future constitution could fail and extremists might take over on either side. Nevertheless the events in this period indicate that even in a situation of severe structural conflict such as South Africa, it was possible to move from confront-ation to negotiations. The steps both sides took opened the door for a potential peaceful settlement.

Among the elements which contributed to this movement were the change of leadership on the government side; the movement away from extreme positions on both sides; the declarations of intent to move toward a peaceful settlement; and the opening of communications between the parties with help from third parties. At the same time, the use of nonviolence in South Africa, and nonviolent sanctions on South Africa, played important roles. The ANC's agreement to abandon the armed struggle, which it could not continue after the change of policy by the Soviet Union, was another step on the way. Violence and the threat of violence was certainly present in the background, and the violent repression of the regime, the riots in the townships and the latent fear of a bloodbath formed the backdrop to these events. Nevertheless, the developments of these two years do suggest that progress towards negotiated settlements is possible even in the most repressive cases of structural violence.

Hendrik van der Merwe, who arranged the first meeting between the ANC and the government, drew these conclusions from his experience of mediating in Africa (Van der Merwe, 1990):

1. empowerment of the weaker party was essential;
2. mediation broke the deadlock when direct talks were not possible;
3. informal facilitation of the conflict was possible when mediation was not possible;
4. coercion and mediation are complementary;
5. incremental and radical steps are compatible;
6. impartiality is compatible with compassion and concern.

Sources: van der Merwe (1989; 1990), International Institute for Strategic Studies (1990), Tjonneland (1990).

peace and justice. It is always possible to pursue one at the price of the other; but a peaceful settlement cannot be wholly peaceful, and neither is it likely to be durable, unless it is just. An outcome cannot be just if is achieved at the cost of human lives.

THE JUST WAR

Is peaceful settlement desirable in conflicts where one side has a just cause? A 'just cause' was one of St Thomas Aquinas' conditions for a 'Just War'. These conditions, which Aquinas set out in the twelfth century, are still widely used in Christian cultures in discussion of the justice of particular wars. They purport to set out restrictions to the types of war in which it is morally permissible to engage. The restrictions cover the decision to go to war and the conduct of military operations.

The conditions are:

1. the war must be waged by a lawful authority;
2. it must have a 'just cause';
3. war must be a last resort (all reasonable prospects of a peaceful settlement must have been exhausted);
4. the war must have a reasonable chance of success (authorities must not risk the suffering of war if the chances of achieving the just cause are slim);
5. the importance of the cause must be proportionate to the losses expected in the war;
6. the war must be discriminate;
7. the innocent must not be directly attacked.

The conditions clearly indicate that it is necessary to exhaust the possibilities of a peaceful settlement before resorting to war, but they are not absolutely clear about how far parties should go before deciding they have reached the last resort. Should a party make concessions from a position it regards as just in order to make a peaceful settlement more likely? If neither side is prepared to make concessions, has a last resort been reached?

The conditions indicate when war is justified from the point of view of one side. But, in most conflicts, the parties have different perceptions of what is just. If each side is entitled to interpret justice in its own terms, both sides are likely to consider they have grounds for a 'just war'. If both sides have just causes, or there is some justice on both sides, is a war between them just?

Justice interpreted by one party or another falls short of the full sense of 'justice'. We need a concept of justice which is true to the situation as a whole. It is mutual justice, or justice for all in the situation, which must be the primary concern.

If justice is interpreted in this way, it is clearly necessary for some process to take place whereby the parties' view of justice is expanded. This is what takes place in efforts to resolve conflict. Well-managed conflict resolution is a process through which parties articulate their fundamental needs and values together, and come to an expanded view of their situation.

Conflict resolution may not succeed if only one of the parties is prepared to see the conflict from both sides. Then it may be necessary to pursue the conflict, but it is still possible to do so in a way that is consistent with a sense of 'the justice of the situation'. Gandhi always insisted that his nonviolent campaigns were an effort to find the truth of the situation through struggle. Both contenders had a place in finding a just outcome, even though Gandhi clearly saw more justice on one side. Similarly van der Merwe (1989) argues that in South Africa both sides have a role to play in finding a just and peaceful end to apartheid, and he advocates both conciliation and sanctions.

In short, situations where one side has a 'just cause' do not negate the value of conflict resolution unless one side has all the justice on its side, and the other none. Few situations are ever so extreme.

CONFLICT AND POWER

The second objection to the notion of peaceful settlement of disputes is very different. Those who make it would regard justice as irrelevant in power politics. They are the so-called 'realist' school who see the play of power as the main factor in conflict.

According to this view, political communities develop separate interests, which their leaders represent and pursue. Clashes between these interests are bound to occur. In these clashes, it is the state with the greater power which will prevail. Since military force is ultimately the decisive form of power in conflict, the use or threat of force inevitably underlies the relations between states. Even when power is not an overt element in conflicts, it lies beneath the surface, and determines events. Consequently, states are obliged to rely on power to protect their interests. Conflicts are tests of power. If conflicts are settled without the use of force, it is simply a sign that both sides recognize from the distribution of power who will win, or that important interests are not involved. But states will resort to force when important interests clash, and power conflicts of this sort cannot be settled peacefully.

E. H. Carr (1939) put this view forcefully in his book (*The Twenty Years' Crisis 1919–1939*, p. 109):

> The supreme importance of the military instrument lies in the fact that the *ultima ratio* of power in international relations is war. Every act of the state, in its power aspect, is directed to war, not as a desirable weapon, but as a weapon which it may require in the last resort to use . . . War lurks in the background of international politics just as revolution lurks in the background of domestic politics.

However, Carr balances this statement by pointing out that power takes a number of forms. Military power is only one of them. There is economic power and power over opinion. Authority, legitimacy and influence are forms of power. Which form is dominant depends on the social or international context.

Speaking of domestic conflict, Carr says, 'Power is an essential factor in every dispute. The settlement of a conflict of interest between British agriculturalists and British industrialists will depend, in part at any rate, on their respective voting strength and the respective "pulls" which they can exercise on the government.' Here he is clearly referring to nonmilitary forms of power.

Since Carr wrote, there has been a great increase in the capacity of military power. It can now destroy more targets at longer distances and in shorter times than ever before. Yet it has become a blunt instrument for achieving limited political ends. Henry Kissinger plaintively asked about strategic superiority, 'what do you do with it?' The record of conflict since 1945 gives some examples of decisive military power, but also others where military power has been ineffective or self-defeating. At its ultimate expression in nuclear weapons, military power has become at the same time almost infinitely powerful and by that token almost completely unusable.

Power in the sense in which it is used by the 'realists' is power for one side. The contest between power on either side settles the contest. But in this sense, power tends to cancel itself out. What matters is not absolute power but relative power, and relative power is volatile. States struggle to match one another's power, and those with power eventually lose it. 'Power over' others tends to produce its own resistance, generating an equal and opposite force. The net result is negative or destructive. Of course, this kind of power is extremely important in today's world.

There is, however, another kind of power. Coercive power can compel, but positive forms of power can move individuals, and unleash the collective power in whole communities and societies. This is the power of great social, religious and political movements, which empower and energize people, and bring about historical change.

There are, therefore, other avenues for the interplay of power than the use of armed force. Force is not necessarily the ultimate arbiter of conflict. It depends on context and circumstance.

In some contexts, and in some parts of the world, military force has been replaced altogether as a means for settling disputes. Other forms of power have supplanted it (Boulding, 1978).

Conflict is both destructive and creative. It breaks down the old and clears a way for the new. It offers an opportunity to find a way to new relationships or a new situation. In this sense, the parties share a potential creative power. This is not 'power over' each other, but 'power to' create something new.

Parties in conflict can choose what kind of power to use, just as they can choose between one-sided and mutual views of justice. The aim of conflict resolution is to seek ways in which the parties can collectively use their power to promote mutual justice.

3 The Meaning of Words: Conflict, Violence, Peaceful Settlement

In ordinary language the terms 'conflict', 'conflict resolution' and 'peaceful settlement' can take many meanings. In order to make an enquiry into how conflicts have been peacefully settled, it is necessary first to define what is to be meant by these terms. This chapter discusses these preliminary conceptual issues.

CONFLICT

The UN and the peace and conflict research community have both struggled to arrive at a satisfactory definition of conflict. It is worth discussing the difficulties they have encountered before setting out the definition to be used in this study.

Definitions by the International Community

Article 1 of the UN Charter states that the first purpose of the UN is

> to maintain international peace and security, and to that end: to take effective collective measures for the prevention and removal of threats to the peace, and for the suppression of acts of aggression or other breaches of the peace, and to bring about by peaceful means, and in conformity with the principles of justice and international law, adjustment or settlement of international disputes or situations which might lead to a breach of the peace.

The notion of a 'dispute' as used in the UN Charter has been defined as a 'conflict between states in which the contesting parties have

36

formulated definite claims, defences and possibly counter-claims' (Bentwich and Martin, 1951)[1]. There may be a prior stage of diffuse tension or friction, where parties have become aware of a clash of interests but have yet to formulate claims, or indeed when organized parties have yet to coalesce. This prior stage is recognized in the phrase 'situations which might lead to a breach of the peace'.

Article 34 empowers the Security Council to 'investigate any dispute or any situation which might lead to international friction or give rise to a dispute, in order to determine whether the continuance of the dispute or situation is likely to endanger the maintenance of international peace and security'. In this respect the UN Charter made an advance on the Covenant of the League of Nations, which had restricted itself to examining 'disputes' only, the assumption being that wars arose from unresolved disputes between nations (Northedge and Donelan, 1971).

Until the Second World War, wars were formally declared between nations in exchanges of diplomatic notes. However, since then virtually all wars have been fought without being declared. There have also been a large number of violent conflicts involving revolutionary organizations, ethnic communities, political parties and other nongovernmental bodies. Consequently the term 'war' has come to be replaced in UN circles by the more general term 'armed conflicts'.

Since Article 27(3) of the UN Charter requires that parties to 'disputes' must abstain from voting on proposals for peaceful settlement, nations have been reluctant to use this term about their conflicts. For this reason the UN Secretariat has no list of disputes since 1945, and in practice the UN deals with whatever situations member states choose to refer to it. These range from major wars such as that between Iran and Iraq, to minor incidents such as a border incursion by a single aircraft. Some continuing conflicts (for example, the Arab–Israeli issue) are dealt with as a succession of episodes. Neither international law nor international practice have clearly defined the boundaries between a conflict and the background situation out of which it can arise.

Definitions by the Academic Community

A number of the seminal works in peace and conflict research were studies of wars, but even wars proved difficult to define. Quincy Wright (1942) confined his *Study of War* to conflicts 'involving members of the family of nations', which 'were recognised as states of war in the legal sense or which involved over 50 000 troops'. This definition is precise but led Wright to omit some important armed conflicts, such as colonial wars. Richardson (1960) invented the concept of deadly quarrels, using it to mean 'any quarrel which caused death to humans. The term thus includes murders, banditries, mutinies, insurrections, and wars small and large.' Singer and Small (1972) count as wars international armed conflicts that caused more than 1000 direct fatalities. Kende (1986) uses the criterion that regular armed forces are involved on at least one side, organized fighting takes place on both sides (this may be by guerrillas), and there is some continuity between armed clashes.

If the definition of war has proved difficult, the definition of conflict in a broader sense is more difficult still. International quarrels range from minor altercations between allies to implacable hostility between enemies who deny each other's right to exist. Within this there is a continuum of situations. Drawing a dividing line somewhere along it and defining as conflicts situations on one side of the line is bound to be an arbitrary exercise. The same is true of relations between groups within states.

The most widely accepted definition of conflict is a situation where the parties have incompatible goals. Michael Nicholson (1971) writes:

> A conflict exists when two people wish to carry out acts which are mutually inconsistent. (They may both want to do the same thing, such as eat the same apple, or they may want to do different things where the different things are truly incompatible, such as when they both want to stay together but one wants to go to the cinema and the other stay at home.) A conflict is resolved when some mutually consistent set of actions is worked out. The definition of conflict can be extended from single people to groups (such as nations) and more than two parties can be involved in the conflict. The principles remain the same.

There has been much controversy among the peace and conflict research community about how conflict should be defined. One school, perhaps best represented in North America, defines conflict in terms of a clash of intrests between interdependent parties. Kenneth Boulding (Matsunaga, 1981, p. 23) writes:

> 'Conflicts over interests' are situations in which some change makes at least one party better off and the other party worse off, each in their own estimation. If the change is 'positive sum', it opens the

possibility that both parties may be better off. If the change is 'zero sum' or 'negative sum' this perception is no longer available. A 'fight' is a situation in which each party to a perceived conflict over interests acts to reduce the welfare of the other.'

Another school, associated with Johan Galtung, argues that injustice and 'structural violence' are themselves situations of conflict, even in the absence of physical violence and confrontation. Adam Curle (1971) defines conflict as any situation where the potential development of one group is impeded by another. This is to include a much broader range of situations than the North American school.

In fact the two schools tend to emphasize different types of conflict. The first is mainly concerned with international conflict. Its primary goal is the avoidance or resolution of armed conflicts between Great Powers. The second school is more concerned with the domination and exploitation of the poor (the periphery) by the rich (the centre), both within particular societies and in world society as a whole.

These two kinds of conflict have been called 'symmetric' and 'asymmetric'. Anatol Rapoport (1974) defines these types as follows:

In symmetric conflict, the participants are roughly similar systems and perceive themselves as such. Thus, two individuals in a fight, say, man and wife, or two comparable nations at war, are typical examples of symmetric conflict. In asymmetric conflict, the systems may be widely disparate or may perceive each other in different ways. A revolt or a revolution is an example of an asymmetric conflict. The system revolted against 'perceives' itself as defending order and legitimacy; the insurgents 'perceive' themselves as an instrument of social change or of bringing a new system into being.

Elsewhere Rapoport (1971) comments further on the difference between the two types of conflicts:

In symmetric conflicts, techniques of conflict resolution seem to be most relevant. The interests of two or more parties clash. Each knows that the resort to force will incur costs far in excess of any benefits of 'victory'. It seems eminently reasonable to seek ways of compromise, of improving 'communication' in order to avoid misperceptions of the other's intentions, etc. The relevance of the conflict resolution approach depends crucially on the assumption of symmetry. Symmetric conflicts are the most visible and understandable in the framework of thought governing the traditional concepts of international relations. The United States and the Soviet

Union are superpowers of comparable magnitude. Israel and the Arab States are comparable, and their grievances against each other, though not centred on the same issues, are comparable. Moreover, both in the case of the superpowers and in the case of the small states, a sober appraisal of the probable consequences of resort to violence will at least give pause to undertaking actions based on the Clausewitzian conception of war as the 'continuation of policy by other means'.

However, the symmetric conception of conflict either ignores or misperceives other types of conflict that have only recently come to the forefront of attention – distinctly asymmetric conflicts whose genesis is not 'issues' to be 'settled' but the very structure of a situation that cannot be eliminated or modified without conflict. Indeed, the suspension of conflict or making conflict impossible is in these instances entirely in the interests of one of the parties – the dominant one. Here, 'peace' is equated to 'pacification'.

In asymmetric conflicts such as this, it is necessary first to bring the latent conflict into the open and to confront it, even though this may seem like starting a conflict. It is then necessary to transform the relationship between the parties. Conflict resolution must be taken in a wide sense to include not merely agreement among parties to a conflict, which may not be possible in asymmetric conflict, but the transformation of a situation so that an existing conflict formation is dissolved.

The Life-cycle of a Conflict

In considering what conflict is and what it means to resolve it, it is helpful to think of conflicts over their entire life-cycle. Figure 3.1 shows a schema of the stages that an armed conflict may go through. It is not intended to represent a typical conflict, but only to assist this discussion.

The conflict begins when some social or political change leads to the emergence of a potential dispute or clash of interests within a society or within the international system. This phase of potential or latent conflict can then lead to the formation of organized parties, or the adoption of the dispute by existing parties. At this stage, when parties perceive that they are in conflict and that the goals they are pursuing are incompatible, there is overt conflict. This may be followed by a phase of noncoercive conflict, when the parties prosecute the dispute

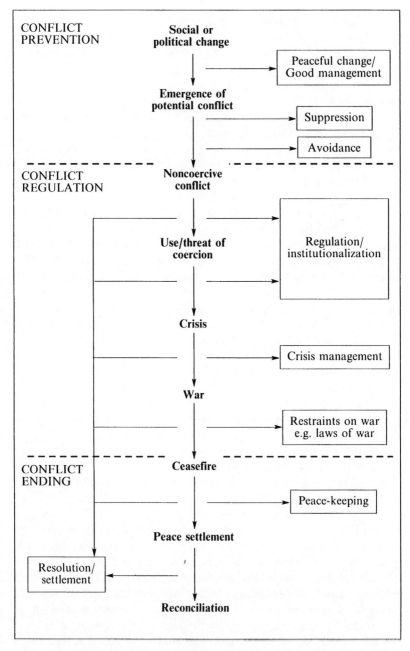

FIGURE 3.1 *Phases in conflict and forms of conflict management*

by methods such as persuasion, negotiation, influence, and so on. If these fail to settle the conflict, there may be a phase of polarization and the use of threat and coercion. Threat can lead to crisis and crisis can lead to war. War may be ended by a cease-fire, which in turn can lead to a peace settlement. This may be followed by reconciliation between the parties.

At any of these stages corrective action may avert the further development of conflict. Figure 3.1 also shows the forms of conflict management that may be used at different times. At the earliest stages, conflicts can be prevented before they have become overt, or good management and peaceful social change can remove the precipitating factors. It is difficult to record a prevented conflict, since by definition it does not come into existence. Just as the prevention of road accidents involves good driving and clear traffic rules, so the prevention of conflict is a matter of the justice and acceptability of a political system which is capable of accommodating change. Other responses to conflict at the early stage are to avoid it or to suppress it.

Conflicts which are overt but noncoercive can be prevented from becoming coercive by 'conflict regulation', the adoption of procedures to limit the forms the conflict takes. For example, institutionalization is a widely used conflict regulation method. It does not resolve conflict, but it serves to prevent conflict becoming violent. At a later stage, if a conflict has become coercive, there are methods of regulating the forms that the coercion takes.

If war is imminent, crisis management can be used to prevent war breaking out. Crisis management does not aim to resolve the underlying conflict at issue, but to limit and contain the intensity of a conflict. Its purpose is to prevent escalation to subsequent stages.

If war has broken out, the first aim is usually to stop the fighting. 'Peace-making' by the UN or the international community usually means reaching a cease-fire and bringing the parties to the negotiating table. It does not necessarily include settling the underlying conflict. 'Peace-keeping' means policing a cease-fire, interposing UN observers or militias between opposed forces, and similar operations directed at preventing a war starting again once it has stopped.

These measures are all distinct from resolving conflict by reaching a political settlement between the parties. This can take place at any time after the stage when conflict has become overt and before the stage of reconciliation. According to this definition, conflict cannot be resolved until it has become overt. Before then, conflict is prevented. This is to distinguish the conditions which bring forth a clash of interests from the behaviour of the parties in response to these conditions. The former is the conflict situation; the latter is the conflict.

The Difference between Conflict Resolution and Conflict Prevention

Conflicts can be prevented from occurring at the outset, through good management, justice and sensitivity. It is arguable that such preventive action is the essence of good conflict management. This is, however, different from conflict resolution. Conflicts which do not have time to form can not be resolved.

Most organizations, communities and polities are constantly engaged in peaceful social change. They arrange and negotiate their affairs so that they take place smoothly, and they try to anticipate and deal with possible conflicts. This is an absolutely normal part of politics, and indeed of the management of any organization. Just as people on the street instinctively avoid bumping into one another, so people in societies conduct their affairs in ways which accommodate each other. Basic co-operation is essential to social functioning, and it takes place all the time.

On the other hand, we have also inherited from the past many 'unpeaceful' relationships. Many groups and communities also exploit others as a normal part of their affairs. To prevent conflict in such situations is simply to maintain the exploitative relationships. In principle it is possible to prevent the exploitative relationships forming in the first place, given a sufficient degree of communication and awareness. If richer and poorer communities, centres and peripheries, advanced and less advanced areas acted in full awareness of each other's needs, on a just and equal basis, they should be able to prevent relationships of domination from developing. This is the equivalent of conflict prevention in asymmetric conflicts. But it does not always happen in practice, and then conflict – and conflict resolution – is needed.

CONFLICT RESOLUTION

The term 'conflict resolution' is used in two senses, one normative, the other descriptive.

In the normative sense, 'conflict resolution' can be defined as a change in a situation which removes a perceived conflict in a manner which is acceptable to the parties. A peaceful resolution is the achievement of such a resolution without violence, and a just resolution is one that is fair to both or all the parties. Peaceful, just resolution is the ideal. In practice many settlements fall short of it.

In the descriptive sense, 'conflict resolution' is often used to mean the way a conflict ends, irrespective of whether all the parties find the outcome acceptable. A wider term is certainly needed, since many conflicts end in outcomes that fail to satisfy one or both of the parties. In the wider sense, 'conflict resolution' would include outcomes which end conflict by coercive means (including for example the total destruction of Carthage by Rome).

To avoid such confusions, in this book the definition of conflict resolution will be taken as a change in the situation which removes the underlying source of conflict. This may come about through the agreement of the parties, but it may also happen through a change in relationships between them, or through the dissolution and replacement of the original parties. If a conflict is settled by the military victory of one side and the other does not accept the outcome and begins organizing another fight, the underlying conflict has clearly not been removed and such a conflict would not be considered resolved.

The term 'settlement' is used to denote conflicts which are ended, either by agreement or by acceptance of the parties, even though the underlying conflict of interest may not have been resolved. A useful way of defining a settlement is that it brings conflict behaviour to an end, though conflict attitudes and an underlying conflict structure may persist (Mitchell, 1981, p. 275).

Settlement suggests finality, but it is not uncommon for 'settled' conflicts to be re-opened. States sometimes find it in their interests to re-activate territorial conflicts that had previously been settled (for example, Iraq–Iran). Interethnic agreements sometimes come unstuck as situations change (the Moldavians in the USSR would be a case in point). One could define a settlement as lasting a week, or a number of years, or up to a certain date. It is difficult ever to be sure that an apparently settled conflicts will not resume. For this reason, it might be sensible to talk merely of 'settlement attempts', recognizing that one conflict might have many settlement attempts. One could never be sure that the most recent settlement was the last. The uncertainty in the definition reflects the real uncertainty in the conflict.

Many conflicts are never settled at all, but simply lapse or become merged into other disputes. Since states are often unwilling to accept outcomes they consider unsatisfactory, but may not wish to actively prosecute conflict, it is common for conflicts to be allowed to lapse.

In other cases some issues are settled, while others remain. These are partially settled conflicts. The parties may continue to prosecute the conflict over the remaining issues or allow them to lapse.

VIOLENCE

Violence is another difficult concept. In situations of injustice, a narrow definition can appear loaded. The powerful party may condemn the violence of a rebellion by the weaker and assert the need for law and order, but injustice is itself a form of violence. This is recognized in ordinary language when we say that unjust acts 'do violence' to the victims.

Different definitions of violence lead adversaries to blame each other for aggression. For example, in South Africa, the Afrikaners regarded themselves as under attack when the black opposition parties, who have taken up armed struggle against them. On the other side the black population saw itself as having been under attack for years from the injustices perpetrated by apartheid.

Many peace researchers advocate a wide definition and would regard violence as anything which prevents the fulfilment and development of human potential. Accordingly, 'structural violence' or 'institutional violence' can include unintentional damage resulting from unequal economic and social structures. This usage does lose some of the word's power for, while one can do violence to someone in various ways, one can hardly 'do structural violence' to them. There is an important distinction between intentional armed violence, intentional exploitation and the haphazard infliction of suffering through economic forces, even if their effects on innocents may be much the same.

Violence is a form of coercion; but not all coercion is necessarily violent. Violence must be damaging and destructive; this is part of the concept. Some forms of coercion can be constructive, especially if they are carried out with the interests of the recipient in mind. It is difficult to say the same of violence. For example, preventing children from running into a road, or preventing mentally disturbed people from damaging themselves and others, are constructive uses of coercion. Virtually all societies accept the legitimacy of some forms of coercion, but some forms are disputed and some are considered illegitimate.

Difficulties arise when different communities attempt to coerce each other, because such coercion is rarely regarded as acceptable. Yet the relationships between communities can become so unjust that coercion may seem fully legitimate to the instigator.

A distinction should then be made between different forms of coercion. The following list, which is not exhaustive, illustrates the range:

1. nonviolent forms of coercion, such as occupations, sit-ins, strikes, lockouts, boycotts, withdrawal of normal services, trade sanctions, and so on;
2. use of legal instruments and legitimate authorities;
3. deliberate use of social or economic structures to exploit and oppress;
4. harassment or small-scale violence (for example, by police of an ethnic minority, or against members of one community by members of another);
5. organized use (or threat) of armed force.

Conflicts involving constructive coercion (as in the first category, and sometimes the second) can be considered as non-violent conflicts; conflicts involving destructive coercion (as in the other categories) can be considered as violent conflicts. A useful further distinction is that between conflicts with hostilities and conflicts without.

PEACEFUL SETTLEMENT

This brings us to the definition of the central topic of this book, 'peaceful settlement' of conflicts. Not surprisingly, this too is used in different ways in ordinary speech. People refer to conflicts resolved both before and after fighting as peacefully settled. A restrictive definition is that the conflict must be settled before violence has taken place. A wider definition is that the conflict is settled in such a way that further violence is averted. For example, one might say that the conflict between Egypt and Israel was peacefully settled by the peace treaty of 1979, because this prevented further wars that would have almost certainly otherwise have taken place, even though it came after four wars had been fought. Another possible definition is that the settlement is reached by pacific means (such as negotiation, arbitration, mediation or judicial settlement), irrespective of when it is reached. A conflict that had previously been violent could be settled by these means.

In this book, 'peacefully settled' conflicts are defined in the restrictive sense, to mean conflicts settled without violence. This is the sense which seems to be intended by the UN Charter and similar international instruments.

NOTE

1. The Permanent Court of International Justice (ICJ) adopted a definition of a dispute as a 'a disagreement on a point of law or fact, a conflict of legal views or interests between two persons: see *Mavrommati's Palestine Concessions (Preliminary objections)*. But H. G. Darwin, writing in *International Disputes: The Legal Aspects* (London: Europa, 1972) says that 'the concept of a dispute should be understood in a wide and non-technical sense. Whenever States advance opposed views about a subject matter of common interest, it may be said that there is a dispute.' He suggests three criteria for an international dispute: (a) it must be between States; (b) it must be active (that is, if it has lapsed through inaction it is no longer a dispute; (c) there must be a defined subject matter in dispute.

Part 2

How can Conflicts be Peacefully Settled?

4   The Theory of Conflict
       Resolution

Is it possible to develop a general theory, or a set of guidelines, which sets out the conditions under which conflicts are peacefully resolved? Such a theory could then be tested against the conflicts of the recent past and used to guide action in the future.

Does such a theory already exist? Important contributions have been made towards a theory of conflict and conflict resolution. Much is known about third-party intervention and negotiations, but we lack a really adequate theory of the dynamics of conflict de-escalation. There is no good general understanding of the conditions under which some conflicts are resolved peacefully.

This chapter presents a set of propositions about factors conducive to peaceful settlement of conflicts in the context of a theoretical approach which is widely accepted by students of conflict and conflict resolution.

CONFLICT THEORY

Galtung (1989) proposed that conflict could be viewed as a triangle (Figure 4.1), with *structure*, *attitudes* and *behaviour* at its vertices.

Structure refers to the conflict situation, the parties, and the conflict of interest between them. Conflict arises where parties come to have incompatible interests, values or goals. These constitute the objective conditions of the conflict, irrespective of the way the parties respond to them and to each other. A conflict is removed only when the situation is changed in such a way that the conflict of interests is dissolved (or transformed). An example of a conflict structure is the system of competing alliances that developed among the Greek city states before the Peloponnesian War. The mutual threat between these alliances

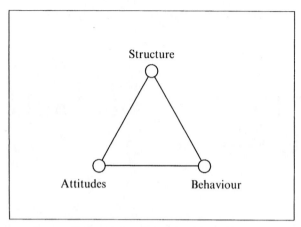

FIGURE 4.1   *The conflict triangle*

constituted a symmetric conflict structure. Another example is the Venetian domination of the Adriatic coastal economy in the fifteenth and sixteenth centuries. The Venetians insisted that all the trade of the Adriatic should go through Venice, thereby enriching themselves at the expense of the other coastal cities. This trading structure created an asymmetric conflict, which led to the outbreak of fighting (Braudel, 1979, pp. 36–8).

Attitudes and perceptions are critical in conflicts. Almost everyone has a tendency to see conflicts from their own point of view, to identify with their own side, and to diminish the concerns of the other. This bias is reinforced by the tendency of leaders to advance their own side's interests. In conflicts, misperceptions increase and understanding of other parties' needs and interests diminishes. At the same time frustration, irritation and anger develop, further blocking communication. Groups develop double standards, seeing their own behaviour as reasonable, but the same behaviour on the part of adversaries as malicious. They form stereotypes of each other, and develop 'enemy images'. The members of the in-group project their own destructive feelings on to the out-group, and see the out-group as aggressive and wicked. The out-group reciprocates. Mutual hostility flares up quickly, each party's hostility feeding the other's. Acts of perceived hostility evoke a fearful, defensive reaction, which itself tends to produce threatening or aggressive behaviour.

Behaviour is the third component of conflict. When groups begin to coerce one another, or damage one another, overt conflict behaviour is present. Behaviour also includes gestures and communications, and these can convey a hostile or a conciliatory intent. The choice parties make between co-operative and coercive forms of behaviour has a clear bearing on whether conflict escalates or not.

Structure, attitudes and behaviour change over time and affect one another. People who perceive a conflict of interest feel threatened and tense, and these feelings may lead to hostile behaviour. Alternatively conciliatory acts soften attitudes and create a basis for changing the structure of the conflict.

Let us look in more detail at how conflict structures can be changed, how attitudes become less antagonistic, and how coercive behaviour becomes co-operative.

THE STRUCTURE OF CONFLICT

Two factors related to conflict structure influence the prospect of peaceful outcomes: the first is what the dispute is about; the second is how successfully the conflict structure is changed.

The Nature of the Dispute

The nature of a dispute is clearly an important factor in how it is resolved. One would expect conflicts in which the parties threaten one another's existence to be more violent and more difficult to resolve than conflicts which do not challenge parties' central goals.

Conflicts can be divided into conflicts of interest, conflicts over values and conflicts over relationships (Mitchell, 1981). For example, a dispute over territory or oil is a dispute over an interest, whereas a conflict over religion, ideology or ethnicity is a dispute about values. Conflicts between a colonial power and the colony's inhabitants, between a minority and a majority, and between a ruling class and a ruled class are disputes about relationships.

The importance of a conflict to a party depends on how much it values the goals which it believes to be under threat. A dispute over a relatively insignificant piece of territory is unlikely to be regarded, in itself, as a major threat to a nation. On the other hand, a conflict over a resource which is perceived as essential for the security and survival of a nation is likely to result in an intense conflict. An interruption of oil supplies to the Western industrialized countries might be seen as such a conflict.

Conflicts over interests may be intense, but the parties usually agree about what the conflict is about and the possible outcomes are fairly clear-cut. The mechanisms for resolving such conflicts are relatively well established. In contrast, conflicts of values are, in principle, more difficult to resolve, because the parties may not agree on what the conflict is about and are usually unwilling to compromise their values. In ethnic conflicts, for example, people who feel that their group identity is under threat are also likely to experience a threat to their individual identity and their sense of self (Horowitz, 1985). Similarly religious and ideological conflicts threaten values by which people define themselves.

Conflicts over values can be resolved by agreeing to live with and respect value differences, by adopting shared values, or by change in one or both of the conflicting values. But such solutions take time to bring about, and while they are unresolved value conflicts engender much hostility and misunderstanding.

Conflicts over relationships are sometimes the most difficult to resolve. They cannot be ended without a change in relationship which affects both parties. Asymmetric conflicts are disputes of this type. If one party is benefiting from a relationship at the expense of the other, it is likely to resist change. Such conflicts sometimes involve the very composition of a society into parties. A resolution then needs to forge a new set of relationships within society, possibly involving the creation of new groups.

Often these three kinds of conflict are mixed up. Jorge Luis Borges described the Falklands conflict as 'a quarrel between two bald men over a comb'. Although the Falkland Islands were of little value to either contestant as territory, both sides turned the conflict into a dispute about values: Argentina treated it as a dispute about decolonization; Britain treated it as a conflict about the principle of resisting aggression. If the 'value' elements in the conflict were separated from the 'interest' elements, it might become easier to resolve. As the Falklands conflict developed the governments on both sides became committed to winning it, so it became a conflict of survival. As these governments pass, the issues involved will probably come to seem less crucial and more tractable.

In asymmetric conflicts, a dispute over a relationship is usually mixed up with a clash in values. 'Bottom-dogs' tend to see conflicts in terms of justice and injustice, while 'top-dogs' see them in terms of law and order and stability. In such disputes parties often fail to comprehend each other and are unable to speak in each other's terms. Each sees the other as a threat to cherished values which can only be dealt with by violence.

However small or great the conflict, what matters is how the parties perceive their situation, not how it might appear to an independent observer. Social psychologists have shown that prior beliefs and assumptions, biases, attitudes and cognitive structures affect perceptions in conflict (Mitchell, 1981, pp. 71–119). Mechanisms like in-group loyalty and projection tend to magnify a sense of threat once groups are in conflict.

Within groups, there is usually a range of perceptions of what a conflict is about and how serious it is. This may be accompanied by disagreement about goals and priorities. In small groups, leaders often promote strong views, even if they simplify the situation, and pressures are brought to bear on the group's members to conform. Within large societies, disagreements are organized around political parties or factions. 'War' parties tend to emphasize the imminence of threats to society's survival. 'Peace' parties have the job of arguing that the conflict is not necessarily so serious and that agreement with the adversary is possible. Whether or not a conflict is resolved peacefully may depend on which party can impose its perception of the situation.

Transforming the Structure of Conflict

Since the basis of conflict is the clash of interests, values and goals, conflicts can only be resolved when these are changed. They can change either because the parties alter their positions, or because of a more fundamental change in the situation.

In conflicts of interest, it is the perceived clash of interests which matters most, and drives parties' behaviour. Even if the parties' real interests are actually reconcilable, this will be irrelevant if the parties act on the assumption that they are not. This is a very common situation, because parties often move quickly into conflict without exploring common ground. There is scope for resolving such conflicts by creating options which open apparently closed situations, and render apparently incompatible positions compatible.

Fisher and Ury (1983) tell a story which illustrates the idea:

> [There are] two men quarrelling in a library. One wants the window open and the other wants it closed. They bicker back and forth about how much to leave it open: a crack, halfway, three quarters of the way. No solution satisfies them both.

Enter the librarian. She asks one why he wants the window open: 'To get some fresh air'. She asks the other why he wants it closed: 'To avoid the draft'. After thinking for a minute, she opens wide a window in the next room, bringing in fresh air without a draft.

Fisher and Ury comment:

> This story is typical of many negotiations. Since the parties' problem appears to be a conflict of positions, and since their goal is to agree on a position, they naturally tend to think and talk about positions – and in the process often reach an impasse.
>
> The librarian could not have invented the solution she did if she had focused only on the two men's stated positions of wanting the window open or closed. Instead she looked at their underlying interests of fresh air and no draft. This difference between positions and interests is crucial.
>
> Reconciling interests rather than positions works for two reasons. First, for every interest there usually exist several positions that could satisfy it. All too often people simply adopt the most obvious position, as Israel did, for example, in announcing that they intended to keep part of the Sinai. When you do look behind opposed positions for the motivating interests, you can often find an alternative position which meets not only your interests but theirs as well. In the Sinai, demilitarisation was one such alternative.

The key to the resolution here is to transform a zero-sum conflict (where interests are incompatible) into a non-zero-sum conflict where the parties have common interests in the settlement. Figure 4.2 shows this in diagrammatic terms. This kind of conflict resolution is creative because, by looking beyond the conflict as the parties currently define it, it aims to find ways in which their interests can be made compatible.

However, there are situations where parties in conflict have real and objective clashes of interest, which they cannot accommodate by finding common ground. For example, the gold-diggers in Brazil have a real conflict with the indigenous Indians of the rain forests; each group's livelihood is in jeopardy if the other's is secure. Such a conflict can only be resolved by one of the groups changing: the gold-diggers have to find an alternative means of livelihood, or the Indians have to give up their traditional habitat and way of life. Given that the gold-diggers' interest is in economic survival, not destroying the habitat of the Indians, an economic policy that created an alternative

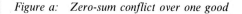

Figure a: *Zero-sum conflict over one good*

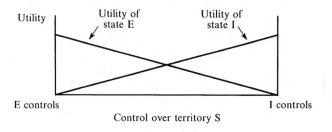

Figure b: *Non-zero-sum conflict over two goods*

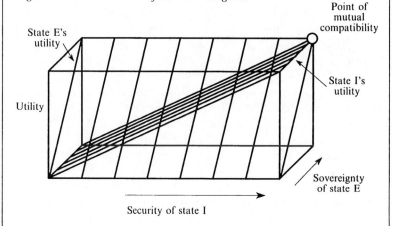

Figure a shows the classic diagram of a zero-sum conflict where states E and I contest control of the territory S. The two sloping lines show the utility or preference curves of the two states. Any gain by one party means a loss for the other. Figure b suggests that the conflict can be resolved if it is disaggregated into the parties' underlying interests. Here the utility curves are two planes, aligned at right angles to one another, so that a point exists which is a maximum for both parties. In this example the conflict over territory S can be disaggregated into state E's need for sovereignty and state I's need for security. Since these can be independent of one another, a mutually satisfactory outcome is possible.

Figure b is derived from figure a by disaggregating the dispute into two issues and rotating them to make them independent.

FIGURE 4.2 *Transforming a zero-sum into a non-zero-sum conflict*

occupation for them would resolve the situation. However, in the absence of such outside help, the conflict is very real.

The 'tragedy of the commons' is another example of a real conflict of interest. Farmers grazing their sheep compete for ever-dwindling common lands. Each farmer, acting on his own, is in conflict with others as the common land diminishes. But if the farmers form a condominium to manage the commons together the conflict is eliminated. The parties redefine themselves and this transforms the conflict structure. This is a common solution in resource conflicts. Indeed, redefinition of identity is a common way of resolving conflicts generally. For example, the conflict between landlords and peasants in China was transformed by both becoming farmers in a collectivized agricultural system. The long conflict in the sixteenth and seventeenth centuries between Protestant and Catholic princes was eventually ended as the principalities evolved into nation states concerned more about trade and colonies than religious affiliations.

Conflict structures are defined by the positions parties take, the situation they are in, and the relationships between them. As parties change their positions, or the situation changes for external reasons, the structure gradually shifts. The purpose of negotiations and mediation is to explore such change of positions. Acts of conciliation, concessions, and reciprocal moves put such changes into effect.

To conclude: conflict structures change by parties reformulating their interests, finding compatibility in their underlying interests, or changing their interests. Alternatively they can change by parties redefining themselves and their relationships. Since these are fundamental changes, they are often resisted. For this reason it is usually harder to bring about changes in structure than in attitudes or behaviour.

ALTERING ATTITUDES

Stereotypes and misperceptions tend to develop in conflicts, accompanied by hostility, anger, hatred and rage. As these emotions build up and conflict becomes more intense, stress and tension are generated. Tension is an almost tangible indicator of conflict, present in impending riots and at moments of crisis between states.

Antagonistic attitudes are less likely to develop if parties are aware of each other's needs, understand each other and have some empathy for each other's positions. In particular, it is important that parties should clearly hear each other's grievances and show that they are prepared to communicate about them. Where this is possible, the development of frustration and anger can be averted. There is plentiful evidence that the mere airing of grievances, for example in negotiations, or pre-negotiation talks, can lead to substantial improvement of attitudes.

Conciliatory acts and co-operative communications are crucial for softening angry attitudes. Powerful unilateral gestures, like the visit of Sadat to Jerusalem, can suddenly alter the prevailing attitudes.

When attitudes are negative and the conflict of interest is severe, parties tend to polarize. People are forced to take sides, communication becomes difficult between people on opposite sides, and subsidiary issues are swept into the main conflict. An example of this process is the polarization that took place between the southern and northern states of America in the period 1800–60 before the Civil War (Miall, 1975). Between countries, polarization takes the form of suspension of trade, reduction in travel and severing of diplomatic exchanges. This happened between Britain and Argentina before the Falklands War (De Reuck, 1989a).

As polarization and tension develop, the likelihood of violence grows. The onset of violence is a sharp turning point, usually associated with a great increase in hostility. Violent acts replace other forms of communication in a destructive drama.

After this point, conflict is harder to resolve. Nevertheless some degree of tension and polarization may be helpful for a settlement, for it is when parties are intensely engaged with one another and recognize that they are at an impasse that they may be willing to change their course.

The existence of tension then provides a pscyhological incentive for settling, since movement towards a settlement releases the tension. Gradual reductions and relaxations in tension provide the momentum that is needed to improve relations and find a settlement.

Just as relaxation of tensions can open a path towards a settlement, so can the building-up of communications: this is the opposite of polarization. A process of 'détente' is typically marked by measures such as improvement of diplomatic facilities, increase of trade, cultural contacts, opening of new transport links and the development of citizen-to-citizen exchanges. These processes help to overcome hostile stereotypes and restore contact between isolated communities. This took place between East and West Germany during the period

preceding the end of the Cold War, and in a number of the other
disputes considered later.

CHANGING BEHAVIOUR: FROM COERCION TOWARDS CO-OPERATION

Research into conflicts at many levels has shown that parties tend to
reciprocate each other's moves. Coercive moves tend to produce
coercive reactions, co-operative moves tend to produce co-operative
reactions (Deutsch, 1973; 1987). When parties coerce each other,
hostility tends to escalate. At a certain point in this cycle there is a
'lock-in' effect, where the two parties effectively lose their freedom of
action and settle down to fight (Smoker, 1969). A similar effect has
been found in gaming experiments with the prisoner's dilemma
(Rapoport and Chammah, 1965, p. 195). It is therefore important
that parties should break out of a cycle of coercive behaviour before it
becomes deadlocked. It is usually much more difficult to resolve
conflict if war has broken out or blood has been shed.

How do people break out of conflicts? Usually one party makes a
move, gesture or signal signifying intent either to co-operate or to
desist from coercion. The other side then reciprocates. A 'benign' cycle
may follow, with moves that undo hostility on both sides.

If conflict has reached a point where both sides have imposed costs
on each other, a shared interest is created in ending the conflict. An
initial stage of confrontation, then, can also be helpful because it
creates this mutual interest. The momentum that the co-operative
moves set up away from conflict may then lead the parties to a
settlement.

It is also possible, of course, that coercive moves by one side may
force the other to submit, or that a coercive move after a sequence of
co-operative moves may smash the possibility of a settlement. Just as
the abandonment of coercive moves can lead towards resolution, so
the failure of moves towards resolution can lead quickly to violence.
Alternatively, a sequence of co-operative and coercive moves may
succeed one another in a complex pattern which makes the outcome
uncertain.

Conflicts can sometimes be defused by measures which are not
directly related to the main issues. For example, the conclusion of
trade agreements, establishment of communications links and restoration of diplomatic ties may foster a steady improvement in relations.

At the end of it, the resolution of the outstanding issues in conflict may seem a foregone conclusion.

How are resolutions reached if one party is willing to co-operate but the other responds with coercion? Must such a conflict slip back into a coercive cycle?

Sometimes it does. However, the most interesting case is where the coerced party resists without itself coercing, and draws the coercing party into a constructive process of engagement. This is a matter of selecting actions which affirm the party's position without attacking the other side, and choosing constructive moves which suggest a way forward. If a threat is made, the response is to withdraw co-operation rather than to retaliate with coercion. Gandhi's campaigns of non-violence always had this affirming character. The skilful campaign of Lech Walesa and Solidarity in Poland succeeded in engaging the government and avoiding a violent conflict.

THE PROCESS OF CONFLICT RESOLUTION

In order to wind down and resolve a conflict, it is necessary to affect structure, attitudes and behaviour together. In practice they all affect one another, and it would be an oversimplification to suggest that movements towards co-operative behaviour or friendlier attitudes necessarily contribute towards resolutions. Generally conflicts take an uneven course, sometimes dampening, sometimes escalating. Structure, attitudes and behaviour are like three great cog-wheels, with structure moving more slowly than attitudes, and behaviour more quickly. Usually the cog-wheels turn together, though with a good deal of slippage and jerkiness. The trick is to find a way to turn them into reverse.

There are two main phases in conflict when resolution is more likely to be achieved. The first is at an early stage, before attitudes become too fixed and behaviour too hostile. The second is at a later stage when the conflict has become a costly stalemate and the parties are exhausted.

At the early stage, the following conditions can be expected to be conducive to peaceful settlement:

1. the existence of channels of communication or fora through which the parties can communicate about their conflict;

2. the opportunity for parties to air their grievances, thus relieving anger and frustration;
3. the presence of third parties capable of engaging the trust of both sides, who can relay messages, reduce misperceptions, interpret one party to another, and make suggestions;
4. the making of gestures, including declarations of intent to settle peacefully, or in some other way the communication of a serious intent to seek a peaceful settlement;
5. the use of existing procedures for settling the dispute, or the creation of new procedures, irrespective of the content of the dispute;
6. the making of reciprocal moves to reduce tension and edge towards settlement.

Channels of communication are essential to explore possible settlements, but they are often difficult to set up. In polarized situations communications are cut, and when there is distrust and violence it can be positively dangerous to communicate with the other side. Among nations, formal diplomatic channels usually exist as well as permanent agencies such as the UN and the regional organizations which have a mandate for assisting in the settlement of disputes. Among non-national groups, even these channels do not exist. It can be extremely difficult for a guerrilla group to communicate with a government, or a liberation movement with a colonial government. If one party denies the other's legitimacy, any communication becomes taboo because it implies recognition. In such circumstances mediation by third parties plays an important role.

Third parties play the crucial role of being impartial, or at least outside the conflict, and it is often easier for parties to communicate with an intermediary than with each other. There is a substantial literature on this type of intervention (Young, 1967; Northedge and Donelan, 1971; E. B. Haas, Butterworth and Nye, 1972; Bailey, 1982; Allsebrook, 1986; Bercovitch, 1986). Essential functions of mediation include carrying proposals and messages between parties, and assisting them to reach the point where they can negotiate directly.

When the parties come together it is helpful to have a phase of 'letting off steam', in which the parties simply vent their grievances and express their anger. When this stage is over, the parties can begin to analyse and explore what the conflict is really about, with the help of questions from the third party. It is usually found that the parties have a poor understanding of each other's positions and there is sometimes more ground for agreement than they expected. The negotiations should allow parties to explore fundamental values and needs. At an appropriate stage, options for reconciling these needs can then be considered (Burton, 1969; 1987; Azar and Burton, 1986).

Unfortunately mediation and third-party intervention often take place only after armed conflict has broken out. Yet it is in the period before potential armed conflict that it may be most needed. In many conflicts, especially at an early stage, international agencies are unable freely to intervene because they might be seen as interfering in the affairs of a sovereign state. Nations rarely regard it as being in the national interest to intervene at an early stage to resolve conflicts in which they are not involved. Moreover, non-governmental bodies lack the resources to become deeply involved in potential conflict situations, especially when ongoing armed conflicts seem more pressing.

At this stage, then, communications are usually left to the parties themselves. Sometimes they are amicable and successful and the conflict is resolved; sometimes they break down in misperception and mistrust. If the parties are not even prepared to negotiate with each other, as is often the case, violence may seem the only recourse.

Decision-making in Conflict

Ultimately conflict will not be resolved unless parties are themselves willing to seek a settlement. A critical question, then, is what makes parties willing to settle? Figure 4.3 shows some of the factors involved.

Considerations of rational decision-making suggest that when the expected costs of conflict are high, compared with the expected costs of settlement, then settlement is more likely to be preferred. The costs of conflict are likely to be seen as high if the party is vulnerable, or if the party is weak relative to the adversary. The cost of conflict is also high if the party values its relationship with the adversary, or if the party dislikes using violence. The costs of settling will be high if the party has to abandon important goals or if concessions undermine domestic support. On the other hand the costs of settling may seem low, and the benefits of settling high, if the settlement meets the goals of the party. The party's evaluation of these costs and benefits and, indeed, its goals may change during the course of the conflict, so that irreconcilable gaps at the outset become narrowed, or narrow differences become irreconcilable.

Decision-makers can rarely predict what course the conflict will take. It is difficult to predict either what costs will have to be borne, or

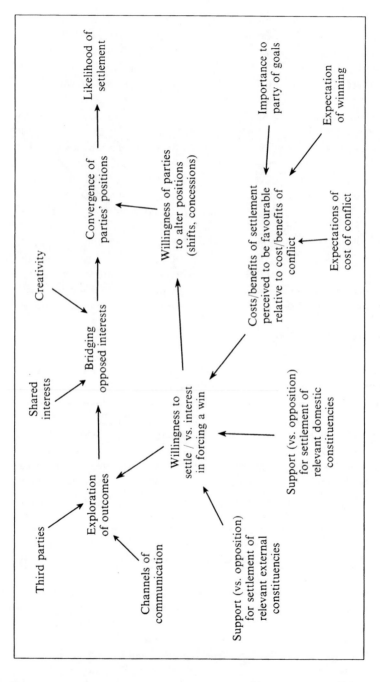

FIGURE 4.3 *Factors influencing conflict settlement*

what benefits will accrue. The conflict may widen, other parties may enter, the domestic repercussions may be larger than expected. Decision-making is therefore a matter of judgement rather than of calculation.

Moreover, outcomes are determined not by the rationality of decision-making on either side, but by joint decisions. It is well established that, especially in conflict, individually rational decisions have collectively irrational results (Rapoport, 1989). It is typical that decision-makers on each side reason as follows: 'I am prepared to offer X (or Y) to move as far as that. But my public won't allow me to go further. So we will offer X (or Y), and if that's not accepted, we go to war. The decision is in the hands of the other side.' Whether war is avoided then depends on whether X and Y intersect.

Of course, the assumption that decision-makers are even individually rational may not always be sustained. Moreover, decision-makers may evaluate costs in idiosyncratic ways. For example, a leadership group may be concerned primarily with its own survival rather than the costs its nation may suffer. Parties' actions in conflict may themselves be outcomes of internal conflicts between factions, which may generate irrational outcomes at the level of the party. A party's willingness to settle is influenced in part by the balance of hawks and doves among the decision-makers, and by the support or opposition of relevant domestic and external constituencies; all these can vary for reasons having nothing to do with the conflict.

Figure 4.3 suggests two routes by which the parties' positions can converge. One is for either or both of the parties to make a sequence of moves which brings their positions closer together. These moves may be forced (as a result of coercion) or voluntary (as part of a co-operative quest for a settlement). Eventually, if there is enough movement, the conflict can be resolved.

The other route is through the discovery of creative outcomes which can bridge the interests of the parties without either having to make concessions. In order to discover such possibilities the parties need channels of communication through which they can explore mutually satisfactory outcomes.

Turning-points in Conflict

The moment when parties stop trying to impose a solution and start to seek a mutually acceptable outcome is a crucial turning-point in conflicts.

Curle (1986) writes that, 'in the slow move towards negotiation, settlement and the eventual restoration of fully peaceful relations, the significant stages are the changes of vision rather than the signing of agreements that result from them, the gradual erosion of fear, antipathy and suspicion, and the slow shift of public opinion'.

Rogers (1984) describes the moment during the Camp David talks when Begin and Sadat exchanged photographs of their grandchildren and, in the emotions of this moment, broke the deadlock. Such psychological turning points also occur in problem-solving workshops – the next chapter describes one of them (see pp. 74–5).

The importance of a vision of conflict as a whole is something that is stressed by statesmen, mediators and spiritual teachers. The Quakers 'tend to sympathise with both sides in an international dispute, as both are usually victims of past mistakes' (Bailey, 1985); Quakers believe there is 'that of God' in people on all sides. Gandhi had a similar idea in his view of the fundamental unity of human beings, which parties would struggle to find in conflict by respecting one another and seeking the truth (Naess, 1958). Buddhists see suffering and conflict as arising from a compartmentalization of reality. Liberation comes from awareness of the integrity of the whole. 'The two sides in a conflict are not really opposing, but two aspects of the same reality' (Nhat Hanh, 1976). Similarly, mediators speak of the necessity of being faithful to the conflict as a whole (Townsend, 1988).

THE CONTEXT OF CONFLICT

The nature of the international system shapes how conflicts are resolved in many ways. First, it still is predominantly an inter-*national* system. The UN is an organization of sovereign states, not a representative assembly for the world's citizens. The dispute settlement system is designed primarily for conflicts between states. It is not so well suited to managing conflicts between blocs or groupings of states, or to the most common conflicts today, which are civil conflicts or mixed civil/international conflicts that arise within states. The international system is founded on the principle of sovereignty, which gives nations, in principle, exclusive powers within their own borders. It is poorly equipped to deal with conflicts within nations.

The structure of power in the international system greatly affects the conflicts within it. During the Cold War, for example, the bipolar power structure made the ideological struggle between West and East an issue in many other conflicts. Recent movement towards a multi-polar system, in which the EC and the newly industrialized states play a larger role, is likely to lead to new patterns of conflict and conflict management.

Another contextual factor is the degree of interdependence between states. The growth of interdependence could make for co-operation or conflict. On the one hand, the costs of conflict become greater, as societies are more vulnerable to disruption and shared relationships are more important. If this leads to a more integrated world community, with shared agreements about how conflicts are to be managed, it may be conducive to peaceful settlements of conflicts. On the other hand, if the world becomes polarized into several large blocs which represent competing concentrations of power, with no common procedures for dispute settlement, then interdependence may make conflicts more likely to be resolved with violence. The global political structure is therefore an important factor.

In the long term, changes in the international system may have more influence on dispute settlement than any other factor. Perhaps there is an analogy in the development of dispute settlement systems within nations. In England, over quite a long period, the 'king's peace' replaced the wars of the barons. The barons were disarmed, a dispute settlement system based on the courts and the justices of the peace was created, and these were backed by a legitimate national authority. Even then the peace was shaky for many years, but since 1685 no further internal wars have been fought.

Radical cultural, economic and technological change is now under way in world society, comparable to the changes that in earlier periods laid a basis for political unification within states. If this leads to a process of international integration, disarmament and the strengthening of international law, a regime could evolve more conducive to the peaceful settlement of disputes than the one we have now.

5 Practitioners of Conflict Resolution

How can peaceful settlements be reached in practice? This chapter examines the views of people who have had direct personal experience in peacemaking, mediation and conflict resolution.

Perhaps the key figures are the diplomats, for it is on them that states place responsibility for reaching peaceful solutions. We begin with an examination of the peacemaking of the UN Secretary-General and his secretariat. Then we examine the practice of diplomats in the service of states. In communal and ethnic conflicts traditional diplomacy does not necessarily have a place. 'Second-track' diplomacy has developed to supplement traditional diplomacy in such situations. Third parties, usually academics or former diplomats with an interest in conflict resolution, invite representatives of opposing parties to attend a workshop to discuss the conflict across a table. A panel of facilitators directs the discussion. Another approach, also involving academics, is the use of new methods of negotiation, as practised by the Harvard Negotiating School. This is directed towards altering the parties' own negotiating behaviour. A rather different approach is mediation, which usually means separate discussions with parties before they have agreed to face-to-face negotiations. The Quakers have developed a distinctive tradition in mediation, and this is touched on here. Others use a mixture of mediation and facilitation.

It is also worth reviewing conflict resolution outside the arena of interstate and major civil conflicts, for the skills of peacemaking in one area may well have lessons for others. For example, industrial conciliation has a long record. The British Prime Minister and Foreign Secretary have advocated that the CSCE dispute settlement role should be based on the model of ACAS, so we shall look at the approach ACAS takes in industrial disputes.

Marital disputes are both common and bitter. While they involve very different considerations from international conflicts, the experience of mediating in disputes which are intensely emotionally charged may suggest insights into peacemaking at other levels. We look at how the Swindon Family Conciliation Service works in this area.

Disputes within and between organizations are also common and costly. A final section looks at the work of a consultant who advises clients experiencing the effects of this kind of conflict.

THE UN AND THE ROLE OF THE SECRETARY-GENERAL

The UN, as the prime body charged with maintaining international peace and justice, plays a crucial role in international peacemaking. Three of the principal organs of the UN share these responsibilities. The Security Council has the primary responsibility for maintaining international peace and security. It has powers under Chapter VI of the Charter to seek pacific settlement of disputes through investigation and by recommending appropriate procedures to the parties. If the parties fail to settle a dispute peacefully themselves, they are obliged to refer it to the Security Council, which may then recommend terms of a settlement. The Security Council also has powers under Chapter VII to enforce its resolutions.

The General Assembly has broad powers to discuss any issue within the scope of the Charter, and specifically to refer to the Security Council situations which are likely to endanger international peace and security. It can make recommendations to particular states and to the Security Council.

The Secretary-General has the power under Article 99 of the Charter to bring to the attention of the Security Council 'any matter which in his opinion may threaten the maintenance of international peace and security'. Due to his status, and because he is independent of any government, the Secretary-General is in a unique position to be a peacemaker. At times when the Security Council has been blocked by vetoes, Secretary-Generals and Assistant Secretary-Generals have been able to play a vital role as brokers of peaceful settlements.

One of the Secretary-General's most valuable powers is the exercise of his good offices. He can make enquiries into disputes, participate in negotiations with both sides, call representatives of parties together at the UN headquarters and dispatch representatives and fact-finding teams (Pecota, 1972). An example of such good offices was the

How can Conflicts be Peacefully Settled?

intervention of Dag Hammarskjöld in the dispute between Saudi Arabia, Abu Dhabi and Oman in 1963 (see Case 63). The intervention did not settle the conflict, but it did help avoid the escalation of violence.

In practice both the Security Council and the Secretary-General have been most conspicuous and most effective in bringing armed conflicts to an end, rather than in settling disputes before they become violent. In his annual report of 1990, the Secretary-General declared that 'the United Nations has had a remarkable success in conducting operations aimed at managing peaceful transition in societies which were the scenes of conflicts or had suffered upheavals' (UN, 1990). He referred to the settlement in Namibia, the new era in South Africa, the cease-fire in Nicaragua, which was verified by UN observers, the partial accord in El Salvador, the plan for a referendum in the Western Sahara, and the steps toward a negotiated settlement of the Cambodian conflict. Previously the Secretary-General had played an important role in negotiating the end of the Iran–Iraq war, among other disputes (Berridge, 1991).

The Secretary-General has also been seeking to strengthen the role of the organization in incipient conflicts. In 1990, and in previous years, Pérez de Cuéllar pointed out that 'the means at the disposal of the Secretary-General for gathering the timely, accurate and unbiased information that is necessary for averting violent conflict is inadequate'. He advised that 'the Organization's mediatory or investigative capacity should not be kept in reserve until it is too late to avert hostilities', and urged member states to 'consider afresh ways of enabling the Secretariat to monitor potential conflict situations from a clearly impartial standpoint' (UN, 1990). The Secretary-General set up a new organization in the secretariat to assist him with this effort, the Office of Research and Collection of Information (ORCI). Working under an Assistant Secretary-General, its role is to assess global trends relevant to peace and security, to prepare country and regional profiles to assist the Secretariat in its conflict resolution functions, and to provide early warnings of conflicts.

There are occasions when the Secretary-General mediates before a conflict has become dangerous. Pérez de Cuéllar's intercession between Libya and Malta in their dispute over their continental shelf was such a case (Skjelsbaek, 1991). However, the Secretary-General still seems conscious of the inadequacy of the UN's role in preventive diplomacy. Studies of the UN's case management effectiveness certainly suggest that the international organization, like the international community as a whole, pays relatively little attention to disputes which have not yet passed the threshold of violence (E.B. Haas, 1983; Sherman, 1987). It is not surprising that major crises and wars take up the majority of the Secretary-General's limited time. Nevertheless, there seems a clear opportunity for the UN, and especially the Secretariat, to extend its role in this area; the Secretary-General is evidently trying to seize it.

DIPLOMATS AS PEACEMAKERS

Diplomats work in the service of states and are therefore not impartial. Nevertheless, it is often in the interests of states to bring about peaceful settlements. The diplomats are the people most engaged in attempting to construct peaceful settlements of international disputes, both as negotiators for parties and as third parties in disputes in which their country has an interest.

The typical process of diplomatic peacemaking begins with an effort to construct an outline settlement. The parties set out their positions, and third parties propose formulae for settlements. They then exchange drafts with the parties and alter them progressively in an effort to close the differences. Often one initiative fails, only for its substance to be taken up in another. This is a learning process in which the parties gradually find out what will be acceptable to each other and alter their positions. Out of it a mutually acceptable settlement may emerge, or diplomacy may fail.

An example of this process is the efforts that US and British diplomats made to bring about the Zimbabwe settlement, (see Case 81). Stephen Low, a former US ambassador who was involved in the negotiations, has described what was done (Low, 1985). The mediating diplomats could not dictate the terms, though they had leverage, because the white government and the black liberation movements both feared that the West might support the other side. The mediators proceeded by putting forward formulae for a settlement, and discussing the points in these formulae with the parties in an effort to find agreement on a 'package deal'. The positions of the parties became clearer to the mediators, even while they remained far apart. When they reached an impasse, the mediators would sometimes give up for a while, but they would then make fresh proposals. If necessary the mediators were prepared to 'twist the arm' of the parties, and Kissinger was especially tough with the beleaguered white leader, Ian Smith. As the conflict continued and the position of the white government weakened, major concessions began to come. The white government first abandoned its hopes of retaining minority rule, and then accepted an internal settlement sharing power with Muzorewa and other black leaders. Again the USA and Britain used leverage. They put pressure on the whites by refusing to recognize the internal settlement, and on the blacks by threatening to recognize the Muzorewa government unless the guerrilla leaders participated in talks to settle the conflict. The combination of these pressures with a costly stalemate in the fighting and patient and sustained diplomacy over a four-year period eventually brought about the agreed settlement at the Lancaster House talks.

Chester Crocker, the US architect of the Namibia settlement (see Case 53), writes on how US diplomacy goes about conflict resolution in regional conflicts. (Crocker, 1990): 'When conflicts were not ripe, we have worked to ripen them. Some of our craftsmanship has enabled us to contain or manage festering conflicts, setting in place the building blocks of an ultimate settlement.' At the same time external powers can help to 'maintain and reinforce military stalemates', if need be through arms sales. In this way the USA worked to create the conditions necessary for a settlement, while persisting for over four years in arduous negotiations over the UN mechanisms for monitoring elections and controlling the local forces for the elections.

The hallmarks of diplomatic mediation, then, are long and patient positional bargaining, combined with a quest for package deals and a willingness to use leverage. It is often successful but, as with the intervention of the UN organs, it tends to be deployed effectively when situations have already reached a stalemate and the parties are willing to compromise, or when one party is near to admitting defeat. Positional bargaining may be less successful in identifying solutions and averting conflicts at an early stage.

NEW METHODS OF NEGOTIATION

Traditionally, diplomats learn diplomacy by doing it, but the skills of negotiation can, in principle, be learned and developed. Ury and Fisher of the Harvard Negotiating School study the process of negotiation and train negotiators. They are interested in both international and industrial disputes and believe that similar negotiating solutions apply.

Governments (and, for that matter, other parties to disputes) usually see the outcomes of conflicts in terms of winning, losing, or reaching a compromise. In contrast, Fisher and Ury are interested in integrative outcomes which can reconcile the basic interests of both sides. They distinguish between 'principles' and 'positions' in dispute, and urge parties to stand on their principles but be flexible on positions.

The idea is that beneath the stated interests or positions of each party are more basic values and principles, which may be reconcilable. One way to discover if they are is to draw an 'interests tree'. In this example (shown in Figure 5.1), a father and son are in conflict over a motorbike: the son wants to buy one, the father refuses. On the surface, the positions are irreconcilable. But, as Figure 5.1 shows, the underlying interests are not. The son wants to gain self-esteem. The father wants to live unobtrusively. These bottom-level interests can be reconciled if the son finds another way to gain self-esteem: perhaps by becoming a soccer star.

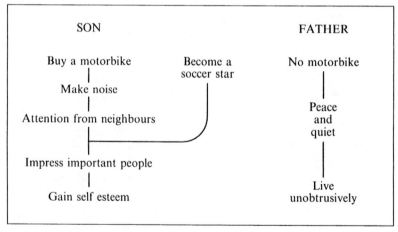

Source: Pruitt and Rubin (1986)

FIGURE 5.1 *An 'interests' tree*

Fisher and Ury also suggested the 'single-text' procedure which President Carter used successfully during the Camp David negotiations. Normally each party sets out its own position in a separate text and diplomats struggle to come to a mutually acceptable draft. In the 'single-text' procedure a third party prepares a draft, to which neither side is committed, and offers it to each side for criticism. The mediator then modifies the draft to incorporate the criticisms and then asks for more criticisms. This process is continued and, if successful, it leads to a draft agreement.

Another approach which aims to distinguish underlying interests from positions is the 'problem-solving workshop'.

PROBLEM-SOLVING WORKSHOPS

Problem-solving workshops aim to bring representatives of parties together in an unofficial setting, to assist them to explore the conflict and possible solutions. The essence of this approach is that the discussion is uncommitted. The parties can explore options in an open, analytical way, outside the framework of traditional diplomatic negotiation.

The technique was invented in the 1950s at University College London, and is particularly associated with the name of John Burton, an Australian diplomat turned academic. In 1965, Burton and others brought together representatives of the Indonesian and Malaysian governments to discuss the then current armed conflict between the two states. A panel of academics supervised the workshop, which lasted for four days. It is difficult to be sure of the effect of this workshop, but shortly afterwards the two sides' governments agreed to resume negotiations and the fighting between them came to an end.

The workshop typically involves four phases (Burton, 1987). In the first, each party states its position. This is the 'grievance-airing' phase, and can be quite noisy and abusive. When this phase has run its course, there is a second phase of questioning and elucidation, where the panel invites each side to pose questions to the other. The purpose is to elicit information and improve understanding of each side's views. Then there is a phase where the parties and the panel analyse the conflict together. In the final phase they attempt to agree solutions.

In the analytical stage, the panel attempts to define the common interests, needs and values of the parties, as well as those that divide them. Often the parties are not aware of what each others' underlying needs are. Consequently in the process of exploration solutions may arise out of the analysis.

There is a psychological dynamic to these meetings. De Reuck (1989b), one of the pioneers of this approach, reports on a moment in one such workshop when, after several days of putting their governments' positions, the parties suddenly stopped making accusations and began to look one another in the face, to laugh and to talk freely. 'Quite suddenly a wave of euphoria went around everybody. The group developed a sense of solidarity and a common task. They began to think of each other as people and not as opponents . . . I believe that at this point, the parties have come to reperceive their situation not as a conflict, but as a predicament.' De Reuck goes on to say:

> In this mood of euphoria the group disperses, thinking that at last we're a group that can talk turkey, that understands one another. We have developed a common language through the analysis and we can proceed along these lines.
>
> When they get back in the morning a catharsis has set in. Everyone is crestfallen. 'Why on earth were we so confident last night? We have achieved nothing. Nothing has changed. It's all an illusion. We're not really making progress.'
>
> However, what then ensued was a new concentration on the task in hand, no longer on analysis, but on concrete proposals and a discussion of what could be done. The tenor of the meeting had moved from ventilation to analysis and from analysis into an instrumental phase of actually trying to solve the problem.

The aim is that the participants should realize that there are prizes that they can conceivably take home: the prize of realizing that they need not continue to prosecute their conflict in the same costly and fruitless way. But one of the difficulties is that those who are so persuaded will not necessarily carry conviction with their colleagues and leaders at home, who have not been through the same process. Nevertheless, it is claimed that the workshop approach shows that parties are willing to co-operate in analysing conflicts, and that in some cases the workshops may stimulate the convening of direct negotiations, in otherwise blocked situations.

Chris Mitchell, a participant in several early workshops, set out the rationale for them (Mitchell, 1989). He says:

> It starts from the assumption that the normal mode of interaction between representatives of parties in intense conflict is dysfunc-tional, that it actually prevents creative thinking, it prevents people emerging from entrenched positions, so there must be a better arena in which adversaries can look at their problems in a quasi-objective way. The basic idea behind the problem-solving workshop is to provide an island of stability to get people to think creatively about

the problem, to realise that they both have a problem and they're both part of each other's problem. The most important effect of the workshops may be to influence attitudes and perceptions towards the conflict.

QUAKER MEDIATION

Another distinctive third-party approach to conflict is Quaker mediation. The Quakers believe that there is 'that of God' in every person, and refuse, in the words of the 1660 peace testimony, to 'fight or war against any man with outward weapons', preferring instead to attempt peacemaking and reconciliation between warring parties. A tradition of Quaker peacemaking goes back to William Penn's efforts to reach a peace agreement with the American Indians living near the new colony of Pennsylvania, in the eighteenth century. Quakers have attempted to mediate in many of the major conflicts since 1945, including work between the two Germanies following the construction of the Berlin Wall, mediation between Pakistan and India, contacts between the parties involved in Zimbabwe's independence, and mediation in the civil conflict in Sri Lanka (Yarrow, 1978).

The purpose of Quaker mediation is to bring the parties in conflict to the point where they are willing to talk to each other. For this reason, Quakers usually approach the parties separately, often shuttling between capitals. If the parties agree to enter into direct negotiation, the mediation phase is over. But it is this initial phase, in which the parties decide to enter into negotiations, which is often the crux of the problem. As Adam Curle (1986) says:

> What mediators do is to try to establish, or re-establish, sufficiently good communications between conflicting parties so that they can talk sensibly to each other without being blinded by such emotions as anger, fear and suspicion. This does not necessarily resolve the conflict; mediation has to be followed by skilled negotiation, usually directly between the protagonists, supported by a measure of mutual tolerance and determination to reach agreement. But it is a good start.

Speaking of his own experience, Adam Curle (1989) says:

> What I can do is to try to clear away some of the mist of anger, fear, rage, all the negative emotions which distort perceptions so much

that they absolutely can't perceive the other side as being human and therefore can't talk to them at all. Any suggestion which side A makes to side B is seen by B as a trap or a trick or an insult . . . What somebody who's not immediately embroiled can do is to help people perceive the truth, and it is only when they perceive the truth that they're able to make a judgement based on rational rather than irrational factors and one hopes that that will lead them to be able to resolve the conflict.

The first stage is for the mediators, usually working in pairs, to obtain access to the leaders of the two parties. They inform themselves about the conflict and speak to government and UN officials. If early soundings favour the possibility of a mediation with some chance of success, a reconnaissance visit is made. The mediators then seek meetings with the leaders. They offer to carry messages to the other side, they try to give a true account of the motives and intentions of one side to the other and, if possible, they befriend the leaders. Above all, they listen carefully, and where they can they supply information and correct misinformation. But they are not negotiators, and they do not try to suggest terms for an agreement.

If the mediation is accepted, the mediators may make a number of trips to and fro between the leaders. This can offer a valuable channel of communications, especially if other channels are blocked by the war. Once a mediation is begun, the mediators make themselves available to go when they are needed. There is evidence that parties in conflict respect the motives of Quaker intervention, and Quakers have been successful in gaining access to decision-makers at the highest levels. In the Middle East, for example, Elmore Jackson shuttled between Prime Minister Nasser of Egypt and the Israeli leader David Ben-Gurion in 1955, at a time when tensions were high between the two states (Jackson, 1983). Jackson's efforts may have succeeded in averting a serious armed engagement in Gaza in 1955. However, there was too much distrust for the two sides to reach a settlement, and war broke out in 1956. Later in 1972–3, Quakers became involved in a further mediation effort between President Anwar Sadat of Egypt and Prime Minister Golda Meir of Israel. On that occasion they passed an Egyptian message to Israel about the 'land for peace' proposal. This message 'contained precisely the elements that the Israelis and Egyptians negotiated through Kissinger and Carter after the war' (Bailey, 1989). The Israelis made no direct response, though subsequent evidence suggests that Golda Meir changed her mind to accept the 'land for peace' formula shortly afterwards (Bailey, 1990b). This was not communicated to Egypt, and the 1973 war ensued. Nevertheless, 'land for peace' became the basis of the eventual peace settlement.

In the end, whether or not the parties come to a negotiated settlement, it is difficult to assess what role the mediation has in the success. To be effective the mediation has to be carried out in confidentiality. Perhaps only the leaders and the mediators know how effective a particular mediation has been; but more likely they do not know themselves. If an agreement is reached, it is the leaders, not the mediators, who take the credit. Similarly, if negotiations break down, it is the leaders who must take the blame. During the Nigerian Civil War, the Quaker mediators travelled to and fro several times between General Gowon, the President of Nigeria, and Colonel Ojukwu, the Biafran leader, but none of their efforts was successful in leading to direct negotiations. In the end, the Biafrans were completely defeated. Many inside Biafra and outside expected genocide. However, to everyone's surprise, General Gowon showed great magnanimity in his victory, and reconciliation followed. We cannot know whether this outcome can be attributed to the efforts of the mediators, but we do know that the mediators were very pleased.

Many attempts at mediation are made to try to bring wars to an end. As Adam Curle says:

> Usually mediation starts too late. It very seldom starts before people are already killing each other and by then the emotions have grown so hot and furious and the feelings have become so distorted that it's very difficult to change anything. What one really needs to do is something long in advance. One needs a kind of early warning system. There need to be people who are really sensitive to the slow, insidious circumstances which lead to violence.

CONSULTANT APPROACHES

Another approach, intermediate between mediation and problem-solving workshops, is the work of 'consultants' or 'facilitators' who go back and forth between parties to an internal conflict and seek to facilitate a process of exploring common ground. Jill Townsend, a management consultant with the Foundation for International Conciliation, practised this approach in South Africa in 1985–6.

Using a single-text procedure, and making separate visits to all the main political actors, she tried to identify features of a constitution which might win broad political assent.

'We try and build a process by which people can come to a table and still keep their constituencies on board,' she said:

There are a lot of constituencies that need to be brought into the process. On the side of the blacks, there are the external groups, the ANC and the PAC, internally AZAPO, UDF, Black Consciousness. The Church and the business community play an important role, both white and black sides. Within the white constituency, you have the government, the parliamentary opposition, the police as another constituency, the civil service as another constituency, and the military as another consituency, and then the extremist groups. For the first six months we ask questions and learn about the complexities of the conflict. The parties suggested 12 topics that they wanted to explore. There would be no commitments. In many cases the constituencies wanted access to the others. So long as this could be done in a safe way, they valued it.

Perhaps you wouldn't bring all the constituencies together at once. You might get several constituencies on one side together, and then constituencies on the other. When the two came together, there was anger and emotion, but useful things came out of it. They also needed to have time to go back to their constituencies and inform them of what was happening.

We got a number of agreements on the question of what a new constitution would look like. Some people including the right wing wanted an entirely new constitution, some wanted to reform the existing one. The meetings addressed a lot of the fears that the whites had.

The facilitator listens to the process, asks questions, and seeks to keep the discussion constructive and analytical. It is often useful to have more than one facilitator, one to watch the dynamics of the group, the other to listen to the content.

As facilitators we don't have a constituency. Our only constituency is the conflict. South African culture doesn't respond well to outsiders who come in with their own solution and try to impose it.

Some people thought that South Africa has got to such a stage that you couldn't have conflict resolution. But it was possible to build contacts and explore relationships and this still has an effect. There is a lot of hope in the situation. A lot of constituencies want to see change with a minimum amount of bloodshed. (Townsend, 1988).

As with other approaches of conflict resolution, facilitators and consultants insist on confidentiality, and for this reason it is extremely difficult to evaluate the practical results. Judging from the accounts that the facilitators give, parties in conflict do value the opportunity such exercises offer for investigating each other's views and exploring possible settlements.

Similar methods appear in efforts to resolve disputes at other levels, such as family, organizational and industrial disputes.

INDUSTRIAL RELATIONS: ARBITRATION, MEDIATION AND CONCILIATION

The strike or lock-out is the industrial equivalent of war. It is costly for both sides, but it is also the ultimate outcome if the parties cannot agree to co-operate.

There is a strong element of 'structural conflict' in industrial relations. Managers are primarily concerned with profitability and the survival of the enterprise, unions with job security, pay and conditions. These interests are sometimes compatible, but they clash when management wishes to shed labour and when unions seek to bid up wages beyond the level that managers regard as economic. Consequently conflict is recurrent in industrial relations, but both sides have a common interest in managing conflict in a way which avoids excessive costs and preserves the viability of the enterprise.

Managers and unions can often resolve their disputes at an early stage through bilateral negotiations, or indeed prevent them from arising through co-operative industrial practices. When serious disputes do occur, however, the parties may find them difficult to manage without coming to deadlock. Then third parties can be of assistance. In Britain the most important provider of third party services is ACAS.

The stated purpose of ACAS is to assist employers and trade unions to reach mutually acceptable settlements. ACAS first tries to uphold established negotiating procedures for avoiding and settling disputes. If these break down, either trade unions or employers can refer a dispute to ACAS.

If the parties agree to submit their dispute to ACAS, the normal procedure is for an ACAS conciliator to meet them, either separately or jointly, at an ACAS office or some other agreed venue. The conciliator discusses the issues informally, without time limits, and encourages the parties to consider their positions in an objective way. Conciliation is a voluntary procedure and the parties are responsible for any agreements they reach. Its aim is simply to help the parties reach agreements. It is up to the parties how they interpret and implement them.

ACAS also offers arbitration, a semi-judicial process. An arbitrator, who is not a member of ACAS staff, listens to the cases of both sides and then makes a binding ruling. Both parties agree to accept the decision in advance.

The third service ACAS offers is mediation, which is different from conciliation, and also differs from mediation as it is understood by private mediators in international conflicts. Mediation starts in the same way as conciliation but, unlike conciliators, mediators formally suggest their own terms for a settlement. These are not binding, and the parties are at liberty to accept or reject them, or to use them as a basis for further bilateral negotiations.

The parties to disputes make the majority of referrals to ACAS. In a little over half of the cases, the two sides agree to refer their dispute to ACAS jointly. In other cases, one side (usually the union) refers the dispute. In a small number of disputes, ACAS itself takes the initiative in inviting parties to come to talks.

In a typical conciliated dispute, a conciliator might see representatives of the parties on several occasions. Sometimes there are separate meetings first. However, on most occasions the conciliator meets the parties for the first time when they attend conciliation talks together, usually in an ACAS office. Normally the parties occupy separate rooms in the same building. The conciliator then meets them, separately, jointly or in caucus, as he or she sees fit. The conciliator plays an active role, making enquiries, identifying the parties' real interests, asking how each party would respond to offers made by the other party, and offering suggestions and proposals. Much of this is done through separate meetings with both sides, although sometimes the process starts with a joint meeting and then splits into separate ones. The conciliator tries to identify the common ground, explores possible solutions, and notes the scope for movement and the sticking points. When the parties are close to an agreement, the conciliator may call lead negotiators from each side together in a caucus meeting to try to clinch it. When the talks are close to a breakdown, the conciliator may also call a caucus to make the negotiators aware of this. The conciliator may bring the negotiating teams together in a joint meeting to ratify an agreement that the lead negotiators have reached, or to put a new proposal to both sides. The exact procedures used are flexible and vary with each case.

One example of a conciliated dispute was a confrontation between an employer and a union over night-time working. A change of legislation had exposed the employer to competition from other employers whose staff were prepared to work at night. In order to compete with them, the employer wanted to introduce compulsory night-time working for its staff. The staff, through their union, resisted this demand, and a strike seemed imminent. ACAS intervened and invited the parties to talks. Through the conciliation process, it transpired that the staff were prepared to offer night-time cover, so long as it was voluntary, and the management was prepared to accept a voluntary arrangement, so long as cover was guaranteed. An agreement based on this principle resolved the dispute.

ACAS is well-established as a dispute settlement agency. It handles more than 1200 industrial disputes a year, and in 83 per cent of the cases the parties either reach a settlement or make progress by narrowing their differences. The vast majority of these disputes are dealt with before the parties take the decision to start a strike or a lock-out.

Increasingly the dispute settlement procedures within industries require the parties to consult ACAS as a last resort before taking industrial action. ACAS also has a 'fire-fighting' role which enables conciliators to take the initiative themselves in important disputes. ACAS staff track the major current industrial disputes in Britain, and they can telephone the parties and invite them to talks whenever they think it is appropriate. ACAS also offers advice to employers and unions about their dispute settlement procedures. The organization has a network of regional offices, and is known and respected by people on both sides of industry.

What techniques do ACAS conciliators use? Basically they are similar to those of mediators and facilitators in other disputes. Conciliators aim to 'find the interests behind the positions'. They must be non-judgemental and pragmatic, avoiding questions about the fairness or unfairness of positions, and instead looking at the conditions which might make an agreement feasible. They need to be skilful listeners, and confident, honest speakers, capable of engaging the trust of both sides. They need a sense of timing and a sense of humour.

FAMILY CONCILIATION

The aim of family conciliation is 'to help couples involved in separation and divorce to reduce the area or intensity of conflict between them, and to work towards reaching agreement, expecially in disputes concerning their children'. As Kate Gardner, of the Swindon Family Conciliation Service says, 'We are here to help couples make the decisions they need to make, about themselves and their children, in the event of the parents separating' (Gardner, 1989).

In this sense conciliation is different from reconciliation. It is not intended to bring couples together, but rather to help the parties 'to explore possibilities of reaching agreement, without coercion'. As such, conciliation is an alternative to the divorce court.

As in the new negotiating methods and the problem-solving workshops, the crux of the problem is to get down to the fundamental, underlying issues. As Gardner explains:

> There are various levels of conflict. There is the overt conflict about whether you pick up Johnnie at ten o'clock or whether you pick him up at eleven thirty, which you can help a couple negotiate on, by defusing it and getting them to suggest compromises. But you've also got to watch what the conflict about time is really about, because it's almost never about time. And you have to take very careful decisions about (a) how you are going to identify it and (b) when you have identified it, what are you going to do about it? We cannot, and it is not part of our brief, resolve all the conflict that may have built up over the years, but we must work with it enough so that it doesn't come out and sabotage arrangements. Quite often, it is sufficient to acknowledge it. Particularly if you can put it as, 'This is something that happened to you both that you both minded about and that upset you both, and it is not going to go away, is it? But it needn't affect what you are going to do from now on in, because that is a different problem. Yes?'. So acknowledging and containing something quite often works and you often have to get the partners to explicitly acknowledge to each other different things they mind about, that they always disregarded.

The first stage of the conciliation is to hold one or more separate interviews with each partner. These are mainly to explore grievances, 'to give them an opportunity to blood-let', but they also enable the conciliators to 'signpost a few unexploded bombs'. 'We would acknowledge and recognise griefs and upsets and then begin to understand what they are asking for and what their backstop will be and how far they are prepared to compromise.'

Then there is a joint interview. Two conciliators conduct it. One of them looks after the substance of what people want to negotiate about, while the other listens and looks after the process. The conciliators are neutral and open. They do not tell the couples what the solutions are, but they work with them to help find them. They can also represent the interests of the children, which the parents are often unable to do, as they are 'locked into great battles as partners'.

The conciliators chair the meeting, choose the agenda and decide the order on the agenda in which to take items. In short, they manage the process, but nevertheless they do not determine the outcome. That is up to the partners. The aim is not to reach a fixed outcome but one that the partners can work with and adapt. Kate Gardner says:

> I can't say what arrangements should be made but my idea of a good settlement is one where the couple – where they were polarised to begin with for one reason or another – have been able to resolve that satisfactorily in a way that is not rigid and is not fixed, so that they have arrangements now that will work for them and their kids, and they are now comfortable and trusting enough of each other as parents to be able to renegotiate these arrangements as everybody's needs change.

Family conciliation has helped many couples in reaching such arrangements, thus avoiding some of the distress and cost of a fought-over divorce. Even in the most bitter and emotional disputes, this suggests, third-party mediation can be helpful. It can help the parties to acknowledge their grievances and lay them to rest, and it provides a process, and neutral ground, through which the parties can seek a mutually acceptable way out of their predicament. The value of trained and sympathetic conciliators, who are sensitive to the emotional and psychological tone of the negotiation, is evident.

MANAGEMENT CONSULTANTS: RESOLVING CONFLICTS WITHIN ORGANIZATIONS

Organizations and businesses do not engage in armed contests, but they do experience destructive conflicts when disputes cannot be settled satisfactorily. Such disputes are a common source of organizational failure and bankruptcy.

Management consultants offer a service to people in organizations which is, in effect, a way of analysing conflicts and exploring possible outcomes. Systems and organization theorists in a number of universities have developed a particular approach to these problems. They are concerned with reframing the problems that people in the organization see in new ways, to help them identify what the basic problems really are.

John Hamwee, a senior lecturer at the Systems Group in the Open University, has several years' experience of this kind of consultancy. He offers his clients a series of exercises and tasks which they use to study the problems and then devise their own solutions. He believes that:

> people in organizations will devise better solutions than any consultant – they know best. However, what the consultant can offer is a process of self-inquiry, which can reveal to the clients the different perspectives each holds. This may give them new insights into the inter-relationships between their problems, and bring into the open what the real problems are. (Hamwee, 1989).

He gives as an example a consultancy with an engineering company.

> The two co-owners, who had been friends for many years, bought the old established company some five or six years before I became involved, and from merely breaking even it had begun to make modest profits. In the spring and summer of 1985 a lot had gone wrong, most notably the failure of a new venture into manufacturing laboratory equipment for bio-technology companies, and the company faced bankruptcy. It was saved by a personal loan, but it was suggested to the co-owners that they needed to hire consultants to help them recover and plan for the future. One of the co-owners knew me personally and was keen to seek my help. The other co-owner was reluctant and commissioned instead a series of studies by marketing consultants.

> The co-owners saw the firm's problems in technical and marketing terms, and the solution they had decided on was to buy a new machine for £200 000 which would enable them to break into new markets. But the consultant saw that the business problems were inseparable from the latent conflict between the co-owners. Hamwee reports:

> In conversations, there were a number of references made to the fact that the partners had not discussed, or had simply failed to resolve, a

number of important issues. Neither partner commented on the absence from the marketing consultant's report of any reference to how they should manage the introduction of the new machine or of the changes it would bring in its wake.

In his sessions with the co-owners, the consultant asked each of them separately to jot down the four most urgent problems the company faced. He then asked each of them to restate the problems, and then to reformulate the restatements. This was done altogether four times. Each co-owner's statements were then put up together on the wall. To their surprise, there was no overlap between them at all. 'They were shocked by it, and that was helpful,' says John Hamwee.

> It made it objective, it moved it from the level of a personal issue to a shared problem to work on. Over two years the fact that they had different perceptions of what was going on had built up to a point where there were real 'no go' areas between them and they actually couldn't discuss them.

This had developed into overtly hostile behaviour between them. As a result of the sessions, the consultant managed to bring the covert conflict into the open and allow the co-owners to address the issues between them. Subsequently the relationship between them changed and the fortunes of the company began to improve.

COMMON ELEMENTS IN THE APPROACHES TO CONCILIATION AND PEACEMAKING

While all of the approaches have their own unique characteristics, there are a number of common features.

1. There is general agreement that effective peacemaking requires a sustained and long-term commitment to the conflict. Third parties have to be prepared to maintain a persistent and active concern.
2. Peacemakers generally insist on confidentiality, and are often unwilling to take credit for agreements, which are of the parties' own making.
3. Peacemaking is a gradual process. There is general agreement that developing and facilitating a process through which parties can communicate is a large part of the battle. The outline of the settlement and its terms arise out of this process, as the parties and the third parties gradually learn what is feasible. The exact nature

of the peacemaking process varies in the different traditions, but this may be secondary. For example, whether the third party deals with the parties through separate meetings or through joint meetings or some combination may depend on the conflict and the circumstances.

4. An important rationale for the peacemaking process is to provide a way for the parties to explore what would happen if they made particular offers or concessions, without actually doing so. Therefore it is important to most schools of peacemaking that there should be no prior commitments, and that the process, whether negotiations, mediation or conciliation, provides a repository for conditional commitments.

5. A good sense of timing is important. Sometimes, for example, a direct meeting between parties can make matters worse. The time and setting for intervention must be carefully chosen.

6. Emotional and psychological factors are important, in conflict resolution as much as in conflict. The different approaches vary in the extent to which they take account of these factors. A procedure which is concerned only with the substance of the dispute, and misses the emotional undercurrents, may miss a settlement.

7. An important difference between the approaches of peacemakers lies in whether or not they are prepared to propose terms. Most of the professionals involved in private conflict resolution avoid offering their own proposals for settlements. They argue that the parties are the only ones who fully know what is acceptable and, as it is their conflict, they can find the best terms, if they are helped through an appropriate process. The intermediary should have a clear understanding of the primary and secondary issues, so as to be able to suggest ways of separating issues or linking them up; but most practitioners would never present a comprehensive draft agreement to the parties. On the other hand, diplomats are much more willing to offer peace plans of their own. Often, as in the Gulf crisis, these are brushed aside as soon as they are made. But sometimes peace plans stick. It may be that they stick best when the third party is itself a powerful actor in the conflict.

Part 3
How Conflicts are Settled

6 Peaceful Settlements in Practice: (1) Case Studies

How do these ideas about the settlement of conflicts square with experience? This chapter examines four examples of peacefully settled conflicts. Through these case studies we can examine whether there are common strands that may have helped to keep them peaceful.

The first is the dispute between Sweden and Finland, over the Åland Islands. Unlike the conflict over the Falkland Islands, this dispute has been settled to the satisfaction of the islanders and both states, and the islands are now autonomous and demilitarized. The second case is Trieste (1945). This territorial dispute between Italy and Yugoslavia seemed likely at one point to become a war, but armed conflict was averted and a peaceful settlement was achieved. The third is the ethnic and territorial conflict over South Tyrol, where a German-speaking minority lives along with an Italian-speaking majority in a province historically contested between Italy and Austria. Unlike similar situations (for example, in Cyprus and Northern Ireland), this dispute has been largely settled without protracted armed conflict. The fourth, and most historically important, is the settlement of the disputes over Berlin and German unification in the context of the end of the Cold War.

THE DISPUTE BETWEEN SWEDEN AND FINLAND OVER THE ÅLAND ISLANDS (1917–51)

The most important decisions in the settlement of this dispute were made in the 1920s, but the dispute was re-opened in the Second World War and finally resolved in 1951. The Åland Islands lie between Sweden, Finland and the Soviet Union (see Figure 6.1). Their population of 23 000 is ethnically and culturally Swedish. The islands were Swedish until 1809, but are now under Finnish sovereignty.

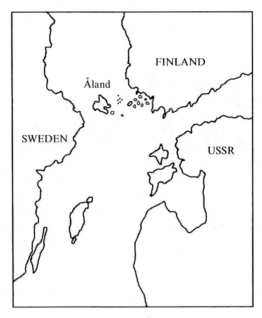

FIGURE 6.1   *The Åland Islands*

Lying at the entrance to the Gulf of Bothnia, near the approaches to St Petersburg, the islands had strategic value in the nineteenth century and earlier, which has now disappeared. In the war between Russia and Sweden of 1808–9, Russia took the islands, together with Finland. The Russian government incorporated Åland into the Grand Duchy of Finland, against the wishes of the inhabitants. Russia regarded Åland as a defensive outpost, and built a fort on the islands at Bomarsund as part of a chain of fortresses around St Petersburg. The Russian army billeted 10 000 troops on the islands and forced the islanders to work on the fortifications.

In 1854, during the Crimean War, an Anglo–French naval force attacked Bomarsund during the Crimean war, and razed the fort. The subsequent peace treaty restored Åland to Russia but demilitarized the islands. In the following 50 years the Russian government respected this treaty, except during the wars of 1905 and 1914 when troops were briefly redeployed on the islands.

In 1917 the Russian revolution gave the islanders what seemed to be an opportunity to break away from Russia. In a secret meeting they decided to seek reunion with Sweden and to elect an unofficial legislature. In December 1917, Finland declared itself an independent republic. It was not prepared to give up Åland, although it offered autonomy to the islanders. Autonomy short of reunion was unacceptable to the islanders, but the Finnish legislature duly passed the Autonomy Act in 1920 and arrested two of the islanders' leaders for their opposition.

At this point Britain referred the question to the League of Nations. The League sent a commission of enquiry to both Finland and Sweden. In June 1921, the League declared that the sovereignty of the islands was Finnish, but that peace required new guarantees for the islanders and the demilitarization and neutralization of the islands. Sweden and Finland accepted the decision and signed a treaty to this effect. The language used in schools was to be Swedish. The islanders alone were to have the right to own and buy land in the islands. Only residents were allowed to vote, and the local Parliament was to have powers over domestic matters. Finland would appoint a County Governor, but the candidate would have to be acceptable to the Åland Parliament. The islanders would be exempt from military service. The islanders accepted autonomy on these terms.

In 1938 and 1939, Sweden and Finland discussed sending troops to the Åland Islands because of the danger from Nazi Germany, but the Soviet Union demanded that the islands remain unfortified. Finnish troops were placed on the islands during the Russo–Finnish war, but were removed after the Peace of Moscow (1940). In 1941 the Swedish armed forces again considered occupying Åland, but the King and Foreign Minister vetoed the proposal. In 1944, the armistice between Finland and the Soviet Union restored Åland once again to its neutral and demilitarized status. The autonomy act was reinstated, with revisions, in 1951.

The islanders have gradually come to appreciate the advantages of their unusual status as inhabitants of an autonomous, demilitarized, neutral territory. The restrictions on the sale of land protected Åland from the fate of Gotland and other Swedish islands near Stockholm, where wealthy city dwellers bought up much of the land at the expense of the local inhabitants. The standard of living on the islands is high and the islanders continue to maintain their own culture and their self-governing status.

In some respects, the outcome of this dispute is a model settlement for ethnic and territorial conflicts of its kind. The award of sovereignty to one side, with autonomy and cultural rights and property rights to the other, has led to a stable settlement. The neutralization and demilitarization of the islands prevented them from becoming a site for further fighting. Even though the demilitarized status was weak in time of war, it was restored with every peace settlement.

TRIESTE (1945–54)

The dispute over Trieste between Italy and Yugoslavia almost brought the two to war in 1945. But a war was averted, and in the end the conflict was settled in a negotiated agreement which has been accepted by the two states.

Trieste was part of the Austro–Hungarian Empire until 1919. In the treaty following the war, the city was awarded to Italy as a reward for joining the war on the Allied side, together with the surrounding territory (see Figure 6.2). The region surrounding Trieste had a mainly Serb and Croat population, while in Trieste itself the majority were Italian. The city and the surrounding region were linked by economic ties.

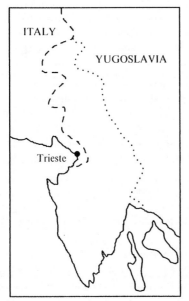

Interwar boundary · · · · ·
1954 boundary   – – –

FIGURE 6.2   *Trieste*

After the Second World War, Italy and Yugoslavia disputed both the city and its surrounding province of Venezia Giulia. Public opinion in both countries supported the government claims.

As German forces collapsed in April and May 1945, Yugoslav partisans entered Trieste. Two days later an Allied force of New Zealanders entered the city and received the surrender of the German garrison. The Yugoslav claim to Trieste, which had been made in April, raised tensions, but all sides agreed to defer the final decision to a peace settlement. Allied and Yugoslav forces on the spot negotiated a temporary division of the region into two zones, one to be occupied by the Allies, the other by Yugoslav forces. The Allied zone included Trieste and a strip of coastal territory connecting it to Italy.

Britain, France, the USA and the Soviet Union continued to negotiate over the final borders. They failed to reach a permanent agreement, with Britain, France and the USA supporting Italian claims and the Soviet Union supporting Yugoslavia. The former allies therefore agreed to make Trieste into a Free Territory under UN administration. According to the Peace Treaty signed in 1947, the Free Territory was to be demilitarized and neutral, with equal rights for all citizens in the area. The Territory was to be administered by a Governor appointed by the UN, but the Security Council could not agree on a candidate. Both Italy and Yugoslavia condemned this solution, and Yugoslavia proceeded to bring the zone it occupied into line with the economic and social reforms under way in the rest of Yugoslavia.

In 1948, the Western Allies proposed to modify the peace treaty, and give the Free Territory to Italy. Yugoslavia objected vigorously, and the Soviet Union vetoed the idea. Later in 1948, however, Stalin and Tito fell out, and Yugoslavia moved away from the Soviet bloc. As a result the Western powers, particularly the USA, grew more friendly to Yugoslavia, and more even-handed in their approach to the dispute. They now abandoned the proposal that the whole Free Territory should be returned to Italy. In 1952, Tito proposed that the territory should be placed under a joint Italian–Yugoslav condominium, or that a neutral governor be appointed. This was unacceptable to the Italians.

An election in Italy in 1953 brought the issue to a head. Election campaigns in support of the Italian position raised Yugoslav fears that Italy would annex the area, and in turn Italy feared that Yugoslavia might formally annex the zone it occupied. Italian troops moved up to the frontier but, after an exchange of diplomatic notes, the crisis eased for a while. In October 1953, however, the British and US governments

announced that they were no longer prepared to maintain responsibility for administering their zone, and proposed to hand it over to the
Italian government. This led to immediate Yugoslav protests and riots
in Trieste. Both Italy and Yugoslavia moved troops to the borders and
Yugoslav threatened to move troops into Trieste if Italy did so.

At this point the Western Allies intervened, and proposed a five-way
conference to pave the way for full negotiations. Both Italy and
Yugoslavia said they were prepared to withdraw their troops simultaneously. Negotiations between Italy and Yugoslavia followed and
resulted in the 1954 agreement, by which:

1. US, British and Yugoslav occupation forces were withdrawn;
2. the zone containing Trieste, with the exception of a small area
    inhabited by Slovenes, was given to Italy;
3. this small area and the Yugoslav-occupied zone were to be part of
    Yugoslavia;
4. minorities on both sides would be protected;
5. Trieste became a free port.

This agreement in fact settled the conflict, although it only became a
legally binding treaty in 1975, when the two parties amicably agreed
some further slight revisions of the border and declared that no further
difficulties existed between the two states.

Factors Contributing to the Settlement

Why was the dispute settled peacefully?

Clearly the presence from the outset of a powerful third party, the
Allies, contributed to averting an armed conflict. Both in 1945 and
1953, Allied troops effectively formed a 'peacekeeping' force separating the two sides.

The tension in 1953 was broken when both sides declared that they
were ready for a negotiated settlement. When the Western powers
proposed a five-way conference, this created a forum in which the
conflict could be settled. Reciprocal troop withdrawals then cleared the
way for the settlement.

At various times, all the main forms of settlement of a territorial
conflict were suggested: control by one side or the other, control by
neither with a third party administration, and a condominium. The
final settlement, a partition with guarantees, has proved effective in

resolving the Trieste dispute. It was clear-cut, and it broadly corresponded to the ethnic divide. At the same time, the parties made provisions for the needs of the minorities on the 'wrong' side of the frontier, and for the management of the economic interdependence between the two areas. Consequently the 1954 settlement proved to be both peaceful and durable.

SOUTH TYROL (1960–71)

Like Trieste, South Tyrol was part of the Austro–Hungarian Empire until after the First World War, when it was ceded to Italy by the Treaty of St Germain. It now forms part of the Italian region of Trentino-Alto Adige. This region consists of two provinces, Bolzano and Trento (see Figure 6.3). Bolzano (South Tyrol) is predominantly German-speaking, with an Italian minority; Trento is almost entirely Italian-speaking. In 1948, about a third of a million people lived in each province.

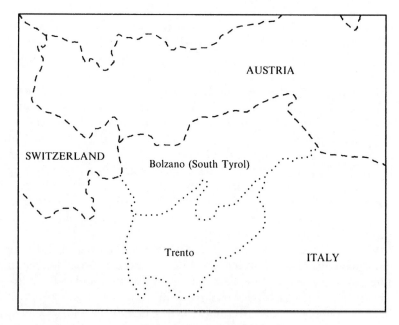

FIGURE 6.3   *South Tyrol*

The structure of minorities has some similarities with Northern Ireland and Cyprus: in each case, two ethnic groups drawn from two nearby 'mother' states have been in dispute about the state to which their shared province should belong (see Figure 6.4). In Bolzano about a third of the population is Italian and is less well off than the German-speaking majority.

The Habsburgs had ruled the Tyrol since the fourteenth century, and retained control of both south Tyrol and Trento in 1870 when Italy was unified. However, Italian nationalists had long wanted Trento to become part of Italy, and in 1919, as a reward for Italy's participation in the war, the Allies gave Italy Trento and South Tyrol. The Italian government promised to respect the customs and language and autonomy of the German-speakers, but when Mussolini came to power he repudiated these promises and attempted to 'Italianize' the province. Italian industries were set up and Italian immigration was encouraged, changing the ratio between German and Italian speakers in Bolzano from 29:1 to 2:1. Italian replaced German in schools and place-names, and even family names were Italianized. Public services were put into Italian hands. The land laws under which Tyrolese farmers held their lands were abolished.

The pact signed by Hitler and Mussolini in 1939 forced the German-speakers and Ladines in South Tyrol to choose between accepting Italian nationality and being repatriated to Germany or Austria. Between a third and a quarter of them left, though some returned later. Those who decided to stay, therefore, stayed in Italy voluntarily. In 1943, South Tyrol was occupied by German troops, with the general support of the local population. Following the German defeat, Austria restated its claim to the province, but at the Paris Peace Conference in 1946, the Allies decided to return South Tyrol to Italy. Austria and Italy then made a bilateral agreement covering the German-speakers in the province. It provided for equal rights for the minority, restoring German family names and the use of German in schools and in local administration. There was to be 'a more appropriate proportion of employment between the two ethnical groups' and an autonomous regional legislative and executive body.

When it came to be implemented, this agreement led to an immediate dispute. The Italian government decided to make not just Bolzano autonomous, but the whole region of Bolzano and Trento. The government called this 'Trentino–Alto Adige'. Bolzano lost most of its autonomy to the government of the new region, in which the German-speakers were a minority. Austria complained that this statute

99

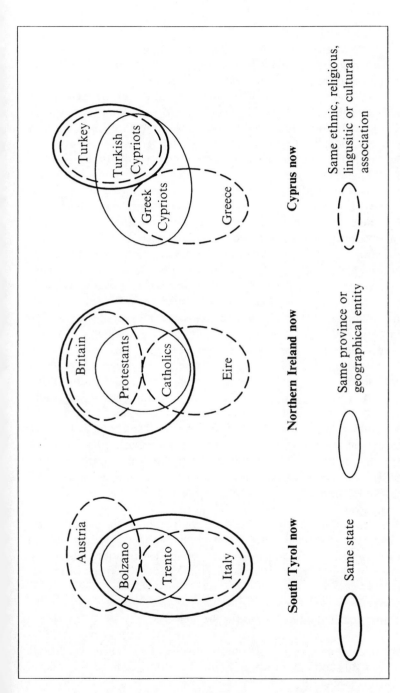

FIGURE 6.4 *Ethnic, state and geographical divisions in South Tyrol, Northern Ireland and Cyprus*

violated the 1946 agreement. The German-speaking minority was particularly alarmed in 1959 when the Italian government decided to set up a housing programme which, it was feared, would lead to large-scale Italian immigration. This decision was taken at central government level and thus flouted the autonomy statute, in the view of the German-speaking South Tyrol People's Party (SVP). Between 1959 and 1961, Austria appealed to the UN about Italy's failure to implement fully the 1946 agreement. The UN called on Austria and Italy to resolve the problem bilaterally, but negotiations with the short-lived Italian governments came to nothing. Extremists in South Tyrol then launched a campaign of attacks against electricity pylons, border posts and Italian soldiers. This culminated in explosions which cut off most of the province's electricity supply in 1961. Italy accused Austria of protecting the extremists and introduced a visa requirement for visiting Austrians to prevent the entry of explosives. Both sides then drew back. Italy created a joint commission, including German-speaking members of the SVP and Italian-speaking Tyrolese, to study the problem. Italy also lifted the visa requirement. Bilateral negotiations resumed in 1963 and a joint commission of experts was set up in 1964. This led to a new agreement in 1969, specifying an agreed sequence of steps towards autonomy. Bolzano was to remain in Trentino–Alto Adige, but it was given new powers, including economic self-management, self-determination in educational and cultural matters and linguistic rights. There were 'internal guarantees' including a permanent commission through which the South Tyrolese could bring grievances to the Council of Ministers in Rome, and a change in an article of the European Convention for the Peaceful Settlement of Disputes which permitted Austria to guarantee the 'internal guarantees'. In other words, Italy accepted an Austrian role in South Tyrol. Meanwhile, the South Tyrolese gave up their demand for reunification with Austria.

This resolution largely settled the dispute, though no timetable was attached to the sequence of steps. By 1986, the measures had still not been completed, and the slow pace of implementation has led to further diplomatic protests by Austria and further terrorist incidents.

Factors Contributing to a Peaceful Settlement

Notwithstanding a certain amount of low-level terrorism, the dispute has been substantially peaceful. South Tyrol has avoided the kind of protracted violent conflict Northern Ireland and Cyprus, for example, have experienced. How has it done so?

It seems clear that the autonomy agreement of 1969, although not perfect, substantially met the minority's needs for recognition of its cultural rights and protection of its identity. The German-speaking minority is not subject to economic discrimination. Moreover, it has some diplomatic protection from Austria, and the Italian government has recognized the legitimacy of Austria's interventions to protect the minority, through the agreements the states have signed. Finally, because there has been little violence, there is no tradition of bitterness or hatred between the two communities.

Figure 6.5 shows a time chart of the major moves in the conflict, divided between coercive or unilateral measures (below the line) and conciliatory or co-operative measures (above the line). The chart shows that a developing pattern of coercive moves in the period up to 1961 was broken by a substantial number of co-operative and conciliatory moves occuring in the period from 1961 to 1969. The momentum of these measures was apparently effective in limiting the escalation of the dispute.

THE CONFLICT OVER BERLIN AND THE END OF THE COLD WAR IN EUROPE (1945–89)

The Cold War in Europe seemed, until 1989, a particularly deadlocked conflict. At the centre of it were Berlin and the antagonism between the two Germanies. Yet in 1989 Germany was unified, Berlin became a single city, and the Presidents of both the USA and the Soviet Union declared that the Cold War was over. How did it come to an end?

The Cold War can be divided into four phases:

1945–75 Cold War I

1975–9 Détente

1979–85 Cold War II

1985–9 Ending of the Cold War

The first Cold War went in waves, alternately more tense and more relaxed. The second Cold War was a period of particularly high tension. The crisis over the Euro-missile deployments badly damaged

102

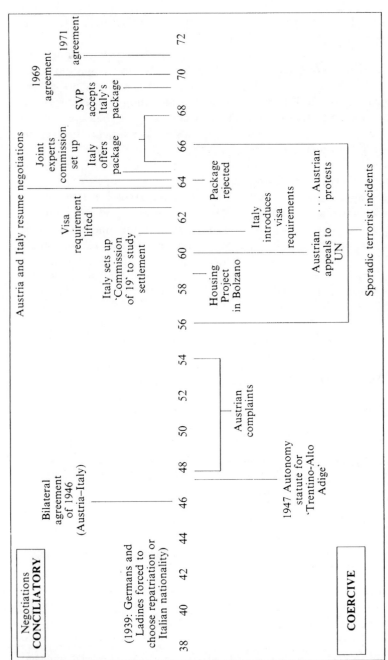

FIGURE 6.5 *The South Tyrol conflict: time chart of coercive and conciliatory moves*

East–West relations, as did the Soviet invasion of Afghanistan. The Reagan Administration's arms build-up and his 'evil empire' rhetoric naturally worried the Soviets, and the deadlock over Star Wars led to a near-breakdown of arms control.

People in both West and East were alarmed. In Western Europe the peace movement mobilized millions of people, and Social Democratic parties developed the philosophy of 'common security' in opposition to NATO policies. But it was in the Soviet Union that the most important reaction made itself felt. Leading thinkers in the KGB and the Party began a fundamental re-assessment of Soviet policies. They concluded that they were failing to meet their objectives, and that reform was essential. Beginning with Andropov, and accelerating greatly under Gorbachev, the Soviet government introduced a wide-ranging programme of reforms. In place of secrecy, there was to be *glasnost*; in place of centralized ossification, a restructuring of Soviet institutions.

In foreign policy, Gorbachev and the reformers decided that neutralizing the danger of world war was the first priority. They made two crucial changes in Soviet security thinking: the first was to perceive that the West did not intend to attack the Soviet Union; and the second was to abandon the view that the West and the East had a total conflict of interest. Instead they saw common interests, particularly in avoiding war, but also in environmental, economic and global issues.

Gorbachev proceeded to make a dazzling series of initiatives in arms control. He began in August 1985 with the moratorium on nuclear tests. In January 1986, he proposed a plan for complete nuclear disarmament by 2000. In August he followed this up with comprehensive proposals on conventional arms control. He accepted intrusive on-site verification, and agreed to Reagan's 'zero option' for the elimination of intermediate range nuclear missiles. Later he accepted asymmetric cuts in shorter-range missiles and, at the Reykjavik summit in 1986, Gorbachev and Reagan came close to agreeing to a global ban on ballistic missiles. On 7 December 1988, Gorbachev announced his 'Christmas present' of unilateral cuts in conventional Soviet forces, including the removal of 50 000 troops and 5000 tanks. Bridge-crossing equipment and other units that would be essential for an offensive were withdrawn. Gorbachev put the Warsaw Pact on a defensive footing and made sharp cuts in military spending. It was a policy of 'graduated reductions in tension' brought about by unilateral initiatives (Osgood, 1962), fired by the vision of 'common security' that the Palme Commission had proposed in 1982. These steps, and the arms control agreements that followed, led to a rapid reduction in East–West tensions.

The second element in the process of de-escalation was the dissipation of ideological conflict, as reform within the Soviet Union gathered pace. This began with *glasnost* and the opening of free discussion and debate. It went on with constitutional changes which gradually eroded the power of the Communist Party and strengthened state bodies. Gorbachev became State President with powers which eclipsed those of the General Secretaryship of the Communist Party, and the Supreme Soviet became a permanent Parliament. Free elections were held in 1989, and resulted in sharp losses for old party officials. These changes took place in an atmosphere of constant political crisis which threatened their continuation, with reformers, conservatives, democrats and nationalists engaged in open struggle. Nevertheless, they were remarkable and irreversible changes in the character of the Soviet state, which sharply altered the 'enemy image' of the Soviet Union that the Western public had held.

A third factor in the de-escalation of the conflict was the Helsinki agreement of 1975, and the 'Helsinki process' of the CSCE, which gradually helped to normalise relations in Europe. The agreement was a product of detente, but its importance was that it set out common principles which all the states of Europe, East and West, agreed to adopt. These included the acceptance of existing borders, the peaceful resolution of disputes, common standards for human rights, and agreements on technical and cultural co-operation. The CSCE also became the basis for a useful set of agreements on confidence-building, and, eventually, for conventional force reductions.

The fourth process moving towards the solution of the conflict was the efforts of the Germans themselves to solve the 'German problem'. 'The barbed wire will not last forever,' declared Willi Brandt, then mayor of West Berlin, in 1961. He became Chancellor in 1969, and launched the *Ostpolitik* to improve relations with the Soviet Union. West Germany renounced the use of force, and gave up its claims to territory east of the Oder–Neisse line. The other strand of this effort was an intensive effort to improve communications between the two Germanies, through people-to-people, city-to-city, trade and political exchanges. German politicians never gave up their desire to unify the two Germanies when it became politically possible.

This came about sooner than expected, as the reforms in the Soviet Union made their impact on the people and governments of Eastern

Europe. In Poland and Hungary, reform movements were already under way, but in East Germany and elsewhere hard-line regimes now found themselves isolated. They were squeezed between the Soviet Union on the one hand, which was moving rapidly away from the kind of Communist system they still represented, and a popular movement for radical change. In Hungary, one of the main popular demands was for freedom of travel, and Hungary opened its border with Austria in the summer of 1989. A flood of East Germans began to leave through this new exit route, destabilizing the country. The reform movement in East Germany set up the 'New Forum' movement and massive demonstrations took place in Leipzig and East Berlin. Gorbachev visited East Germany and warned Honecker that if he failed to respond to popular pressures he would put himself in danger. With this clear signal that the Soviet government would not support a crackdown, Honecker fell, to be replaced by a reforming government. Further emigration forced the government to allow free travel and, on 9 November, it opened the Berlin Wall. Free elections followed, and parties supporting re-unification won a sweeping victory.

In this way, the conflict over the two Germanies and the two halves of Berlin came to a spectacular end, eventually through the efforts of the Germans themselves who insisted on unity. Two central parties to the conflict had suddenly become one. The city at the centre of Europe's divisions now opened the way towards its potential unification.

Of course, many problems remained, and new conflicts opened up. The course of change in the Soviet Union made further conflict between East and West quite possible. The major Western states (with the exception of Germany) had made few fundamental changes in their positions to correspond with those that had been made in the East. The conflict therefore came to an end in a one-sided way, and there were seeds of new conflicts within Germany and between Western and Eastern Europe. Nevertheless, an old conflict, which had generated the largest arms build-up in the history of the world, and sometimes seemed the most likely setting for a third world war, had reached a resolution through integration instead of war.

CONCLUSIONS

What conclusions can be drawn from these four cases? In many ways the conflicts were very different, although there are points of similarity.

They all involved, to some degree, ethnic and territorial issues. In all of them groups of people were divided from others of the same people by borders between states. The East–West conflict, of course, dwarfs the others in terms of its historical significance, and involved issues of ideology and superpower rivalry which the others did not. The Åland Islands and South Tyrol in this period were principally internal conflicts of an ethnic character, while Trieste was primarily an interstate conflict, although with an ethnic dimension.

How important were the issues at stake to the principal parties? The size of the groups involved varied from the very small in the case of the Åland Islands, to the very large in the case of Germany. The importance of the disputes to the principal states also varied. In each case, the local people whose future was at issue were critically involved – the Ålanders, the inhabitants of Trieste and its surrounding area, the Tyrolese and the Germans – but the stakes for the governments were not necessarily so high. The Åland Islands had lost their strategic importance and so were not a security issue for Sweden and Finland. Neither was South Tyrol a matter of vital interest to Italy and Austria. Trieste was more important to Yugoslavia and Italy, but more in the context of nationalism than vital interests. The future of Germany, on the other hand, had certainly been considered a critical security issue by both superpowers.

Did third parties play an influential part in the settlements? The League of Nations had played a key role in the settlement of the Åland Islands dispute. Over Trieste, the Allies were powerful third parties that the disputants could not easily ignore. The presence of their occupation forces in the city meant that Yugoslavia and Italy had to consult them before using force, and had little choice but to attend the negotiations they called. In the South Tyrol the Austrian government, although in a sense a party to the conflict, nevertheless played an important third party role, first of all by accepting that South Tyrol would remain Italian, and second by insisting on guarantees for the German-speaking minority. In the East–West conflict, oddly enough, it was the Germans themselves who played the most influential third-party role, bringing their country together despite the best efforts of the superpowers to stabilize their confrontation along its inner border.

Were unilateral gestures or conciliatory steps important in these conflicts? Was a 'peace process' started, and were reciprocal steps made to find a solution? These seem most strikingly clear in the ending of the Cold War. Here Soviet moves included unilateral gestures and gradual steps towards a reduction in tensions. Taken together with reform in the Soviet Union, and the reciprocated trust-building measures in the Helsinki process and the arms control talks, these steps broke the tensions generated by the Cold War and gradually eroded the hostility between the superpowers. Meanwhile *Ostpolitik* and citizens' diplomacy were developing a similar process across the Germanies. In the case of the Åland Islands, Finland's offer of autonomy to the islanders perhaps signalled that a peaceful settlement was possible, but the primary process was the settlement through the League Commission, which made enquiries in both Sweden and Finland before it reported. In Trieste, there were no clear signals of an intent to settle until the final negotiations. South Tyrol shows a rather complex pattern of moves, although Italy's setting up of the 'Commission of 19' seems to have been the event that altered the course the dispute was taking. Once the parties agreed to study the conflict together, they moved towards a negotiated settlement.

Did attitudes shift in the course of these conflicts? We have no good evidence of attitude change for the earlier disputes. It is clear that the progress towards agreement softened attitudes in the South Tyrol and the Åland Islands; this was important in the South Tyrol because it permitted the SVP to accept Italy's package of proposals. The East–West conflict became much less severe with the dissipation of earlier ideological hostilities, and public attitudes (including greater communications between East and West) certainly played a part in this process. Yet the shift was largely one-sided: it was particularly the East that changed its view of the West, and of itself. The attitudes of elites in the West showed much less sign of change.

Finally, did these conflicts reach integrative solutions? Did the settlements truly reconcile the real interests of the parties? The settlements of the Åland Islands, South Tyrol and Trieste all incorporated guarantees for the ethnic minorities. The settlement in the Åland Islands was perhaps the most integrative, for it managed to combine Finnish sovereignty with a remarkable degree of self-management for the Ålanders. With time, these guarantees have proven more or less satisfactory. In the case of Germany, integration was achieved for German citizens, though in a way which left those of the East unprotected against the superior economic strength of the West. The larger process of integration of Eastern and Western Europe still remains on the agenda.

To conclude, these case studies suggest that the factors which the theory has identified do play a role in peaceful settlements. But factors which are prominent in some conflicts may be less prominent or absent in others. Moreover, we cannot generalizce about the influence of these factors without looking at whether they also operated in other conflicts which had violent outcomes. To make a fuller evaluation of what factors operate, we need to look at a larger group of conflicts.

7 Peaceful Settlements in Practice: (2) A Comparative Study

A limited number of case studies can suggest some of the factors that are conducive to peaceful settlement but, in order systematically to test theories about what these factors are, it is desirable to consider a much larger set of conflicts. Ideally the study should examine all post-1945 disputes, but this is a dauntingly large population. This chapter presents the results of a study of 81 international and civil conflicts in the period 1945–85. The cases, which are drawn from Africa, Europe, and the Middle East, include peaceful and violent conflicts and resolved and unresolved disputes.

Most published work on conflict resolution concentrates on violent conflicts, but there is a set of studies which examine both peaceful and violent conflicts. Northedge and Donelan (1971) examined 50 international disputes between 1945 and 1970, of which over half were resolved peacefully or became quiescent without a resort to force. Holsti (1966) analysed 77 major international conflicts between 1919 and 1965; all of them involved at least the threat of force, if not its use. In 49 of them (64 per cent) there was some form of third party intervention, and these conflicts showed least evidence of destructive violence. E. B Haas, Butterworth and Nye (1972) and E.B. Haas (1983) assessed the effectiveness of the UN and regional conflict management organizations in 146 international conflicts between 1945 and 1970. Among Haas's findings were that in the period 1945–70 the UN had helped to settle about a third of the cases referred to it, but that the organization had shown relatively little interest in conflicts in which there was no fighting. Butterworth (1976; 1978) expanded this data set to include cases without conflict management in order to ask the question: do conflict managers make a difference? Brecher, Wilkenfeld and Moser (1988) looked at factors influencing peaceful and violent outcomes of international crises. Alker and his co-writers (1972; 1982) further developed the Haas/Butterworth data to examine the UN. Recently Sherman (1987), in his dissertation on the UN's effectiveness, has compiled a fuller data set than his predecessors. This includes domestic as well as international conflicts, and many disputes which were not referred to international organizations. The notes to this chapter quote some of the findings of this literature, using different sets of conflicts from those in this study.

FACTORS CONDUCIVE TO PEACEFUL SETTLEMENT

Chapter 4 canvassed a number of factors which may be conducive to peaceful settlement of conflicts. They include three propositions which can be tested against the available data.

The Nature and Intensity of the Conflict

The first proposition is that some conflicts are inherently simpler to resolve peacefully because the degree of conflict of interest is less, or the threat to the goals and values of the parties is minimal. A conflict in which parties threaten one another's existence is more likely to be violent than one which does not affect a party's central goals. It is suggested that conflicts over interests may be easier to resolve than conflicts over justice or power (Ury, Brett and Goldberg, 1988), so that one strategy for seeking peaceful resolution should be to reformulate a conflict apparently over power or justice in terms of interests.

Agreed Procedures and Early Third-party Intervention

The second proposition is that conflicts are more likely to be peacefully resolved if parties choose agreed procedures to deal with them (irrespective of the substance of the disagreement). Even signalling an intention to accept some form of mutually agreed procedure can help to create the momentum for a settlement. Accepting third-party intervention is such a signal, and it is widely held that early third-party intervention – for example, mediation – makes peaceful resolution of conflict more likely.

'Integrative' Outcomes

The third proposition is that outcomes should integrate the interests of the parties. Common to many theories of conflict resolution (see Fisher and Ury, 1983; Burton, 1987) is the idea that what is perceived as a zero-sum conflict should be transformed into a positive-sum situation in which the parties have common interests in a settlement.

A simple version of this theory is the idea that peacefully resolved conflicts should have 'win–win' outcomes. A rather more sophisticated version is that while parties' overt positions may clash, their underlying interests may be reconcilable (Pruitt and Rubin, 1986). Parties should be helped to explore the conflict in order to identify the potentially integrative outcomes.

METHODOLOGY

Research Design

The initial plan was to classify conflicts into four categories, by whether they were peaceful or violent, and by whether they were resolved or unresolved.

	Resolved	Unresolved
Peaceful	a	b
Violent	c	d

Theories about factors which are conducive to peacefully resolved conflicts could then be tested by comparing differences between the resolved and unresolved conflicts, and between the violent and peaceful conflicts. Cases in all four categories need to be examined in order to confirm or disprove propositions about how conflicts are peacefully resolved (Richardson, 1952).

However, a large number of conflicts are neither full wars nor free of military coercion, and besides 'resolved' and 'unresolved' conflicts there are those that were partly, but not wholly resolved by the cut-off date of the study (1985), and those that lapsed without being resolved. To accommodate these, a three-by-three classification was adopted, as in Table 7.1.

TABLE 7.1   *Classification of conflicts by level of violence and type of resolution*

Peaceful

Peaceful/Resolved
Algeria–Tunisia (1961–70)
Cameroons (British) independence (1955–63)
Cyrenaica (1949–51)
Gadaduma Wells (1955–70)
Ifni (1964–9)
Liberia's boundaries (1958–61)
Mauritania–Morocco (1958–70)
Wadi Halfa (1958–9)
Åland Islands (1808–1947)
Albania–Greece (Northern Epirus) (1945–85)
Austria (status of) (1945–55)
Belgian–Netherlands border (1957–9)
Minquiers Islands (1951–3)
Norway–UK fishing (1949–51)
Saar (1950–7)
Bahrain–Iran: Bahrain independence (1970–1)
Kuwait–Saudi Arabia (1957–65)

Peaceful/lapsed, quiescent or interim
German unification (1945–72)
Romania–Soviet Union (1964–76)
South Tyrol (1960–71)

Peaceful/unresolved
Gibraltar (1964–)

Minor violence

Minor violence/resolved
Gabon–Congo (1960–2)
Ghana–Ivory Coast, Niger, Upper Volta, Togo (1965–6)
Ghana–Upper Volta (1964–6)
Malagasy independence (1947–60)
Malawi independence (1959–64)
Mauritania–Mali (1960–3)
Niger–Dahomey (1963–5)
Sudanese independence (1946–56)
Tunisia's independence (1922–56)
Denmark–UK fisheries (1961–4)
Iceland–UK fisheries (1952–61)
Poland (1956)
Trieste (1945–75)
Saudi Arabia–Oman, Abu Dhabi (1949–75)
Syria–Lebanon (1949)

Minor violence/lapsed, quiescent or interim
Malawi–Tanzania (1964–)
East German uprising (1953)
Iceland–UK: cod war (1971–3)
Syria–Turkey (Hatay) (1945–)

Minor violence/unresolved
Albania–Yugoslavia (Kosovo) (1963–)
Albania–Soviet Union (1960–)
East–West confrontation in Europe (1945–)
Greece–Turkey (1970–)
Hungary–Romania (N. Transylvania) (1945–)
Bahrain–Qatar (1971–)
Kurds–Turkey (1945–)

Major violence

Major violence/resolved
Algeria–Morocco (1962–70)
Algerian independence (1945–62)
Cameroun's independence (1948–61)
Morocco's independence (1943–56)
Mozambique's independence (1962–74)
Nigerian Civil War (1967–70)
Tunisia–France (Sakiet and Bizerte) (1958–63)
Zaire's independence (the Congo) (1960–5)
Zimbabwe: independence and majority rule (1963–80)
South Yemen–North Yemen (1969–73)
Yemeni civil war (1962–70)
Yemen: conflict over Aden and independence of S.Yemen (1948–67)

Major violence/lapsed, quiescent or interim
Tutsi–Hutu (1958–)
Berlin (1948–)
Czechoslovakia (1968)
Hungary (1956)
Egypt–Israel (1948–79)
Jordan–Palestinians (1970–1)
Oman–Imam's rebels (1954–71)

Major violence/unresolved
Angola (1956–)
Ethiopia–Somalia: the Ogaden (1950–)
Ethiopia–Eritrea (1946–)
Mozambique civil war (1981–)
Namibia (1946–)
South Africa (1946–)
Sudan civil war (1956–)
Uganda (1971–)
Western Sahara (1964–)
Cyprus (1954–)
Northern Ireland (1968–)
Iraq–Iran (1969–)
Iraq–Kuwait (1973–)
Israel–Palestinians (1920–)
Oman–Dhofar rebels (1963–)

The Selection of Conflicts for the Study

It was decided to include domestic, international and mixed conflicts. A strict distinction between internal and international conflict is difficult to maintain, since much conflict starts within states and then spills over their borders, while international conflict often exacerbates domestic conflicts.

One of the main methodological difficulties of the study was to define a population of conflicts. Scholars have had difficulty establishing clear and agreed criteria for defining wars. It is even harder to find a boundary for a population of peaceful conflicts. The schema on p. 41 suggests that conflicts that have reached or passed the stage of overt non-coercive conflict should be the focus of study. But distinguishing overt conflicts from situations of potential conflict is not a straightforward task.

The following criteria were adopted for defining the relevant population of conflicts:

1. the participants must perceive that they are in conflict;
2. the conflict must have a focus (there must be a clash over interests, values, relationships or goals);
3. the conflict must be between nations or must involve significant elements of the population within a nation (that is, they must be international or major civil conflicts);
4. the outcome must be important to the parties.

Domestic conflicts were included only if the outcome was important to the society as a whole, and if their resolution required something other than the normal functioning of an existing political institution. Industrial conflicts, *coups d'états* and institutionalized political conflict between political parties were excluded. Terrorist incidents were excluded, as were incidents of tension created by overflights of aircraft or movements of naval ships in foreign waters.

Distinguishing One Conflict from Another

Any method of classifying and counting conflicts requires distinctions to be made between conflicts. The difficulty is that often one conflict leads to another, and separate conflicts become linked and entangled. Sydney Bailey (1988b) speaks of the 'hybrid nature of many conflicts'. The Arab–Israeli conflict, for example, began as a conflict between Jewish underground groups and the British administration. As soon as the UN Partition Resolution was passed on 29 November 1947, it became a conflict between underground Arab organizations and the Jewish communities. When the State of Israel was declared on 15 May 1948, the Arab states intervened and it became an inter-state conflict.

Butterworth (1976) deals with this problem by splitting conflicts into separate cases whenever a change of party or issue occurs. This means his list has more cases than conflicts. This seemed inappropriate in a study focusing on how conflicts are settled. For this purpose it is preferable to treat conflicts as wholes, so if a conflict has several different phases, but the same basic issues are involved and the same parties participated, it is treated as a single case. For example, successive wars between Egypt and Israel are treated as a single Egypt–Israeli conflict. On the other hand the conflict between Syria and Israel is treated as a separate dispute.

The List of Conflicts

The decision to adopt a broad definition of a political conflict, covering a longer phase than simply an armed conflict, meant that a new list of conflicts had to be compiled. Although there are existing lists of armed conflicts (Singer, 1988), crises (Brecher, Wilkenfeld and Moser, 1988), cases that have been referred to the UN (Allsebrook, 1986) and general international conflicts (Butterworth, 1976), no good lists yet exist of peacefully resolved conflicts. A list of about 350 nonmilitarized and armed conflicts was drawn up, using reference sources and existing lists. The lists consulted include those of Allsebrook (1986), Beer (1981), Bebler (1987), Brecher, Wilkenfeld and Moser (1988), Butterworth (1976), Day (1987), Holsti (1966), Kende (1986), Luard (1986), Northedge and Donelan (1971), Small and Singer (1982), Sivard (1987) and Zacher (1979). Sherman's (1987) comprehensive list was not available to the author at the time of the study. The main list used was Butterworth's.

The Conflicts Selected for Analysis

Due to the difficulties of establishing a complete population, no attempt was made to draw a random sample. Instead, conflicts were selected from three continents – Africa, Europe and the Middle East.

Several cases which represent the same conflict over several periods were collapsed into one case, yielding 120 cases. Of these, 81 were selected for analysis. This set includes peaceful and violent, resolved and unresolved conflicts. Once the conflicts are broken down into these categories, it is possible to analyse factors which discriminate between them. However, because the selection was non-random, caution must be used in generalising statistical conclusions.

THE DATA BASE

A computer data base was constructed with standardized information about the conflicts and their outcomes. This information appears in the reference section, together with brief profiles of the conflicts. The following paragraphs describe the categories used in the data base and are important for interpreting the results.

Data base Categories

Start and End Years
These dates signify the years when a conflict becomes overt and when it is settled or terminated.

Area
This indicates where the main action of the conflict took place. In cases of colonial conflicts, the location of the colony rather than the metropolitan power is taken. This tends to weight the incidence of armed conflicts towards the Third World, and so not too much significance should be ascribed to this variable. If African colonial conflicts were classified as European, for example, a different picture of the regional incidence of armed conflict would appear. This caveat also applies to cases where European and American states directly or indirectly intervene.

International and Civil Conflicts
International conflicts are only those between states; civil conflicts only those within states. Others are classified as mixed.

Parties to the Conflict
Only the principal parties are listed. No attempt has been made to list the names of all the parties in complex internal conflicts.

Third Parties
This entry includes third parties who intervened to help manage or settle the conflict, not interventions in support of one side.

Classification of Conflicts by Issue

It was planned to divide the conflicts into types, such as territorial, minority and ethnic conflicts, on the assumption that there are categories of conflicts about similar issues where outcomes can be compared. If peacefully resolved conflicts appear in these categories, their outcomes may be relevant to the solution of other conflicts of the same type.

The complexity of most conflicts, and their tendency to spread over several issues, defies exclusive classification. Instead a record was made of the principal issue which appears in each case. Conflicts could then be classified into groups in which a particular issue was involved, although the groups would not be mutually exclusive. The issues chosen are listed below, with brief explanatory notes:

Class:	A conflict between social classes was a major issue
Control of government:	A civil contest for power
Ethnic:	A conflict between ethnic groups, or between ethnic groups and a government
Fishing:	A dispute over fishing rights
Great Power:	A power contest between Great Powers
Ideology:	A dispute between adherents of clashing ideologies (clashes between republicans and royalists are included in this category)
Independence:	A dispute over the independence of colonies or states from former rulers
Jurisdiction:	A dispute between two powers over who is to exercise authority in a disputed area as distinct from a dispute over territorial sovereignty
Minority:	A dispute between a minority and a majority
Post-independence:	A conflict arising from a struggle for power following independence

Religion:	A dispute between adherents of different religions, or between adherents of one religion and another party
Resources:	A dispute over oil, minerals or other natural resources
Secession:	A dispute over an attempt to secede from a state, excluding colonial independence struggles
Territory:	A dispute over the delimitation of borders or the sovereignty of a disputed territory

Whenever conflicts are referred to in the text as 'ethnic' or 'territorial', what is meant is that ethnic or territorial issues were involved.

Violence and Coercion

A simple distinction between 'peaceful' and 'violent' conflicts is difficult to sustain in practice. Three variables were included to represent peacefulness/violence: the degree of coercion used, the extent of hostilities and the number of fatalities.

Following Butterworth (1976), coercion was indicated as one of six categories: no coercion, nonmilitary coercion, threat of force, display of force, use of minor force, use of major force. Here non-military coercion includes measures such as economic sanctions intended to achieve a political objective. Display of force includes the mobilization or deployment of armed forces for demonstrative purposes, but not its use to secure an objective. The category of 'minor force' indicates the use of very limited military force, with no attempt to make a major attack on an adversary's military forces. 'Major force' indicates the use of substantial military forces to secure objectives by military means.

Hostilities

This indicates the amount of fighting that took place, ranging from none through 'minor' (small-scale skirmishes) to 'major' (substantial military engagements).

Fatalities

Figures are given for the number of military and civilian casualties attributable to the conflict, including civilian losses through starvation caused by war. The figures are given as logarithms of the number killed, following Richardson (1960). This suggests the magnitude of violence without suggesting spurious accuracy. The main sources were Sivard (1987), Butterworth (1976) and SIPRI (1969).

Classification of Conflicts by Level of Violence and Type of Resolution

The following definitions were adopted in the three-by-three classification (see Tables 7.1 and 7.2):

Peaceful:	Conflicts in which no hostilities took place and there was no use of coercion
Minor violence:	Conflicts that involved some coercion or some hostilities but not the use of major force
Major violence:	Conflicts involving major hostilities or the use of major force by at least one side
Resolved:	Resolved conflicts as of 1985, where the major parties accepted the conflict was over
Lapsed, quiescent or interim:	Conflicts which had reached interim settlements as of 1985 (some major issues settled, others left outstanding), and conflicts which lapsed or became quiescent without being resolved
Unresolved:	Unresolved conflicts as of 1985

FINDINGS

This section summarizes the findings of the analysis of all 81 conflicts. Subsequent chapters focus on conflicts involving territorial, ethnic, minority and resource issues.

Association between whether a Conflict is Peaceful and whether it is Resolved

Table 7.1 gives a listing of all the conflicts by whether they were resolved, partially resolved or unresolved and whether they were peaceful, violent to a minor degree or violent to a major degree. Table 7.2 shows the number of conflicts in each category. This suggests that there has been a tendency for the peaceful conflicts to be easier to resolve: 80 per cent of the peaceful conflicts had been resolved, compared with 35 per cent of the more violent conflicts; 44 per cent of the conflicts involving major violence remain unresolved, compared with 5 per cent of the peaceful conflicts and 27 per cent of the conflicts involving minor violence.[1]

TABLE 7.2 *All conflicts: level of violence by type of resolution*

	Resolved	Partially resolved	Unresolved	Total
Peaceful	17 (21%)	3 (4%)	1 (1%)	21 (26%)
Minor violence	15 (19%)	4 (5%)	7 (9%)	26 (32%)
Major violence	12 (15%)	7 (9%)	15 (19%)	34 (42%)
Total	44 (54%)	14 (17%)	23 (28%)	81 (100%)

Conflict Resolution by Area

Tables 7.3–5 show a similar breakdown by violence and type of resolution for conflicts by area. Europe has significantly more peaceful conflicts and fewer violent conflicts than the average for all cases. Africa has significantly more violent cases. The Middle East is not significantly different from the average for all conflicts.

TABLE 7.3 *Europe: level of violence by type of resolution*

	Resolved	Partially resolved	Unresolved	Total
Peaceful	7 (26%)	3 (11%)	1 (4%)	11 (41%)
Minor violence	4 (15%)	2 (7%)	5 (19%)	11 (41%)
Major violence	0 (0%)	3 (11%)	2 (7%)	5 (19%)
Total	11 (41%)	8 (30%)	8 (30%)	27 (100%)

TABLE 7.4   *Africa: level of violence by type of resolution*

	Resolved	Partially resolved	Unresolved	Total
Peaceful	8 (22%)	0 (0%)	0 (0%)	8 (22%)
Minor violence	9 (24%)	1 (3%)	0 (0%)	10 (27%)
Major violence	9 (24%)	1 (3%)	9 (24%)	19 (51%)
Total	26 (70%)	2 (5%)	9 (24%)	37 (100%)

TABLE 7.5   *Middle East: level of violence by type of resolution*

	Resolved	Partially resolved	Unresolved	Total
Peaceful	2 (12%)	0 (0%)	0 (0%)	2 (12%)
Minor violence	2 (12%)	1 (6%)	2 (12%)	5 (29%)
Major violence	3 (18%)	3 (18%)	4 (24%)	10 (59%)
Total	7 (41%)	4 (24%)	6 (35%)	17 (100%)

Relationship between Type of Conflict and Peaceful Conflict Resolution

Are some types of conflict more likely to be peacefully resolved than others? The conflicts were classified into eight types (see Tables 7.6–13) according to whether they involved the following issues: control of government, ethnic issues, ideology, independence, jurisdiction, minorities, resources and territory (the categories are not mutually exclusive). The breakdown in each type by level of violence and type of resolution was then compared with that of all conflicts.

TABLE 7.6   *Conflicts over control of government*

	Resolved	Partially Resolved	Unresolved
Peaceful	0	0	0
Minor violence	0	0	0
Major violence	4	4	6

Total = 14

TABLE 7.7   *Conflicts over ethnic issues*

	Resolved	Partially resolved	Unresolved
Peaceful	3	1	0
Minor violence	4	1	4
Major violence	3	2	10

Total = 28

TABLE 7.8   *Conflicts over ideology*

	Resolved	Partially resolved	Unresolved
Peaceful	0	1	0
Minor violence	1	1	4
Major violence	3	2	7

Total = 19

TABLE 7.9   *Conflicts over independence*

	Resolved	Partially resolved	Unresolved
Peaceful	4	0	0
Minor violence	4	0	0
Major violence	6	1	6

Total = 21

TABLE 7.10   *Conflicts over jurisdiction*

	Resolved	Partially resolved	Unresolved
Peaceful	3	2	1
Minor violence	4	1	1
Major violence	1	4	4

Total = 21

TABLE 7.11 *Conflicts over minorities*

	Resolved	Partially resolved	Unresolved
Peaceful	0	2	0
Minor violence	0	1	4
Major violence	1	2	4
	Total = 14		

TABLE 7.12 *Conflicts over secession*

	Resolved	Partially resolved	Unresolved
Peaceful	0	0	0
Minor violence	1	0	1
Major violence	3	1	4
	Total = 10		

TABLE 7.13 *Conflicts over territory*

	Resolved	Partially resolved	Unresolved
Peaceful	5	3	1
Minor violence	6	2	4
Major violence	3	1	8
	Total = 33		

This comparison shows that territorial conflicts were significantly more peaceful than average, having more peaceful cases and fewer cases with major violence than would be expected. Territorial conflicts did not differ significantly from all conflicts in their distribution between resolved, partly resolved and unresolved. Resource conflicts were only slightly different from average in terms of peacefulness, but slightly more than average were resolved.

Conflicts involving a struggle for control of government and ideological issues were more violent than average. Indeed, all the cases involving contested control of government involved major violence. All the conflicts involving an attempted secession were also violent, with more cases of major violence than the average. Among minority conflicts, there were few resolved conflicts. Fewer ethnic conflicts were peaceful and resolved than average.

To summarize, territorial and (to a lesser extent) resource conflicts appeared to be more likely to be peacefully resolved, whereas ideological conflicts, struggles for control of government, ethnic and secession conflicts appeared more likely to be associated with violence.[2] Conflicts involving higher levels of threat to central values are also more likely to be violent.[3]

Association between Peaceful Outcomes and International Disputes

The conflicts were classified into those that were purely international, and those that were either civil or a mixture of civil and international. The association between this attribute and the type of resolution and level of violence is shown in Table 7.14. There was a strong association between international disputes and peaceful outcomes: 85 per cent of the international conflicts were conducted without major violence, compared with only 32 per cent of the civil conflicts. There was no significant association between whether the conflicts were international and whether they were resolved, partially resolved or unresolved.

TABLE 7.14   *Level of violence by whether international or civil*

	Number of international conflicts	Number of civil or civil/international conflicts	Total
Peaceful	17 (43%)	4 (10%)	21 (26%)
Minor violence	17 (43%)	9 (22%)	26 (32%)
Major violence	6 (15%)	28 (68%)	34 (42%)
Total	40 (100%)	41 (100%)	81 (100%)

Duration of Conflict and Violence

The median duration of the resolved conflicts was examined in the three categories of peacefulness/violence. The results are shown in Table 7.15. Conflicts involving major violence had a higher median duration than peacefully resolved conflicts, but conflicts involving minor violence had the lowest median duration. Even in the peacefully resolved conflicts the median duration was seven years.

TABLE 7.15   *Median duration of resolved conflicts by level of violence*

	Median duration (years)
Peaceful	7
Minor violence	3
Major violence	10

Early Third-Party Intervention and Peaceful Resolution of Conflict

There is a growing interest in the idea that the international community should make an effort to catch emergent conflicts at an early stage. If third-party intervention helps to settle disputes, then it is desirable that the intervention come sooner rather than later, and in particular before hostilities have broken out. Was it the case that there was early third-party intervention in the peacefully resolved disputes considered here?

The data base collected by Butterworth (1976) includes information about the types of intervention carried out by third parties in conflicts, and the timing of their interventions. From this it is possible to isolate the conflicts in which interventions aimed at resolving a conflict were made (namely, conciliation, mediation, good offices, arbitration and investigation), as distinct from interventions such as coercion or exhortation. The conflict-resolving interventions were then divided into those made before hostilities had broken out, and those made after. All other cases were counted as no intervention. Insufficient information was available on 12 conflicts.

Table 7.16 shows the resulting classification by level of violence and timing of intervention. The first, second and third columns suggest an association between peaceful resolution and early intervention. Excluding cases where information is missing, 44 per cent of all peacefully resolved conflicts had some form of third party intervention, by definition at a peaceful stage of the conflict. In contrast only 12 per cent of the violent conflicts had early third party intervention. Less than a third of the cases with third party intervention at the phase of peaceful conflict became wars, while half of the cases without early intervention ended in war. No significant association was found between timing of intervention and whether conflicts were resolved, partially resolved or unresolved.[4]

TABLE 7.16 *Number of conflicts with third-party intervention before and after the outbreak of hostilities by level of violence*

	Intervention during peaceful phase of conflict	Intervention after hostilities	No intervention	Information missing
Peaceful	8	N/A	10	3
Minor violence	2	5	12	7
Major violence	4	20	8	2
Total	14	25	30	12

Association between Level of Violence and Power Disparity

Did differences in the relative power of the parties affect how their conflicts were resolved? It was not possible to investigate this subject in detail, but Butterworth (1976) gives an index of power disparity based on the Cox–Jacobson scale, which classifies nations into smallest powers, small powers, middle powers, large powers and superpowers. The scale cannot be used for non-state actors. Table 7.17 shows differences in power compared with level of violence. There is no significant association.

TABLE 7.17   *Level of violence by power disparity*

	Roughly equal	Somewhat unequal	Very unequal
Peaceful	8	5	6
Minor violence	8	2	9
Major violence	10	11	11
Total	26	18	26

Association between Level of Violence and Previous Antagonism

Butterworth also provides data about the previous relationships of the parties in dispute. Table 7.18 classifies conflicts into those in which the previous relationship was antagonistic, and those in which it was not. There was a signficant relationship between previous antagonism and the likelihood of a dispute being violent.

TABLE 7.18   *Level of violence by previous relationship*

	Previous relationship non-antagonistic	Previous relationship antagonistic
Peaceful	8	10
Minor violence	10	9
Major violence	6	26
Total	24	45

NOTES

1. Sherman (1987) reports somewhat comparable results. He groups conflicts into four categories: (a) 'mere disputes' (disputes which never became violent); (b) 'mere crises' (disputes in which one side considered using force, or there was a display or threat of force, but force was not in fact used); (c) 'diffused hostilities'; (d) 'tenuously terminated hostilities'. The last two are treated together here.

He looks at their resolution in terms of five categories: 'complete settlement', 'new case evolution', 'dissipated', 'defeated parties' and 'ongoing cases'. Merging 'new case evolution' and 'ongoing cases' into a category of 'unresolved', and relabelling 'dissipated' as 'lapsed', this gives the following table:

TABLE 7.19   *Conflicts in Sherman's data set (numbers and row percentages)*

	Settled	Lapsed	Unresolved	Defeated	Total
Mere disputes	138 (58%)	59 (25%)	41 (17%)	0 (0%)	238
Mere crises	43 (22%)	80 (41%)	69 (35%)	3 (2%)	196
Hostilities	53 (18%)	104 (35%)	94 (32%)	43 (15%)	295
Total	234 (32%)	243 (33%)	204 (28%)	46 (6%)	729

Source: Sherman (1987).

The 'mere disputes', in which there was no threat or use of violence, were much more often settled than the 'mere crises' and the cases with hostilities (36–40 per cent difference). A smaller percentage of 'mere disputes' remained unresolved. This supports the finding in this study that peaceful disputes are more likely to be resolved. Sherman comments, 'Once conflicts escalate into and through a crisis phase, complete settlement is unlikely. Other than among mere disputes, dissipation is the most likely outcome.'

2. Sherman's data for violence by type of conflict are worth comparing with these results, though Sherman uses different categories, namely:

- colonial;
- borders/territory;
- international personality (disputes over diplomatic status, espionage and treaty revisions);
- anti-regime;
- human rights;
- resource;
- navigation;
- terrorism.

His data also show that territorial and resource conflicts were more likely than average to be peaceful, while anti-regime (corresponding to this study's 'control of government' category) and colonial conflicts were more likely to be violent. There are cases of peaceful conflict in every issue type.

TABLE 7.20   *Hostilities by type of conflict: Sherman's data (number of cases and row percentages)*

	Mere disputes	Mere crises	Hostilities	Total
Colonial	18 (24%)	14 (19%)	43 (57%)	75
Territory	78 (40%)	44 (23%)	72 (37%)	194
International personality	30 (61%)	16 (33%)	3 (6%)	49
Anti-regime	10 (6%)	32 (21%)	114 (73%)	156
Human rights	32 (49%)	22 (34%)	11 (17%)	65
Resource	36 (57%)	21 (33%)	6 (10%)	63
Navigation	34 (38%)	38 (42%)	18 (20%)	90
Terrorism	0 (0%)	9 (24%)	28 (76%)	37
Total	238 (33%)	196 (27%)	295 (40%)	729

Source: Sherman (1987).

3. Sherman's data suggest that there is an association between the degree of threat to a party's values and the likelihood that it will resort to violence. He classifies cases by the perceived intensity of threat, ranging from a threat to existence to a limited threat to property or persons. The categories are:

- threat to existence;
- threat to political system;
- threat of loss of colonial territory;
- threat to territorial integrity;
- threat (limited) to population and property;
- threat to diplomatic personnel and process;
- threat to influence in international system;
- threat to economic interests.

Threats to a party's existence or to a political system are associated with a relatively high level of resort to violence, whereas lesser threats are more likely to remain disputes. Yet in all the categories, even in the cases of threats to existence, there are some conflicts which do not become violent.

TABLE 7.21 *Level of violence by threat: Sherman's data (number of cases and row percentages)*

Threat	Mere disputes	Mere crises	Hostilities	Total
Existence	5 (9%)	9 (17%)	40 (74%)	54
Political	7 (5%)	32 (24%)	97 (71%)	136
Loss of colony	21 (34%)	10 (16%)	31 (50%)	62
Territory	83 (39%)	57 (27%)	73 (34%)	213
Population	36 (32%)	39 (35%)	36 (32%)	111
Diplomatic	30 (52%)	21 (36%)	7 (12%)	58
Influence	20 (57%)	11 (31%)	4 (11%)	35
Economic	36 (64%)	16 (29%)	4 (7%)	56
Total	238	196	295	729

Source: Sherman (1987).

4. Bercovitch (1986; 1991) studied mediation in a set of 79 international disputes between 1945 and 1989 which involved more than 100 fatalities. There had been 284 mediation attempts in the 79 disputes. Of these, Bercovitch assesses that 5% led to a full settlement of the dispute, 9% led to a partial settlement, and 8% led to a cease-fire. He treats these as successes. The parties refused the offer of mediation in 22% of the attempts, and 47% were unsuccessful.

    Bercovitch found that the likelihood of successful mediation falls as the number of fatalities in a dispute increases. In disputes with 100–500 fatalities, mediation was successful in 42% of the attempts, compared with only 17% in disputes with more than 1000 casualties. This finding supports the suggestion that early mediation is desirable.

    Bercovitch's study showed that mediation is more likely to be successful between parties of roughly equal power, especially if the parties are both weak states. In disputes between previously friendly states, mediation was twice as likely to be successful as in disputes between previous adversaries.

8 Conflicts Involving Territorial Issues

There were once two men living next door to one another in a comfortable suburb who quarrelled over the ownership of a flower that was growing between their properties. The quarrel began amicably enough, but little by little the men began to argue, raise their voices and insult one another. One of them built a fence to enclose the flower in his garden. The other tore the fence out and built another to make the flower part of his garden. The men then donned terrifying war paint and began to use the fence posts to attack one another. Unable to prevail, one of them struck at his neighbour's wife. The other picked up his neighbour's child and hurled it to the ground. Eventually in their fury the men killed each other's wives and children, each other, and even the flower.

This story, which comes from Norman McLaren's 1952 film *Neighbours* (Hughes, 1962), is a simple parable, but it highlights a universal tendency. We associate borders with security, and attacks on those borders as attacks on ourselves. Throughout history, disputes over borders and territory have precipitated warfare, and many current armed conflicts or threatened conflicts involve territorial disputes. For years huge Soviet and Chinese armied have faced each other along their disputed land frontier, occasionally engaging in minor clashes. In the Himalayas a frontier dispute has caused war and numerous incidents between China and India. India is in dispute with Pakistan over Kashmir, which has been the cause of several wars between them. The eight-year war between Iran and Iraq was ostensibly caused by a dispute over whether their border at the Shatt al'Arab should be along the 'thalweg' line (in the middle of the river) or along the eastern bank. Britain and Argentina, whose people appear to have few interests in conflict, were nevertheless drawn into war over the territorial dispute regarding the Falklands. Even in deserts the need to establish a border has brought war to Algeria and Morocco, North and South Yemen, Iraq and Kuwait. And in Africa the ill-drawn colonial boundaries have contributed to wars and famines in Nigeria, Ethiopia, Chad, the Sudan and elsewhere.

Of course, territory is usually not the only issue in these conflicts. Border disputes are inflammatory, but they can be fanned or quenched by governments. As Downing (1980) says:

> Border disputes rarely have an independent life of their own. They do not suddenly spring into existence, complete with incompatible claims, enraged governments and casualty lists. Rather they resemble cases of high explosives left carelessly behind by the indifferent progress of human history. They need fuses to be dangerous, and someone has to light those fuses for them to explode.

Governments can also choose to defuse the explosives. Territorial disputes do not have to be resolved by war. It is striking how many of the cases in this study were in fact peacefully settled. Table 8.1 shows the breakdown of conflicts involving territorial issues, by the level of violence they involved and by how they were resolved.

TYPES OF OUTCOME

Galtung (1984) outlines some of the outcomes that are possible in territorial conflicts with a hypothetical example: 'Let us imagine that there are two brothers, who agree on one thing, they both want to be King of Milan: if necessary using a battle and military victory as the decision mechanism.' He uses the layout shown in Figure 8.1 to illustrate the possible outcomes.

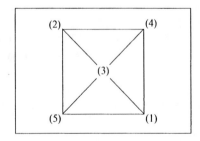

FIGURE 8.1   *Images of lordship in Milan (after Galtung)*

In position (1) Brother 1 lords it over Milan; there is nothing to Brother 2 – in position (2) it is the other way round. But it is easily seen that there are at least three clear alternatives to these rather classic monarchic outcomes. Thus, there is position (3); a compromise whereby they would divide Milan, for instance along the river

TABLE 8.1   *Conflicts involving territorial issues: listing*

	Peaceful	*Minor violence*	*Major violence*

Resolved	Algeria–
	  Tunisia
	Cyrenaica
	Gadaduma Wells
	Ifni
	Liberian
	  borders
	Mauritania–
	  Morocco
	Wadi Halfa
	Åland Islands
	Albania–Greece
	  (N. Epirus)
	Austria
	Belgian–Netherlands
	  border
	German borders
	Minquiers Islands
	Saar
	Bahrain–Iran
	Kuwait–Saudi
	  Arabia
		Gabon–Congo
		Ghana–Upper
		  Volta
		Mauritania–
		  Mali
		Niger–Dahomey
		Trieste
		Saudi Arabia–
		  Oman, Abu Dabi
			Algeria–Morocco
			Algerian
			  independence
			Yemen (Aden)

Partially
resolved
	Romania–Soviet
	  Union
	South Tyrol
		Malawi–
		  Tanzania
		Syria–Turkey
		  (Hatay)
			Egypt–Israel

Unresolved	Gibraltar	Albania–
		  Soviet Union
		Greece–Turkey
		Hungary–
		  Romania
		Bahrain–Qatar
			Ethiopia–Somalia
			Namibia
			Western Sahara
			Cyprus
			Iraq–Iran
			Iraq–Kuwait
			Israel–
			  Palestinians
			South Africa

Po, one ruling to the North and the other to the South of that river.
Then there is position (4) which is considerably more imaginative,
similar to the biconsular solution to Rome some time ago: the two
brothers rule together. Of course, like position (3) this means a redefinition of the situation since the point of departure, the struggle
for outcome (1) or outcome (2) was clearly in terms of either brother
ruling Milan, and all of Milan, alone, to the exclusion of the other
brother. Positions (3) and (4) mean that both have yielded . . . And
then, on top of this, there is also position (5) where neither brother
lords it over Milan.

The suggestion here is that along the 2–1 diagonal there is zero-sum
conflict, but along the 5–4 diagonal lie other solutions which may
peacefully resolve the conflict.

It was found that the outcomes of the territorial conflicts could be
divided into four categories: those in which the territory was awarded
to one side, those in which the territory was awarded to one side but
the other was compensated, those in which the territory was partitioned, and those in which the territory was shared.[1] One conflict
(Bahraini independence) resulted in neither of the original contestants
(Britain and Iran) getting their way but this has been classified as an
award to one side since Bahrainis – who were really one party in a
three-party struggle – ended up ruling their own territory. The
distribution of peaceful and violent conflicts into these categories of
outcome was then examined.

COMPARATIVE ANALYSIS: FINDINGS

Table 8.2 shows the breakdown of peaceful conflicts, conflicts
involving minor violence and conflicts involving major violence by
types of outcome. The table includes both resolved and partially
resolved conflicts, but of course excludes unresolved conflicts. The
conflicts involving violence are defined as those in which armed force
was deployed by at least one side, even though no hostilities may have
occurred.

The table shows that in all the conflicts, including those which were
peacefully resolved, a clear award of territory to one side was the most
frequent outcome. An outcome other than this occurred in only a third
of the peaceful cases. One of the four cases resolved after major
violence involved an outcome other than an outright award to one

TABLE 8.2 *Resolved and partially resolved territorial disputes by level of violence and type of outcome*

	Territory to one side	Territory to one side, compensation to other	Partition	Condominium
Peaceful	12	5	1	0
Minor violence	4	2	1	1
Major violence	3	1	0	0
Total	19	8	2	1

side; this was the Egypt–Israeli settlement. The most common alternative outcome was the award of territory to one side, with some form of compensation to the other; this might take the form of shared rights in minerals or oil in the disputed territory (Algeria–Tunisia) or an agreement to share the use of a disputed river (Liberian boundaries).

This analysis was repeated with the conflicts classified in a different way on the peaceful/violent dimension. Table 8.3 shows a breakdown of territorial conflicts by type of outcome and by level of hostilites. Here 'hostilities' means the engagement of the armed forces of both parties. The outcomes can be divided into 'wins' and 'non–wins'. The first is where one side wins the disputed territory outright, the second is where something else happens: one side gets the territory but the other gets compensation, the territory is partitioned or the territory is shared.

TABLE 8.3 *Resolved and partially resolved territorial disputes by level of hostilities and type of outcome*

	Territory to one side	Territory to one side, compensation to other	Partition	Condominium
No hostilities	14	6	2	1
Minor hostilities	2	1	0	0
Major hostilities	3	1	0	0
Total	19	8	2	1

Nine out of 23 (about 40 per cent) of the conflicts involving no hostilities were 'non-wins'. One out of three (33 per cent) of the conflicts involving minor hostilities were 'non-wins'. One out of four (25 per cent) of the conflicts involving major hostilities were 'non-wins'. There is a suggestion of a tendency for outcomes involving compensation, partition or sharing to be more frequent among the conflicts with less hostilities, but the tendency is not very strong.

The means parties used to reach a settlement were also compared. A number of methods appear in several of the settlements summarized in Table 8.2. One is that the parties agree on a procedure for settling the conflict. This may mean, for example, that they agree to set up a joint boundary commission to look into a frontier dispute as with (Kuwait–Saudi Arabia), that they agree to submit the dispute to the (Belgium–Netherlands), or that they agree to set up a joint study commission (South Tyrol). Yet another means of settling a conflict is to hold an election or plebiscite in the disputed territory. Another is to involve third parties, sometimes as mediators. Some agreements are reached in stages, following a sequence of small co-operative moves. Sometimes a change of government results in a change in the policy of one of the parties which leads to the resolution of the dispute.

Table 8.4 shows the percentage of conflicts in which one or other of these methods of settling was important, broken down by the level of violence in the conflict.[2] No single factor would predict for peaceful resolution: that is, no one factor was present in all the peacefully resolved cases and absent in the violently resolved cases. The involvement of third parties turned out to be the single most important factor of those examined in resolving conflicts. Third parties had an important role in 16 out of the 30 territorial conflicts examined. They were important in half of the conflicts resolved without major violence, and in three out of four of the conflicts resolved after major violence. Change of government was a significant factor in seven out of the 30 conflicts, including two of the four conflicts involving major violence and five of the 18 conflicts resolved without violence.

Finding an agreed procedure was important in one-third of the peaceful conflicts, and moving to an agreement in stages was important in another third. Elections and plebiscites were significant in three of the peacefully resolved conflicts, and the granting of autonomy or cultural rights was important in six of the 26 conflicts resolved without major violence.

TABLE 8.4 *Percentage of resolved and partially resolved territorial conflicts in which particular settlement strategies played a significant role*

Percentage of resolved conflicts in which a significant role was played by:	Peaceful	Minor violence	Major violence
Third parties	50	50	75
Agreed procedure	33	17	25
Agreed reached in stages	33	17	25
Granting of autonomy or cultural rights	22	33	0
Elections/plebiscites	17	0	0
Change of government	28	0	50
Compensation *or* agreed procedure *or* autonomy *or* elections	78	50	25

Although no single factor accounts for the difference between the peacefully and violently resolved conflicts, the picture is different if factors are taken in combination. Table 8.5 also shows the percentage of conflicts which were resolved through the compensation of one side, the acceptance of an agreed procedure, the granting of autonomy or the use of a plebiscite. All of these represent co-operative or integrative solutions to some degree. It was found that at least one of these was present in 14 of the 18 (78 per cent) peaceful conflicts, in four of the eight (50 per cent) conflicts involving minor violence, and in one out of the four (25 per cent) of the conflicts involving major violence.

DISCUSSION AND CONCLUSIONS

This analysis suggests that while no particular method of resolving a territorial conflict is likely to determine a peaceful outcome, the use of some kind of co-operative measure may make a peaceful outcome more likely. Several measures have been used to resolve conflicts peacefully, and they are therefore worth considering in the case of emergent conflicts which are at an early stage. One or more of the following measures may be helpful.

1. The parties should use an accepted procedure for settling the conflict, or invent one if one is not available. An expectation or a declaration that parties seek to settle is a useful preliminary to settling. It can take the form of agreement to submit a dispute to arbitration, to enter into bilateral negotiations, or to set up a joint study group. This does not of itself resolve the conflict, and neither does any party have to abandon its position. However, it is a way for parties to signal intent to settle peacefully.

2. Most outcomes of territorial conflicts are a clear-cut award of the disputed territory to one side. However, it is possible to give both sides a stake in the outcome by some form of compensation to the loser.

3. Third parties often play an important role in resolving this type of dispute.

4. Where territorial conflicts are bound up with disputes over resources, it is often helpful to agree to separate the issues. In several cases a territorial dispute was resolved (or at least allowed to lapse) when it was agreed to deal with the resource conflict separately.

5. Where territorial conflicts are bound up with ethnic disputes, the offer of autonomy, political and cultural rights, or some other form of protection to minority groups can lead to an acceptable resolution of the territorial dispute.

6. In complicated conflicts, a gradual process of resolution is sometimes necessary. Either the parties may agree on a sequence of steps to resolve the conflict, or the parties make gradual moves towards a settlement. Parties need to work for and wait for a resolution in a process that is difficult precisely because it depends on mutual adjustment, and on communications between parties in an already fraught situation.

Nevertheless, territorial conflicts appear to have a higher proportion of peaceful outcomes than some other types of conflict. It is noticeable that in Europe the proportion of peacefully resolved territorial conflicts is particularly high. West European borders have been unchanged for a long time in most areas and are widely accepted as settled. Some eastern and south-eastern European borders are less so. All the European states (except Albania) agreed to regard Europe's boundaries as fixed and inviolable in the Helsinki Final Act (1975). In contrast, many or most of the borders in Africa and the Middle East are creations of colonialism, and have left states divided by serious ethnic, religious and cultural rifts. In Western Europe the coming of the Common Market and the forthcoming changes of 1992 are making borders of less and less importance. Consequently territorial conflicts within Western Europe become of less importance too. When Spain joined the EC, for example, a number of co-operative steps were taken in the dispute over Gibraltar. If there were a greater level of integration and interdependence in the world community as a whole, the importance of territorial conflicts might begin to diminish.

NOTES

1. The following conflicts were ones in which the outcome was that one side won the disputed territory: Cyrenaica, Ifni, Mauritania–Morocco, Åland Islands, Albania–Greece (Northern Epirus), Belgium–Netherlands, Minquiers Islands, Saar, Bahrain–Iran (Bahraini independence), German unification, Romania–Soviet Union, South Tyrol, Ghana–Upper Volta, Mauritania–Mali, Malawi–Tanzania, Syria–Turkey (Hatay), Algeria–Morocco, Algerian independence, Yemen (Aden).

   The following conflicts were ones in which one side won the disputed territory but the other was compensated: Algeria–Tunisia, Gadaduma Wells, Liberian borders, Wadi Halfa, Austria, Gabon–Congo, Saudi Arabia–Oman, Egypt–Israel.

   The following conflicts were settled through partition of the disputed territory: Kuwait–Saudi Arabia, Trieste. In the Niger–Dahomey conflict the disputed territory was shared.

2. The list below gives the conflicts in which various methods of settling were significant:

   (a) separation of territorial from other issues: Algeria–Tunisia, Wadi Halfa, Minquiers Islands, South Tyrol, Gabon–Congo, Trieste, Egypt–Israel;

   (b) agreement on procedures to settle the conflict: Belgium–Netherlands, Minquiers Islands, Saar, Bahrain–Iran, Kuwait–Saudi Arabia, South Tyrol, Trieste, Egypt–Israel (in the cases of Saudi Arabia–Oman and Algeria–Morocco such agreements were made but then broken by one side);

   (c) granting of autonomy or cultural rights: Åland Islands, Albania–Greece, Romania–Soviet Union, South Tyrol, Trieste;

(d) plebiscites or elections: Austria, Saar, Bahrain–Iran (in this case a UN representative made soundings of public opinion although formal elections were not held);

(e) agreement reached in stages: Cyrenaica, Gadaduma Wells, Ifni, Albania–Greece, Saar, South Tyrol, Syria–Turkey, Egypt–Israel;

(f) change of government: Liberian borders, Mauritania–Morocco, Wadi Halfa, Austria, German unification, Algeria–Morocco, Algerian independence;

(g) third-party intervention: Cyrenaica, Mauritania–Morocco, Wadi Halfa, Åland Islands, Belgium–Netherlands, Minquiers Islands, Saar, Bahrain–Iran, South Tyrol, Gabon–Congo, Ghana–Upper Volta, Niger–Dahomey, Saudi Arabia–Oman, Algeria–Morocco, Algerian independence, Egypt–Israel.

9 Conflicts Involving Ethnic Issues

Ethnic issues are at the heart of some of the most dangerous and protracted disputes in the world today. The conflict between Palestinians and Israelis, for example, has been described as a struggle about 'ethno-nationalism' (Heraclides, 1989). The Lebanon conflict involves struggles between Maronite, Arab and Druze ethnic groups. The current struggle for reform in the Soviet Union is going on against a backdrop of ethnic conflict.

Ethnic divisions are those based on differences between peoples. In principle, they can be measured scientifically by genetic analysis, but in practice what matters is groups' perceptions of differences between themselves. As such, ethnic differences may not be sharply distinct from other intercommunal differences, such as those between religious groups. Physical differences are the most obvious discriminators, but differences in language, accent, clothing or behaviour may be sufficient for individuals to be seen as belonging to a different people. In this sense, as Horowitz (1985) says, ethnic differences are ascriptive.

Most ethnic conflicts involve the rights of ethnic groups to maintain their identity, to have equal status with other groups, and to have equal access to decision-making. Societies with ethnic differences often divide along ethnic lines in such a way that some ethnic groups are permanently excluded from power. If the excluded groups are forced to integrate into the national culture of the state in which they find themselves, the threat to their identity can readily lead to frustration, polarization and violence. Since ethnic conflict involves whole communities, it makes itself felt not only in disputes between elites, but also at the level of popular stereotypes and mass antagonisms. If polarization takes place, it feeds on existing differences which are already widely recognized.

Table 9.1 gives a breakdown of the conflicts involving ethnic issues included in the study. Within the category of ethnic conflicts, the table includes several sub-categories. One cluster is situations where people are ethnically different from the nation in which they live, but share the same roots as the people of another nation. They may have become separated by conquest, by the drawing and redrawing of boundaries through history, by colonialism, or for other reasons. The separated group usually aspires to be returned to the government of the ethnically similar nation. Examples of this type are the Åland Islanders, ethnically Swedish but subject to Finnish sovereignty, the Greeks living in Northern Epirus (now part of Albania), the Germans in the Saar while this territory was held by France, the German-speaking ethnically Austrian people in the South Tyrol (part of Italy), the Hungarians living in Romania (Case 33), and the Somalis living in Ethiopia (Case 24). The Kosovo conflict in Yugoslavia (Case 2) is similar, with the complication that a minority of Serbs in Kosovo is protesting against the concessions the government has made to the Albanian majority in the province, who are themselves a minority in Yugoslavia.

TABLE 9.1 *Conflicts involving ethnic issues*

	Peaceful	*Minor violence*	*Major violence*
Resolved	Åland Islands Albania–Greece (N. Epirus) Saar	Gabon–Congo Mauritania–Mali Sudanese independence Trieste	Nigerian Civil War Zaire (Congo) Zimbabwe
Partially resolved	South Tyrol	Syria–Turkey (Hatay)	Tutsi–Hutu Jordan–Palestinians

Unresolved		Albania–
		  Yugoslavia
		  (Kosovo)
		Greece–Turkey
		Hungary–
		  Romania
		Kurds–Turkey
			Angola
			Ethiopia–Somalia
			Ethiopia–Eritrea
			Namibia
			Sudan
			Cyprus
			Iraq–Iran
			Israel–Palestinians
			South Africa
			Uganda

Another cluster involves situations where two ethnic groups, derived from two nations, live in a disputed area. Examples of this type are the conflict between Greek Cypriots and Turkish Cypriots in Cyprus (Case 16), the conflict between Italians and Yugoslavs in Trieste, and the Syrians and Turkish in Hatay (Case 69). Another cluster is of conflicts within one nation divided by ethnic fissures. Examples are Sudan (Case 66), which straddles the North–South divide in Africa between Moslem and 'traditional' groups; Zaire (Case 80), where the sudden granting of independence led to a power struggle between the major ethnic groups; Nigeria (Case 55), an inchoate colonial incorporation of different ethnic groups, also plunged into rivalry following independence; Zimbabwe (Case 81), where the conflict between ZANU and ZAPU reflected Shona–Ndebele divisions; and Uganda (Case 74).

South Africa and Zimbabwe together belong to a category on their own of conflict between white colonial regimes and black majorities. In some ways the conflict between the Tutsi and Hutu in Rwanda and Burundi (Case 73) might be put in this category too, because it is a legacy of the Tutsi conquests of territory previously occupied by Hutus, and of the resentments created by an ethnically stratified society, where one ethnic group ruled the other.

The Greece–Turkey (Case 31) and Gabon–Congo (Case 25) examples are not classic ethnic conflicts. Both involved expulsion of nationals of one country resident in the other. The Mauritania–Mali conflict (Case 47) was primarily territorial, although the ethnic conflicts of traditional societies in the disputed area was a precipitating factor.

HOW THE CONFLICTS WERE RESOLVED

The cases of the Åland Islands, South Tyrol, Trieste and Northern Epirus are cases where such conflict was resolved without hostilities. In the Åland Islands case, the conflict was resolved by granting the Swedish islanders autonomy and self-government, although the islands remained Finnish. The islanders use Swedish for education and government, and are proud of their islands' status as autonomous, neutral and demilitarized. (They even have advantages over other islands which remain Swedish because their protected land rights mean that wealthy Stockholmers have been unable to buy holiday cottages and drive the house prices up.) In the case of South Tyrol, the 1969 agreement gave the German-speaking minority self-determination in educational and cultural matters, linguistic rights and some autonomy of economic management. The Trieste dispute was resolved through a territorial partition, with cultural guarantees for the minorities created on either side. The Northern Epirus dispute (Case 3) between Greece and Albania appears to have been resolved through Albanian acceptance of Greek cultural and political rights. The Greek minority is taught Greek in schools and is well represented in the Albanian political system. Indeed, it was a Greek Albanian who negotiated the end of the notional 'state of war' between Greece and Albania in 1985. In the cases of South Tyrol, Hatay and Northern Epirus, members of the ethnic groups involved were also given the option to leave if they wished.

If a settlement is to last, it must give the ethnic groups a fair stake in the political system. These cases suggest that one of the options which offers prospects for a durable settlement is the granting of autonomy and cultural rights to an ethnic minority, possibly within the framework of a federal system.

How were the violent ethnic conflicts eventually resolved? There are three cases of resolved conflicts following major violence: the Nigerian Civil War, Zimbabwe and Zaire. In the case of Zaire, the effort of the Katangans to secede was crushed and a strong unitary government was established, which then became a military dictatorship. This kind of resolution may work if the defeated group is either completely destroyed or reconciled to its defeat, but if it is only dispersed or driven underground, resentments may linger and resurface at a later time; in this sense the conflict may not be fully resolved. (Indeed, if the recent fighting in Shaba by Katangan exiles is interpreted as a continuation of the conflict, this conflict has not been resolved.)

In the Nigerian and Zimbabwean cases, although there was a clear victor, the victor pursued a policy of reconciliation. In the case of Zimbabwe, the conflict was ended before any party had been utterly defeated. Certainly the white minority government did not give up without being exposed to a great deal of pressure. The combination of international sanctions, greater isolation following Portugal's withdrawal from her colonies, the South African calculation that it was better to have a moderate black government than a protracted civil war and the pressure from Henry Kissinger eventually forced the white government to accept the principle of majority rule. Having conceded this, the further steps taken by the Muzorewa government towards free elections on a one-person, one-vote basis presented an alternative to a fight to the finish in the guerrilla war. It is also true that the settlement was marred by ethnic fighting between the Shona majority and the Ndebele minority. However, Mugabe followed a policy of conciliation, working with both the whites and Nkomo to form the new state.

In the case of Nigeria, despite the utter defeat of Ojukwu's Biafra, General Gowon did not slaughter the Ibos, as had been feared, but instead pursued a relatively conciliatory policy towards them. When power returned to civilian hands in 1969, the framers of the new federal constitution set up a system which represented the ethnic groups with reasonable fairness. More states were created and more executive powers were given to the states. This tended to enhance the representation of all the ethnic groups at the local level, while containing and reducing the struggle for power at the centre (Horowitz, 1985). The new constitution treated the Ibos on a par with other ethnic groups.

COMPARATIVE ANALYSIS: FINDINGS

First, of all the ethnic conflicts studied, the only ones which were resolved peacefully were those in Europe.

Second, of the ethnic conflicts which were resolved without major violence, all also involved a territorial dispute (Sudanese independence may be counted as an exception, although this conflict involved contested jurisdiction over Sudan). In contrast, none of the conflicts resolved after major violence involved issues of territory or jurisdiction. Of the violent ethnic conflicts which remain unresolved, half also involve territorial disputes.

This rather surprising finding suggests that ethnic conflicts which also involve territorial claims are more likely to be resolved. It would be dangerous to press this too far, however. Irredentism is well known as a cause of war. A familiar case is Germany's pre-war aspirations to German-speaking areas; and Somalia's irredentist conflict with Ethiopia is the source of a continuing, costly armed conflict.

The finding directs attention to the nature of governments' involvement with ethnic conflict. If territorial issues are involved, conflicts may become a matter of intergovernmental relations, and they may be more easily defused at this level.

Third, in the peacefully resolved conflicts, governments were not fully aligned and identified with the interests of the ethnic groups. Indeed, ethnic passions seem to have cooled when the focus of the dispute shifted toward intergovernmental negotiations in the cases of

South Tyrol, Trieste, Northern Epirus, Mauritania–Mali and Sudanese independence.

In contrast, in the conflicts which led to major violence, there was often either an identification between the government and one ethnic group or a struggle between ethnic groups for the control of government. For example, in the Nigerian Civil War, it was the capture of government by a coalition of parties from the North and West which led the Ibos to feel excluded and to mount a coup in 1966; the Ibo-dominated government they formed then led to resentments in the North and massacres of Ibos.

Sudan is a classic case of a government identified with one ethnic group imposing its values on another. The decision to make the Shari'a (Islamic law) compulsory even in non-Moslem areas has been one of the southerners' most bitter grievances. Similarly, the effort of the Ethiopian government to impose an Ethiopian national identity and the use of the Amharic language in Eritrea has led to violent resistance, as have Iraq's efforts to impose Arabic culture on the Kurds. South Africa and Israel are well-known cases where the government is wholly identified with one of the groups involved in an ethnic conflict.

There seems to be a chance that ethnic conflicts can be contained in cases where governments either stand aloof or at least remain less involved than the ethnic groups themselves. Governments may then play a third party role and act as a channel of communication between the disputing parties. Moreover, governments are subject to the diplomatic energies of the international community. On the other hand, where governments themselves become identified with an ethnic group, they clearly became parties themselves, and may make an existing dispute more violent.

Fourth, all the ethnic conflicts which became a struggle for control of the government led to major violence, usually civil war.

Finally, all the ethnic conflicts in which secession was attempted led to violence. Six secession attempts are included (Biafra, Katanga, Eritrea, the Ogaden, southern Sudan and the Kurds). All involved major violence. Indeed, these conflicts accounted for a total of over 3.2 million civilian and military casualties.

CONCLUSIONS

In the cases of peacefully resolved ethnic conflicts, the parties on each side were ultimately prepared to acknowledge and take account of each other's interests. In the cases of South Tyrol, Northern Epirus, the Åland Islands and Trieste, the ethnic minorities were prepared to accept the sovereignty of the nations in which they found themselves. In turn these nations were prepared to acknowledge the ethnic minority's special needs for identity, granting cultural guarantees and a measure of political autonomy.

In contrast, when ethnic groups attempted to impose a settlement – either by making a secession attempt, or by using control of the government to dominate an ethnically divided society – violence was the result. Neither attempting secession nor seeking to establish a dominant national identity by excluding ethnic groups is likely to result in peaceful resolution of conflict.

In the cases where violent conflicts were finally resolved, societies needed to find a settlement which acknowledged the reality of the interests of the divided groups. The Nigerian case is interesting precisely because, although Biafra was destroyed, the subsequent federal constitution acknowledged and balanced the interests of all the groups that the parties in conflict had comprised.

10 Conflicts Involving Minorities

Most states include minorities within their populations. Some may be religious, some ethnic, some linguistic. Two main types of conflict can be distinguished: those where the minority is excluded from power by the majority and those where a minority has power and excludes the majority.

Much of the discussion in the previous section applies to minorities too; it is common for ethnic issues and minority issues to arise together.

In conflicts where the majority community holds power, the minority seeks to preserve its group identity and assert political rights, while the majority group tends to rule in its own interests. In democracies divided between majority and minority groups which operate majority voting, the minority can be permanently frozen out of power, and this creates inevitable tensions.

Where a minority holds power, the majority usually seeks to assert its rights and establish majority rule. Such conflicts are overtly about majority rule, but the question of the rights of the minority in the event of a transfer to majority rule is also a latent issue.

A classic case of a majority ruling a minority is Northern Ireland (Case 56), where the minority (Catholic/Nationalist) community comprises 37 per cent of the population and the majority (Protestant/Loyalist) community 63 per cent. The roots of the conflict lie in the seventeenth century, when the 'plantation' of English and Scottish settlers created a local majority in Ulster at odds with the Irish Catholics. In its present form, the conflict goes back to 1921–2, when Ireland was partitioned into the Irish Free State and Ulster. In the subsequent decades the Catholic minority refused to participate in the political system in the North because it was dominated by Protestant parties, and consequently the Protestants governed on their own.

When young Catholics demanded equal political rights through the Civil Rights movement of 1969, the Protestant leaders refused to make concessions, and sectarian violence broke out. The British government decided to deploy British troops in the province, and the IRA (Irish Republican Army) stepped up its campaign of terrorism. The conflict remains unresolved because the Catholic and Protestant parties are unable to agree on power-sharing or on any other system of government which meets the minority community's demands.

Turning to situations where a minority rules a majority, a classic case is South Africa (Case 64). This conflict also goes back to the seventeenth century, when Dutch settlers established a colony at the Cape. In 1806 Britain captured the Cape from Holland, and the Boers left on their 'Great Trek' to create two new republics in the interior. The Boers were defeated by the British in the Boer Wars, but after 1948 the Afrikaner nationalists won power in South Africa, and set up a tightly controlled system for preserving white minority power. On the basis of the doctrine of apartheid, the minority government created separate homelands for blacks where they suffer massive deprivation, and denied them civil and political rights in South Africa. Having dealt harshly with the black majority for many decades, the white minority community clearly fears the consequences of majority rule.

HOW THE CONFLICTS WERE RESOLVED

Table 10.1 shows a classification of conflicts involving minority issues by type of resolution and level of violence. Only three of the 14 cases were either resolved or partially resolved (Romania–Soviet Union, South Tyrol and Zimbabwe) and only two were peaceful (Romania–Soviet Union and South Tyrol).

The conflict between Romania and the Soviet Union over the Romanian minority in the Soviet republic of Moldavia appeared to have been peacefully resolved following Ceauşescu's recognition of Soviet territorial rights in 1976. Romania had distanced itself from the Soviet Union since 1956, and in 1964 republished Marx's *Notes on the Romanians*, in which he had condemned the Tsar's annexation of Bessarabia in 1812. Romania had also followed an independent ideological line, calling for the dissolution of the Warsaw Pact and NATO, and denouncing the Soviet invasion of Czechoslovakia. There were fears that the Soviet Union might also invade Romania, but these did not materialize, and in 1976 Ceauşescu announced that Romania

TABLE 10.1   *Conflicts involving minority issues*

	Peaceful	*Minor violence*	*Major violence*
Resolved			Zimbabwe
Partially resolved	Romania– Soviet Union South Tyrol	Syria–Turkey (Hatay)	Tutsi–Hutu Jordan–Palestinians
Unresolved		Albania–Yugoslavia (Kosovo) Greece–Turkey Hungary–Romania Kurds–Turkey	Northern Ireland Iraq–Iran Israel–Palestinians South Africa

had 'no territorial or other problems with the Soviet Union', while Brezhnev declared that there were 'no important problems between our countries'. In 1976 new constitutions were promulgated in the Soviet republics which extended the rights of national minorities.

Recently, however, the issue of minority rights has surfaced again in Moldavia. In 1989 the Moldavian Soviet introduced a draft law to make Moldavian the official language, and this prompted a strike among the Russian minority. A newly formed Moldavian Popular Front is demanding a Moldavian flag, a Moldavian Church, democracy, closer links with Romania and an end to Russian immigration. President Gorbachev secured an agreement on the issue of language, whereby Moldavian would become the official language but Russian would remain the language of use between the two communities. It remains to be seen whether the difference of views between the nationalists and Russians who favour centralism will become more serious.

In South Tyrol, the 1969 agreement provided protection for the German-speaking minority by guaranteeing equal access to employment, an autonomous regional assembly and cultural rights in language and education. The minority has also been protected by the Austrian government, which took part in drawing up and monitoring the agreement. Although the implementation of the agreements is still not complete, the parties have accepted the principles of equal treatment for minorities and co-operation (even in 'internal affairs') between concerned states.

The case of Zimbabwe, partly covered in the previous section, is a resolved conflict in which a dominant minority was replaced by majority rule. The process by which this was achieved involved both political pressure on the white government by the international community – notably Britain, the USA and later South Africa – and an armed struggle. However, the Lancaster House talks came to an agreed procedure for passing power to a majority government that was acceptable to the black nationalist parties, the white government and black moderate leaders. This procedure included the holding of elections, and a constitution which provided some protection and electoral privileges for the white minority, notably the reservation of 20 out of 100 seats in the Lower Assembly as 'white seats'. These seats were later to be scrapped, but the acceptance by both sides of an interim period, in which power was transferred and black politicians and white officials worked together, undoubtedly made for a more peaceful transition. The white minority recognized the rights of Zimbabweans to majority rule, but the new government also recognized the need to co-operate with the white minority.

DISCUSSION AND CONCLUSIONS

A helpful and considered treatment of minority conflicts can be found in the report of the British Council of Churches Working Party on Human Rights and Responsibilities in Britain and Northern Ireland (Bailey, 1988a). The focus of the report is Northern Ireland, but its canvas is much wider.

The report insists on the need to strike a balance in minority conflicts between rights and responsibilities. One group's rights, says the report, are another's responsibilities. Both minorities and majorities have rights, and they also have responsibilities to one another:

> It is not in accord with human dignity that one people should rule over another; it is desirable that peoples should be responsible for their own destinies. But, like other rights, self-determination needs to be balanced by a regard for responsibilities. The majority in any state has a duty to respect the rights of local minorities, and minorities have a duty to respect the democratic wishes of the majority' (Bailey, 1988a, p. 59)

The report outlines three conditions that are necessary for the peaceful resolution of minority conflicts. The first is that political dialogue and intercommunity relations develop in a stable framework; it has to be accepted on all sides that territorial changes will not be brought about by violent coercion. Second, solutions will last 'only if adopted by the free and willing consent of the people concerned'. Third, 'a fair and reasonable attitude of mind is fundamental to the successful resolution of tensions in society. There must on all sides be a willingness to treat other communities with the same fairness as one expects for one's own' (Bailey, 1988a, p. 64).

Where minority conflicts have been resolved, the principles of equal status and respect for minority rights are accepted, and backed by legal or constitutional measures. Switzerland is often cited as a successful case. It manages its ethnic and linguistic diversity through a federal system in which the cantons have considerable self-government. There is also proportional representation in the Cabinet. According to polls, most people now identify themselves first as Swiss, despite their ethnic differences, and the French and Italian minorities are more satisfied with Swiss government than the German majority (Horowitz, 1985). (This balance was not achieved without armed conflict in the nineteenth century, when there was a brief war between the 'liberal' and 'Catholic' cantons.)

In 1979 the UN Subcommission on the Prevention of Discrimination and the Protection of Minorities published the Caportiti report (Caportiti, 1979). It suggested that, when dealt with well, minorities could form bonds between states:

> History shows that the minority problem can poison international relations. However, with the new standards set by the United Nations in the framework of human rights, minority groups can now play a positive role in international relations. When their rights are guaranteed and fully respected, minority groups can serve as a link between States. The Special Rapporteur believes that bilateral agreements dealing with minority rights concluded between States where minorities live and States from which such minorities originate (especially between neighbouring countries) would be extremely useful. It must be stressed, however, that co-operation with regard to the rights of members of minority groups shall be based on mutual respect for the principles of the sovereignty and the territorial integrity of the States concerned and non-interference in their internal affairs.

Bailey (1988a) observes that 'in all the successful solutions to conflicts involving minorities, one common cluster of features is an unqualified acceptance by all the states concerned of each other's sovereignty and of secure and recognised boundaries between them, and an unqualified renunciation of territorial claims upon each other'.

The cases of South Tyrol, Northern Epirus and Romania–Soviet Union all seem to support this view. In the Northern Epirus case, the formal state of war between Greece and Albania was ended by Greece dropping its territorial claim, and the members of the Greek minority in Albania were influential in bringing about the rapprochement between the two states. In the South Tyrol case Austria's willingness to abandon a territorial claim, and Italy's willingness to accept an Austrian role in relation to South Tyrol, were important factors in creating the peaceful settlement. In the Romania and the Soviet Union, Romania's willingness to forswear its territorial claims defused the conflict.

It is encouraging to note, in this context, that the territorial element of the Northern Ireland conflict has effectively been dropped, at least in terms of relations between the governments. Articles 2 and 3 of the Irish Constitution asserted the Republic's claim to the North:

2. The national territory consists of the whole island of Ireland, its islands and territorial seas.
3. Pending the reintegration of the national territory, and without prejudice to the right of the Parliament and Government established by this Constitution to exercise jurisdiction over the whole of that territory, the laws enacted by that Parliament shall have the like area and extent of application as the laws of Saorstat Eireann (i.e. the twenty-six counties of the Republic) and the like extra-territorial effect.

In 1967 an all-party Irish committee agreed to reformulate Article 3 to indicate that the reintegration of Ireland was an aspiration, to be achieved through agreement and by peaceful means (Boyle and Hadden, 1985). The claim was dropped in both the Sunningdale agreement of 1973 and in the Hillsborough Accord of 1985 (the Anglo–Irish Agreement). The former declared that there could be no change in the status of Northern Ireland until a majority in Northern Ireland wanted it. The latter reiterated this principle, and observed that at present the majority has no wish for such a change. The principle of consultation between the two governments has been agreed, but the task of securing equal political rights, equal opportunities to employment and an acceptable basis for administration remains to be achieved.

While the two communities are unable to agree on a political settlement, the conflict continues. Meanwhile the claim to territorial sovereignty continues to play a powerful role in popular Nationalist folklore. Here it is put in Tommy Makem's lyrical folk song, 'Four Green Fields' (the fields in the song are the four provinces of Ulster, Munster, Leinster and Connaught, and the fine old woman is Ireland):

> 'What did I have', said the fine old woman
> 'What did I have', this fine old woman did say
> 'I had four green fields, and each one was a jewel
> But strangers came and tried to take them from me.
> I had fine strong sons and they fought to save my jewels
> They fought and died, and that was my grief', said she.

> 'Long time ago', said the fine old woman
> 'Long time ago', this fine old woman did say
> 'There was war and death, plundering and pillage
> My children starved, in mountain, valley and sea
> And their wailing cries, they shook the very heavens
> My four green fields ran red with their blood', said she.

> 'What have I now', said the fine old woman
> 'What have I now', this proud old woman did say
> 'I have four green fields, and one of them's in bondage
> In strangers' hands, who tried to take it from me
> But my sons have sons, as brave as were their fathers
> My four green fields will bloom once again', said she.

11 Resource Conflicts

There can no longer be the slightest doubt that resource scarcities and ecological stresses constitute real and imminent threats to the future well-being of all people and nations. These challenges are fundamentally non-military and it is imperative that they be addressed accordingly. If this is not recognised . . . there is a grave risk that the situation will deteriorate to the point of crisis where, even with low probability of success, the use of force could be seen as a way to produce results quickly.

(Thorsson et al., 1982)

Pressure on resources and the competition it generates has always been a source of disputes. For Greece in the sixth century BC, it was the growth of the population of Athens beyond the carrying capacity of its hinterland which drove the city into developing trade, colonies and an empire, leading ultimately to the war with Sparta. In the Middle Ages, kings and knights struggled over land, the key resource in an agricultural society. In the sixteenth and seventeenth centuries, England, Spain, Portugal and Holland struggled for control of gold, spices and other traded commodities. In the early industrial age, regions rich in coal and oil became the sources of disputes.

Now, with industrialization spreading around the world, and the world population growing rapidly, both renewable and non-renewable resources are under increasing pressure. At the same time urban populations have grown dependent on a constant flow of resources supplied from outside national boundaries. As states and peoples seek to enrich themselves and assure their security, the risks of competition over resources are evident.

This competition is most dangerous over the resource which now fuels all the world's major cities, industries and transport systems. Oil is universally required, but very unevenly distributed, and it is not

surprising that people have struggled over its control since the earliest
days of the oil industry. The Great Powers were already alert to the
security aspects of oil by the First World War, when oil-fired warships
were entering their fleets. British policy in the Middle East during and
after the war had the protection of oil supplies as one of its aims
(Venn, 1986). In the Second World War, the US decision to embargo
Japanese oil influenced the Japanese decision to go to war, with the
aim of seizing territory to establish a large 'Co-Prosperity Sphere'
which would be self-sufficient in natural resources. In the West too, oil
played a major role in strategic planning, particularly in the German
attack on the Caucasus. After the war, the USA took over the British
role in the Persian Gulf. By 1950, President Truman was assuring King
Abdul Aziz of Saudi Arabia that 'no threat could arise to your
kingdom that would not be of immediate concern to the United
States'. In 1973, at the height of the first oil crisis, Henry Kissinger
threatened to use force if necessary to secure the supply of oil from the
Middle East. President Ford was asked about this in an interview:

Q. Can you tell us more about the idea of using force in the Middle
    East?
A. I stand by the view that Henry Kissinger expressed . . . Now the
    word strangulation is the key word. His language said he
    wouldn't rule out force if the free world or the industrialised
    world would be strangled. I would reaffirm my support of that
    position.

President Sadat of Egypt was asked about these American threats:

Q. Do you take seriously the threats of Mr. Gerald Ford and Mr.
    Henry Kissinger concerning the possibility of American military
    intervention in the Middle East?
A. Henry was wrong to use such language . . . Do you think we
    would remain with our arms folded in the face of American
    military intervention? The United States has been warned: the
    Arabs will set fire to the oil wells if they are the victims of armed
    aggression.

Later President Carter warned again that the USA would be
prepared to use force to protect the supply of oil. He stationed a
Rapid Deployment Force off the Gulf. Subsequently the protection of
oil supplies became a central role for the US Central Command. In

1990–1, following the Iraqi invasion of Kuwait, these plans and warnings became a reality. The USA now appears to be committed to increasingly open military intervention to maintain the security of supplies.

Oil is the most prominent disputed resource, but it is not the only one. The supply of natural gas has been less contentious than oil, but the Soviet pipeline from Alaska to Western Europe led to a dispute with the USA over America's fears that Western Europe would become too dependent on Soviet resources. Uranium and coal supplies have been factors in the conflicts over Namibia and South Africa.

Minerals have also been at stake in these and other conflicts in southern Africa (Maull, 1984; Hveem, 1986). The discovery of manganese nodules on the seabed has led to disputes over this new source of minerals.

Water is a scarce resource in arid regions, and it is under increasing demand in Africa, the Middle East, South Asia and elsewhere (Falkenmark, 1990). Disputes over water have become a growing issue, especially in the Middle East. Israel and Jordan are in sharp contention over the use of the River Jordan. In 1990, King Hussein of Jordan declared that water was the only issue over which Jordan would be prepared to go to war with Israel. The Nile is also becoming a focus of dispute. Egypt and Sudan have shared the waters for years but, as demand rises, tensions are mounting. In 1985, Egypt's foreign minister predicted, 'The next war in our region will be over the waters of the Nile, not politics.' The control of the Nile has also become an issue in the Sudanese Civil War. In southern Asia, India and Bangladesh have been in dispute over the sharing of the Ganges. Bangladesh feared that India's plans to divert water from the river would adversely affect its agriculture, as indeed it did when India built a dam upstream of the frontier. Bangladesh submitted the dispute to the UN, but it remains a source of contention. Falkenmark estimates that 35 per cent of the world's population lives in river basins which flow through more than one country and, as populations grow, occasions for disputes will increase. Rivers which are already subject to actual or potential disputes include, besides those already mentioned, the Euphrates, Zambezi, Niger, Senegal, Medjerda, Brahmaputra and Mekong (Falkenmark, 1986).

Food resources are also under increasing stress. Fishing disputes between states are now common, especially as existing stocks suffer from overexploitation. Disputes over cattle and land are common both within and between states. Besides the competition for resources, industrial development and population growth is putting stress on the natural environment, threatening a global 'tragedy of the commons' (Hardin, 1968). This is a 'social trap' which can readily lead to serious disputes. It applies, for example, to atmospheric pollution, overfishing and deforestation.

Most of these resource disputes do not give rise directly to international and civil disputes. The more usual pattern is that resource disputes become an additional issue in existing conflicts which combine numerous issues. For example, oil was undoubtedly a critical factor in the Gulf conflict, but other issues overlaid it (in particular a territorial dispute, the background grievances between poor and rich Arabs and the particular ideological and nationalist aspirations of the Ba'athist regime). In the Middle East water issues become conflicts by being combined with existing ethnic and nationalist conflicts. Within states conflicts over food generally appear as disputes about the wealth and status of different social and economic strata. The social, cultural and historical background always mediates the conflict of interest, so that resource conflicts show up in a variety of complex forms.

How have disputes involving resources been resolved in the past? Table 11.1 shows the disputes involving resources in the 81 conflicts of this study.

TABLE 11.1   *Conflicts involving resources*

	Peaceful	*Minor violence*	*Major violence*
Resolved	Gadaduma Wells Mauritania– Morocco Wadi Halfa Austria Kuwait–Saudia Arabia	Gabon–Congo Mauritania– Mali Saudi Arabia– Oman, Abu Dhabi	Algeria–Morocco Algerian independence Zairean independence
Partially resolved			
Unresolved		Greece–Turkey	Sudanese Civil War Western Sahara Iraq–Kuwait

Four of the disputes were over water. Of these, the Gadaduma Wells (Case 26) and Wadi Halfa (Case 75) disputes were peacefully resolved. In the former, British colonial boundaries had deprived nomads on the Ethiopian side of the Kenyan border of access to traditional sources of water. When Kenya became independent, the government agreed to revise the border to correct these difficulties. Kenya was compensated with several smaller wells. In the latter, Egypt flooded land in Sudan by building the Aswan dam. This came close to armed conflict but, after Ethiopian mediation, the parties agreed to a resolution which compensated Sudan with money and water. These disputes illustrate one way in which resource conflicts are relatively easy to resolve. Where the resources are divisible they can be partitioned, or one party can make side payments to the other. The Mauritania–Mali dispute (Case 47) was similar to the Gadaduma Wells one, in that colonial boundaries had been drawn across old routes of access to water. In this case the dispute involved fighting between local tribes, but the states avoided a serious armed conflict by Mauritania's agreement to revise the border. Water is also an issue in the civil war in Sudan, although it is subsidiary to other issues. Attacks by southern Sudanese guerrillas stopped the construction of a new canal, which they feared would be used to divert water to the north (Falkenmark, 1986).

The Mauritania–Morocco (Case 48) and Western Sahara (Case 76) disputes involved the rich phosphate reserves in the Rio de Oro (formerly the Spanish Sahara, and now known as the Western Sahara or Saharwi). Both Morocco and Mauritania made claims on this territory, which contains the world's richest deposits of phosphates. Morocco already held large phosphate reserves and was anxious to increase them. This became part of the project of establishing a 'greater Morocco', including both the Western Sahara and the whole of Mauritania. These claims led to sharp tensions between Mauritania and Morocco but, after Algerian mediation, the Moroccan government agreed to drop its claim to Mauritania, and the two states signed a treaty of friendship in 1970. They submitted their claims to Western Sahara to the ICJ, but before the Court had reached a judgement they agreed to partition Western Sahara and the phosphate reserves between themselves. In 1975 Spain agreed to hand over its colony to the two states, and they duly partitioned it, with Morocco taking two-thirds and Mauritania one-third. This resolved the Mauritania–Morocco dispute, but left the Saharwi nationalists out of the reckoning. Polisario had already been fighting the Spanish for independence, and now its liberation struggle turned into a war with Morocco and Mauritania. Mauritania could not sustain the war and abandoned its claims in 1980. Morocco, however, succeeded in occupying most of Western Sahara, including the coastal region and the phosphate deposits, despite a prolonged and continuing war.

The Gabon–Congo (Case 25) and Algeria–Morocco (Case 5) disputes both involved territories rich in minerals. In the former, Congo (Brazzaville) abandoned its claim and hostilities were avoided. In the latter, Moroccan claims led to war. After the cease-fire and an inconclusive arbitration, Morocco abandoned its effort to take the disputed territory by force. Eventually, seven years after the fighting, the two states agreed to set up a joint company to exploit the iron ore deposits. The civil war in Zaire (Case 80) also involved minerals. Katanga's rich copper deposits fuelled the province's drive for secession, and the determination of the Congolese government to resist.

Several disputes involved oil. The dispute over the status of Austria (Case 9) was rather a special case, as the Soviet demand for oil was for reparations after the war. The dispute between Greece and Turkey over oil drilling rights on their continental shelf has not yet led to war but, while it remains unresolved, it adds to the stakes of a dispute that is already bitter for other reasons. The Kuwait/Saudi (Case 42), Saudi/ Oman (Case 63) and Iraq/Kuwait (Case 38) disputes are more readily comparable as they were all direct conflicts over oil between Arab states. The first case was peacefully resolved through a Kuwaiti–Saudi agreement to share the oil in the disputed territory. The second, which involved small-scale fighting, was resolved by Saudi Arabia dropping its claim in return for compensation with two small pieces of territory. The third reached deadlock and led to war. The disputed oilfield remains in Kuwait and remains in dispute. At the time of writing, almost all the remaining oil wells in Kuwait are on fire. The following chapter discusses whether this dispute could have been resolved along the lines of the other disputes over oil discussed in this section.

Is there a pattern in these disputes? It appears that when a dispute is between states and is primarily about resources, or resources and territory, it is not too difficult to find ways to resolve it. Dividing the resources or offering compensation are feasible and common outcomes. Greater difficulties arise when resource conflicts are embedded in disputes over other issues, especially if these involve nonstate actors with whom states are reluctant to negotiate. Then the presence of scarce resources can increase the stakes in the conflict (as in the

Sudanese Civil War, the Western Sahara and Zaire) without making the dispute any easier to resolve.

Table 11.2 shows the fishing disputes. Most of these arose out of extensions of territorial waters. Sometimes this gave rise to sharp confrontations, as in the Cod War (Case 35), but most of these disputes were resolved without serious violence. They were of great importance to the fishing industries concerned, and the importance of fishing in Iceland made the issue of high importance. For the British government the loss of traditional fisheries was not so vital a national interest that it was prepared to commit itself to more than a limited use of force. In each case, after shorter or longer periods of negotiations and deadlock, the principle that the coastal state is responsible for managing its own territorial waters was accepted, and the state claiming high seas fishing rights could not prevent the gradual extension of territorial limits. In the disputes over Iceland, Britain was compensated by agreements to permit British trawlers to fish within the disputed periods at certain times of the year, or for a limited future period. Other fishing disputes have been resolved by similar joint arrangements. For example, Norway and the USSR have agreed to establish exclusive economic zones in the Barents Sea and to set quotas jointly for their catches in an area where the border is disputed (Peterson and Teal, 1986).

TABLE 11.2 *Fishing conflicts*

	Peaceful	Minor violence	Major violence
Resolved	Minquiers Islands Norway–UK	Denmark–UK Iceland–UK: 1952–61	
Partially Resolved		Iceland–UK: Cod War	
Unresolved			

The Law of the Sea conferences have established a framework within which further fishing disputes can be managed. States have generally accepted the 12-mile limit, and the exclusive rights of coastal states to manage fisheries within that area. The 1982 Law of the Sea conference extended this principle by establishing exclusive economic zones up to 200 miles from the coast, and coastal states are to have authority for managing and conserving resources within this zone. Outside these zones, the conference declared the oceans a part of the 'common heritage of mankind'. Fishing in these areas is unrestricted, although a number of international agreements regulate the exploitation of particular species. The 1982 Law of the Sea agreements have not been universally ratified, and neither are the other agreements fully effective in protecting species. The International Whaling Commission, for example, has reduced but not prevented the hunting of whales. Nevertheless, these agreements establish the principle of a regime of co-operative agreements covering the exploitation of natural resources in an important area of the 'commons'.

This seems to be the way ahead for disputes involving resources in areas outside national jurisdiction. It is necessary to establish a joint regime to manage resource extraction, and under this regime states need to set quotas and limits to which they will agree to adhere. The difficulty is to make the regime sufficiently stringent but, in the absence of a common authority, a balance has to be struck between stringency and the willingness of parties to observe the regime.

The Antarctica Treaty is another example of a co-operative regime governing natural resources. It has provided a basis for the demilitarization of the continent and for setting aside disputes over territorial rights. However, it remains fragile, partly because it is limited to a few states and partly because of the failure to develop an adequate agreement covering the continent's mineral resources.

The value of regimes is not limited only to the 'commons'. In areas which are territorially divided, co-operative management arrangements provide a valuable alternative when partitioning of resources is not accepted. For example, bilateral or multilateral river management commissions have helped to institutionalize co-operation and prevent or resolve disputes over water. Falkenmark (1986) cites the Senegal, Danube, Columbia and Nile as river basins where commissions have functioned well in the past.

Even in oil supply, co-operative arrangements have a part to play in preventing conflict. The most important conflict over oil since the Second World War was that between OPEC (the Organization of Petroleum Exporting Countries) and oil consumers, starting in 1973. This was resolved entirely peacefully, in part by market mechanisms (which removed the conflict from the political domain), and in part by the willingness of OPEC states to recycle their massive windfalls into the Western economies. Japan, which was considerably more dependent on Middle Eastern oil than the USA, showed the feasibility of a non-military response to oil security by investing heavily in the economies of its Middle East suppliers, and signing long-term bilateral trading agreements.

As yet no regime applies to the global atmosphere, although a number of states have agreed to limit emissions of sulphur, nitrogen and chlorofluorocarbons (CFCs). A regime to control carbon emissions is clearly needed, and if one can be established it will help to anticipate and prevent disputes which are otherwise likely to occur. In any situation where interests are in conflict, the practical difficulties of establishing and maintaining a co-operative regime are substantial (Young, 1989). Nevertheless this approach offers the prospect of a framework in which emergent conflicts can be peacefully managed.

12 Lithuania and the Gulf

It is interesting to consider how the general points about peaceful settlement of conflicts apply to two contemporary conflicts, even though they are by no means resolved at the time of writing. Both these disputes involved a phase of protracted crisis. Both involved a serious clash of interests and values. They were, of course, very different situations: one was an international conflict over territory, sovereignty and resources; the other an internal conflict over secession. The contrast in the way they have been managed may nevertheless be suggestive.

LITHUANIA (1989–OCTOBER 1990)

The conflict between Lithuanian nationalists and the Soviet government was an important test for Mikhail Gorbachev's policy of *perestroika*. The stakes were high. On the one hand, if the Lithuanians won their demand for immediate independence there was the danger that other republics might also secede, causing a rapid break-up of the Soviet Union. On the other hand, if the Soviet Union used force to suppress the independence movement, *perestroika* and 'new thinking' would be undermined. Gorbachev would no longer be able to claim that he had made a decisive break from the days of Stalin and Brezhnev, and East–West relations would have taken a sharp turn for the worse. Gorbachev's domestic political position was also at stake, for he could not be sure of support either from the 'hard-liners' on the Communist Party's central committee, or from the army.

Background

Lithuania, Latvia and Estonia lie on the Soviet Union's western borders (see Figure 12.1). Once part of the Hanseatic League, they

had fallen under the control of the Teutonic Knights, Poland, Russia
and Germany as these larger powers held sway over the region. In 1917
they became independent of Russia. In 1940, following the Nazi–
Soviet pact, they were incorporated into the Soviet Union.

FIGURE 12.1   *The Baltic States*

Lithuania has a population of 3.7 million. About 20 per cent are
non-Lithuanian, including Russians, Poles and Belorussians. The Poles
seek their own autonomous region. Lithuania's economy is principally
agricultural. It depends on the Soviet Union for oil, raw materials and
industrial goods. The population is traditionally Catholic.

Development of the conflict

Gorbachev's policy of *glasnost* allowed nationalist parties throughout
the Soviet Union to express demands for independence. In Lithuania,
the Sajudis (Popular Front for Perestroika) campaigned for immediate
independence on the grounds that the Soviet occupation in 1940 was
illegal. Lithuania had suffered '50 years of political repression,

economic mismanagement and cultural stultification', they charged. Support for the Sajudis grew rapidly. In December 1989 the Communist Party of Lithuania, led by Algirdas Brazauskas, declared its support for secession and asserted its independence from the Communist Party of the Soviet Union (CPSU).

Following a stormy meeting of the Central Committee of the CPSU, Gorbachev decided to visit Lithuania personally. He was met by a rally of 300 000 people demonstrating for independence in Vilnius. In a speech, Gorbachev ruled out the use of force, but warned of serious consequences if Lithuania should attempt to secede unconstitutionally. He declared support for 'self-determination short of secession', and promised to introduce a draft law enabling republics to leave the Soviet Union. The law would require a two-thirds majority and there would be a transition period of 'up to five years' before full independence. The chairman of the Sajudis, Vyautas Landsbergis, responded that this law, and other Soviet laws, would not apply to Lithuania.

In February 1990 the Sajudis won 80 per cent of the seats in the Lithuanian elections. Landsbergis was duly elected chairman of the Lithuanian Supreme Soviet. He declared Lithuania's independence and the restoration of the Lithuanian constitution of 1938. He called for 'interstate talks' with Moscow to settle outstanding matters. Meanwhile Lithuanian conscripts began to refuse the Soviet draft, and volunteers came forward to form a Lithuanian border guard.

The Soviet government rejected Lithuania's declaration of independence, stating that it was invalid and illegal. The Foreign Minister, Shevardnadze, repeated that force would not be used. However, Soviet army commanders in Lithuania demanded that 'deserters' should return to their units and threatened to use force to get them back. Gorbachev issued a decree that Lithuania should stop recruiting its own border guards. The Soviet government declared a ban on private weapons in Lithuania, and the KGB began to seize hunting rifles and other weapons from Lithuanians.

Things came to a head on 24/25 March. Lithuanian nationalists attempted to seize the offices of the pro-Moscow rump of the Lithuanian Communist Party. They were rebuffed by detachments of workers. On the morning of 25 March, before dawn, a column of armoured personnel carriers and army trucks rumbled through the centre of Vilnius, passing the Parliament buildings. The population remained calm, and the army column took no action.

Soviet troops began a clampdown on the 'deserters', rounding up a number of conscripts who were in hiding. Soviet troops also occupied the offices of the Lithuanian Communist Party and a Communist Party print works. On 5 April, Soviet troops occupied the State Procurator's office, evicting the Lithuanian State Procurator who was refusing to enforce Soviet laws.

Despite these coercive measures, both sides seemed concerned to limit the possible escalation of the dispute. Landsbergis publicly assured Gorbachev that Lithuania would not arm volunteers or set up militias. Gorbachev repeated his promise that force would not be used. In Vilnius, Lithuanian government leaders met Soviet army commanders. They discussed the matter of the 'deserters' and agreed to establish a co-ordinating committee to maintain contacts. Landsbergis stated that he believed that the army column was ordered to move by a local faction of the Lithuanian Communist Party.

While the immediate crisis of 24/25 March passed, tensions remained high and neither side retreated from its basic position. Gorbachev warned of 'grave consequences' if Lithuania failed to retract its independence declaration. Landsbergis denounced continued Soviet 'aggression against Lithuania'. Gorbachev stated that force would not be used 'unless lives were threatened', a change of wording that Landsbergis interpreted as a prelude to the use of force. Among the people, there was fear that hard-line army officers and neo-Stalinists in the Party might precipitate military action. At the same time, working class Lithuanians and many governments in the West were worried that Landsbergis was going 'too far, too fast'. European governments called for restraint and negotiations, as did the Pope. The US government warned that if force were used there would be a 'significant negative impact' on bilateral relations. Soviet troops of the Interior Ministry occupied the main printing press in Vilnius and prevented the printing of nationalist newspapers. Gorbachev accused the Lithuanian leadership of 'leading matters into a dead end' and 'blocking any exit to the crisis'.

The impasse continued for the first weeks of April. Landsbergis called for negotiations, but refused to rescind the declaration of independence. Gorbachev refused to talk until this had been done. Nevertheless, talks took place between the Lithuanian leadership and the Defence Ministry. People continued to remain calm. A split developed in the Lithuanian leadership group, with Brazauskas and the pro-independence Communists urging the suspension of the declaration of independence and a referendum. Landsbergis was not prepared to countenance the former condition. The Lithuanian Supreme Council introduced a provocative law requiring citizens of

Lithuania to pledge their support to the independence constitution, on pain of loss of certain legal rights.

On 13 April, Gorbachev issued an ultimatum threatening economic sanctions unless the Lithuanian Parliament rescinded its declaration of independence and all subsequent laws. The Lithuanian Council refused. The blockade began a week later. Soviet oil supplies and raw materials were cut off, bringing much of Lithuania to a standstill. In protest, a Lithuanian factory worker committed suicide by setting himself on fire outside the Bolshoi Theatre in Moscow.

The Supreme Soviet in Latvia followed Lithuania in declaring independence in May. More cautiously, it went on to suspend the application of the declaration until after negotiations with the Soviet Union. Both Latvia and Estonia took the position that Soviet laws would continue to apply so long as they were not in conflict with the domestic Latvian and Estonian laws. The Soviet government responded that these declarations of independence were also illegal, but did not threaten to apply sanctions. Strikes against independence took place in Estonia, which has a large Russian minority (only 64 per cent of the population is Estonian; in Latvia the proportion is only 53 per cent). The strikes were suspended after an appeal by Gorbachev.

Western reaction was generally sympathetic to the Lithuanian cause, but critical of the nationalists' tactics. It was clear that Western governments were not prepared to break the blockade. President Mitterland of France and Chancellor Kohl of West Germany offered to mediate and proposed that Lithuania suspend its declaration of independence to get negotiations started.

Movements of position on both sides now began. After talks between the Prime Minister of Lithuania, Kazimiera Prunskiene, and the Soviet Prime Minister, Nikolai Ryzhkov, the Lithuanian Council decided to suspend all laws passed since the declaration of independence. Gorbachev insisted that the declaration of independence should be suspended as well, but this was a shift from his earlier position that it be rescinded.

The deadlock continued until the middle of June. Kazimiera Prunskiene suggested a moratorium on the declaration of independence, but Landsbergis and the Sajudis were opposed to this move. By the end of June a formula acceptable to the nationalists was found and the Lithuanian government suspended the application of the declaration of independence for 100 days. Twenty-four hours later, Moscow resumed oil supplies to Lithuania.

From this point on, Lithuania's position came into line with the other Baltic republics, and they agreed to negotiate with Moscow together. Other developments in the Soviet Union began to over-shadow the drama over Lithuania. Boris Yeltsin came to power as president of the Russian Federation, and he announced that Russia too declared itself independent of the Soviet Union. The old centra-lized structure of the Soviet Union was becoming unsustainable. Gorbachev responded by proposing a plan for a new confederation of sovereign republics to replace the old Union. Negotiations between Lithuania and Moscow continued intermittently, without any agree-ment on the fundamental issue of independence.

Factors Influencing the Avoidance of Violence

1. Both sides made it clear from the outset that they preferred a peaceful settlement. Medvedev, for the Soviet Central Committee, said, 'our Party uses political, not military means'. On the Lithuanian side, rallies and demonstrations were non-violent and people remained calm. The Lithuanian Council did not attempt to set up armed militias or to seize Soviet weaponry (as the Azerbaijani nationalists had in Baku, with violent results).
2. The Soviet government rounded up weapons as a precautionary measure.
3. Both sides held power in the situation. The Lithuanians had the power of mass popular support and control of the republic's government and Parliament; the Soviet Union controlled the borders and security forces and had the power of blockade, and ultimately of military force.
4. At times of crisis, both sides held talks. The dangerous issue of 'deserters', which threatened to precipitate military action, was defused through talks between the Lithuanian leaders and the Army. Following the blockade, the Lithuanian and Soviet Prime Ministers met for direct talks.
5. Both sides interspersed unilateral or coercive moves with con-ciliatory acts or statements. After the periods of crisis (24/25 March and the blockade) the sides drew back from extreme positions. The subsequent course of the conflict was protracted and involved further confrontations, but it seemed that, at this stage at any rate, both parties intended to avoid a violent outcome if they could.

THE GULF CONFLICT

The occupation of Kuwait by Iraq precipitated one of the most extraordinary crises since the Second World War, leading to the outbreak of war on 17 January 1991. Could this conflict have been peacefully resolved and, if so, how?

From the time of the invasion, it was too late for a peaceful settlement of the conflict. A peaceful settlement, in the sense in which the term is used in this book, would have had to have come *before* 2 August. Two questions arise: first, could the conflict have been resolved before the invasion? Second, after the invasion, was an opportunity lost to find a settlement to avert a full-scale war?

The roots of the dispute

The territorial dispute that existed between Iraq and Kuwait was one of the disputes over borders which lie around the world like cases of unexploded ammunition. The dispute arose as soon as Kuwait became independent in 1961, but Iraq had regarded the colonial boundaries between Iraq and Kuwait as invalid ever since Iraq became independent in 1932 (Figure 12.2).

The roots of the dispute go back to a period when Kuwait and Iraq were both under Ottoman rule. An Arab tribe from the Najd (now central Saudi Arabia) built the settlement which was to become the town of Kuwait in the early eighteenth century. For geographical and cultural reasons, Kuwait's history was closely tied to developments in Mesopotamia (now Iraq) and the Najd (now Saudi Arabia). In the eighteenth century, Kuwait was nominally subject to the Ottoman Empire, but in practice it was virtually independent. The Ottoman Empire administered Mesopotamia as the three *vilayet* (provinces) of Mosul, Baghdad, and Basra; Kuwait formed one of the districts of Basra.

As the Ottoman Empire began to disintegrate in the late nineteenth century, Britain became the dominant power in the Gulf region. Kuwait, along with other sheikhdoms, sought British protection. In 1899 Sheikh Mubarak signed an agreement with Britain under which he retained administrative control of Kuwait, and Britain took over its external affairs. When the Ottoman Empire was dissolved in 1918 Britain took over the mandate for Mesopotamia, and ruled it until it became independent as Iraq in 1932. British colonial rulers were therefore in a position to set the borders between Kuwait and Iraq.

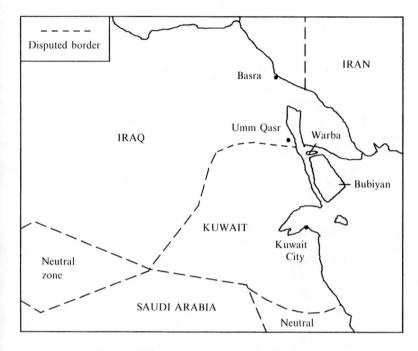

FIGURE 12.2 *The Iraq–Kuwait border dispute*

Sir Percy Cox, the British High Commissioner for Iraq, fixed these boundaries in a meeting with King Ibn Sa'ud (of Najd) in 1922. His purpose was to fix the boundaries between Iraq, Kuwait and Saudi Arabia (in part to stop incursions by Bedouins, who paid little attention to the artificial borders). Sir Percy Cox drew the new borders himself (using an inaccurate map). The boundaries had always been unclear. The Sheikh of Kuwait wrote at the time to a British official, 'I still do not know what the frontier between Iraq and Kuwait is, and I shall be glad if you will kindly give me the information so that I may know it.' With British encouragement, the Sheikh claimed an extensive northern boundary, including the two islands of Warba and Bubiyan.

Sir Percy Cox, who had previously agreed to give an area claimed by Kuwait to Najd, endorsed this claim. The effect was to reduce Iraq's access to the sea. This demarcation seemed to Sir Percy Cox to fit the realities of power at the time. Unfortunately it also gave rise to a prolonged and ultimately costly dispute.

Crises and Negotiations: 1938–90

August 1990 was not the first time Iraq had massed troops on its borders with Kuwait. When Iraq became independent, under a monarchy established with British approval, its first Prime Minister wrote to the Sheikh of Kuwait and recognized Cox's boundaries. However, Iraqi nationalists opposed the boundaries and wanted Kuwait to be integrated with Iraq. They appealed to the Kuwaiti people to win civil rights and overthrow their Sheikh. Influenced by the nationalists, King Ghazi of Iraq massed troops on the border. His death in a car crash in 1939 forestalled an invasion.

The next threat came in 1961, when Kuwait became independent of Britain. By this time Kuwait's population had quadrupled, following the spectacular growth of its oil industry. Kuwait, which had been poorer than Iraq, was now much richer. General Kassim, who had overthrown the monarchy in a coup in 1958, ordered troop and tank movements on the border.

Iraq based its claim on the grounds that Kuwait had been part of Basra province in the Ottoman days, that Britain had recognized this, that the 1899 agreement between the Sheikh of Kuwait and Britain was invalid because it had not had Ottoman authority, and that the British agreement to give Kuwait independence was also invalid. Kuwait responded by claiming that it had never been subject to Turkish sovereignty, and that the al-Sabah dynasty had ruled Kuwait since 1756 without Turkish interference.

The British embassy in Baghdad heard of Iraq's plans for mobilization and warned the British government. Britain, in consultation with the Sheikh of Kuwait, moved rapidly to place troops in Kuwait. At the same time Egypt made it clear that Kuwait would be welcome to join the Arab League, and that Egypt supported its independence. These moves pre-empted Kassim's plans. With armed conflict a possibility, the UN Security Council met but failed to defuse the crisis. The Soviet Union vetoed the Security Council's resolution. Instead the Arab League took over the case, and agreed to place its own force in Kuwait to replace the British troops. The League also agreed to commit itself to Kuwait's independence, and to extend a collective security arrangement to Kuwait, under which an attack on Kuwait would be regarded as an attack on any member of the League. Kassim gave up his attempt to invade Kuwait. In 1963 he was overthrown and the first Ba'athist regime which followed recognized Kuwait's independence. Iraq also agreed to supply Kuwait with fresh water.

However, the border was still in contention. Iraq refused Kuwait's request to set up a joint border commission, and in 1965, Iraq reopened the dispute by making claims to the islands of Warba and Bubiyan and other territory near the Iraqi border. Kuwait replied that it would consider leasing the islands to Iraq. However another military coup took place in Iraq, and the issue lapsed for a period.

In 1973, the Iraqi government (now the second Ba'athist regime) again raised its claim, with Soviet support. Shortly before this, Iraq and Kuwait had been negotiating over water and loans, and Kuwait had refused to give Iraq a large loan. Iraq sent troops into the disputed area, resulting in minor clashes with Kuwaiti troops. The Iraqis built a number of huts in the disputed area and the Kuwaitis responded by building mosques around the huts. At this point the Arab League offered to mediate, but Kuwait was not prepared to allow mediation until the Iraqi troops had withdrawn. Saudi Arabia moved troops into Kuwait, and the Shah of Iran also offered support to Kuwait. In the face of this, the Iraqi government decided to withdraw. After the withdrawal, both sides accepted mediation from Yasser Arafat. In the negotiations, Kuwait refused to cede or lease the islands, although there was some discussion about splitting Bubiyan into two. No agreement was reached on the territorial issue, although Iraq agreed to increase its supplies of fresh water to Kuwait.

In 1975 Iraq again occupied the disputed border area and each side again built huts and mosques. In the subsequent negotiations, Kuwait offered Iraq a 100-year lease on Warba if Iraq would agree to a final demarcation of the disputed frontier. Such an agreement would have allowed Kuwait to retain the populated parts of the border, and Iraq to build a deeper channel for its port at Umm Qaşr. However, no formal settlement was reached.

In 1978 Iraq again suggested that Bubiyan might be divided. Two years later, Saddam Hussein decided to attack Iran, and attention shifted away from the dispute with Kuwait for the next eight years.

At the end of his long and unsuccessful war with Iran, Saddam Hussein's attention turned back to the dispute with Kuwait. Iraq had ended the war with a huge military machine, but massive debts. Of its 16 million people, 1 million were in the army. Iraq's debts totalled $80 billion (almost twice its 1989 gross national product), and it faced a bill of $230 billion for reconstruction after the war. Since Iraq was spending some $23 billion a year abroad ($3 billion on food, $9 billion on other imports, $5 billion on arms, $5 billion on debt servicing and $1 billion on foreign workers' transfers), and receiving oil revenues of $13 billion a year, the country had a deficit of $10 billion a year to find even before it could cover reconstruction. This was an extremely serious prospect for the regime, especially because of popular expectations that things would get better now that the eight year war with Iran had come to an end.

Iraq owed Kuwait about $13 billion, and Saudi Arabia $22 billion. The Iraqi government argued that the Gulf States should write off these debts, since Iraq had been acting as a buffer for them against Iranian fundamentalism. The Saudis agreed, but Kuwait did not. Iraq then demanded a further $10 billion from each state to help rebuild its shattered economy. Kuwait offered only $500 million, repayable over three years. This angered Saddam. More seriously, he was angered by Kuwait's policy of raising its oil output above its OPEC quota. Iraq claimed that it was losing $89 billion of revenue because of low prices due to this overproduction. Kuwait was waging 'economic warfare' against Iraq, claimed Saddam. When in July 1990 the Saudis persuaded Kuwait and the United Arab Emirates to cut their output, Saddam saw only a conspiracy against himself. The foreign minister, Tariq Aziz, said to a meeting of the Arab League in Tunis, 'We are sure some Arab states are involved in a conspiracy against us.' Iraq went on to accuse Kuwait of stealing oil by drilling in the area of the Rumailah oilfield that Iraq claimed. Kuwait countered that Iraq had been stealing Kuwaiti oil.

Saddam now stepped up the pressure. He made a fierce speech on television, openly threatening the Kuwaitis. Kuwait could avoid a crisis only by making payments to Iraq and ceding the oilfield. To add to the threats, Saddam massed troops and armoured divisions near the border. He then met the US Ambassador, who failed to communicate to him any warning about how the USA would respond. The Saudis, by now thoroughly alarmed, encouraged Kuwait to agree to a rise in the oil price at the OPEC meeting on 26 July, though not as large a rise as Iraq demanded. This agreement appeared to defuse the oil price issue. Next, Iraqi and Kuwaiti representatives met at Jeddah to discuss Iraq's territorial and financial demands. According to a Kuwaiti account, the Kuwaiti side said they were prepared to write off Iraq's debts, and lease Warba to Iraq (Darwish and Alexander, 1991). However, Kuwait remained defiant on Iraq's financial demands. In any case, it was too late. The talks broke down with the Iraqi spokesman withdrawing. Iraqi forces invaded Kuwait the following day.

The best time to have settled the dispute would clearly have been before the invasion. The dispute had been rumbling for a long time, and there were clear previous warnings of danger. If a firm border had been agreed in 1938, 1963, 1965, 1973, 1975 or 1978, the dispute might have been laid to rest. The talks in 1973 offered a real opportunity, as did the talks in 1975. Kuwait, though convinced of its own sovereignty and threatened by a stronger neighbour, probably made a mistake in allowing the issue to lapse after negotiations failed, without trying more strenuously to settle the issue. Iraq's reliance on using force first and negotiating afterwards was scarcely calculated to produce a co-operative response. The international community, busy with larger issues, failed to back up local mediation efforts, or to read any danger signals in what seemed an intractable local dispute.

After the Invasion: 2 August to 17 January

In his State of the Union speech on 29 January, President Bush said that every effort had been made to find a diplomatic way out of the crisis. The British Prime Minister made a similar statement in the House of Commons. Had every effort been made, and was a diplomatic settlement possible?

An early opportunity came in the first 72 hours after the invasion. During this period there was silence in much of the Arab world, and the Saudis in particular refrained from condemning Iraq. The Arab League was meeting in Cairo. King Fahd of Saudi Arabia called King Hussein of Jordan to inform him of the invasion and urge him to do what he could to convince Saddam Hussein to withdraw. King Hussein immediately flew to Baghdad, where he held two meetings with Saddam Hussein. According to Jordanian and French sources (Salinger and Laurent, 1991), Saddam agreed to hold talks with King Fahd over his dispute with the Kuwaitis. He said that if the talks succeeded, he would withdraw from Kuwait. But he warned that if Arab states attacked him for invading, he would not meet King Fahd. King Hussein returned to Jordan to contact President Mubarak of Egypt, but he was too late. Egypt, at the behest of the USA, had already condemned the invasion. Saddam was now unwilling to meet King Fahd.

With the failure of these early efforts to reach an Arab solution, the crisis settled into a confrontation between the USA and Iraq. On 6 August the UN imposed mandatory sanctions to reinforce Security Council Resolution 660, which demanded Iraq's immediate and unconditional withdrawal from Kuwait. On 8 August, Iraq declared that it was annexing Kuwait. The following day US troops began to arrive in Saudi Arabia. President Bush listed the US objectives as being:

1. immediate and unconditional Iraqi withdrawal from Kuwait;
2. restoration of the legitimate Kuwaiti government;
3. the security of the Gulf, including the oilfields;
4. safeguarding American lives in the region.

During the first phase of the crisis, once the coalition's *cordon sanitaire* was in place, a debate took place in the USA and Britain over the future conduct of policy. On one side were those who argued for negotiations and sanctions; on the other were those who favoured the threat of military action. For example, at a conference in Washington in October 1990, Peter Rodman (a former assistant to Kissinger and Schultz) argued that the USA should rely on the threat of force as the most potent means of making Saddam withdraw. On the other side, Hal Saunders (a former Assistant Secretary of State during the Carter Administration, who had been involved in the Camp David talks) suggested that the USA should explore the possibility of a settlement using third-party channels or intermediaries. He did not advocate rewarding Iraqi aggression or deviating from the UN resolutions, but proposed using an intermediary as a repository for commitments on both sides. If Iraq signalled its willingness to withdraw, it could then find out through the intermediary what reciprocal steps the USA might take, such as the withdrawal of some of its forces. This would begin a reciprocal winding-down, lasting some months. At the same time it would be possible to look beyond the crisis at some of the questions of economic justice in the Middle East, other regional conflicts and the question of disputed boundaries.

American public opinion was at first evenly divided, but it soon became clear that the Administration had chosen the hard-line position. George Bush and Margaret Thatcher said that there was nothing to negotiate about. Iraq would have to get out of Kuwait. To enforce this demand, Bush relied on the threat of military force. The hope, in both the USA and Britain, was that a policy of threat would induce Iraq to withdraw and hence settle the dispute without hostilities.

Iraq claimed that it was prepared to negotiate 'without preconditions', but at no time did it indicate willingness to withdraw immediately and unconditionally, as required by Security Council Resolution 660. Moreover, Iraq kept up a stream of inflammatory actions and rhetoric which further breached international law and created the worst possible basis for negotiations including holding foreigners hostage, operating the human shield policy, besieging the embassies, mining Kuwaiti oilfields and making threats against Israel, Saudi Arabia and the Americans. Despite all this, Saddam Hussein did give indications that he was prepared to bargain. His offer of 12 August, linking his occupation of Kuwait to Israel's presence in the occupied territories, implicitly accepted the principle of withdrawal. The offer proposed that all the occupations in the region should be reversed, in the order in which they had taken place. This would mean that Iraq would withdraw from Kuwait only after Israel had withdrawn from the occupied territories and Syria had withdrawn from Lebanon. If other states failed to withdraw, the UN should impose sanctions against them. Meanwhile, the UN should freeze its resolutions applying sanctions to Iraq, and an Arab force should replace the US forces in Saudi Arabia. The USA rejected the proposal immediately.

Was it possible to bridge the gap between the UN demand for unconditional withdrawal and the Iraqi hint of withdrawal on conditions? The way to do so seemed to be by seeking progress on other issues in the region, but without explicitly linking them to Kuwait. The UN had a number of resolutions relating to Palestine and the occupied territories already on its agenda. On 4 September the Soviet Union reiterated its longstanding proposal for a conference on the Middle East. Had this proposal advanced further, it might have offered openings in the search for a settlement. However, the USA, supported by Israel, rejected the proposal.

On 21 August Iraq offered direct talks with the USA without preconditions. The USA refused. Its refusal was consistent with the policy of relying only on threats; but it was not a policy aimed at maximizing the chances of averting hostilities.

With the principal actors deadlocked, it was left to third parties to find some way out of the *impasse*. King Hussein attempted to mediate between Saddam Hussein and President Bush, but found no way to break the deadlock. Saddam Hussein made his efforts no easier by rounding up British and American hostages on the day he was meeting President Bush.

The PLO (Palestine Liberation Organization) was equally unsuccessful with its efforts to find an Arab solution. First the PLO proposed a three-stage plan, involving a freeze on the build-up of Western forces, mutual Iraqi and Western force withdrawals, and subsequent talks through the Arab League on the territorial dispute. This plan found little favour with either side. Subsequently Jordan and the PLO put forward a joint plan, under which Kuwait would become like Monaco: an autonomous zone under Iraqi protection. There should be simultaneous withdrawal of forces, a plebiscite in Kuwait and an Arab peacekeeping force. Iraq said it was prepared to consider this formula, but it fell short of the UN demands, and was unacceptable to the USA and the coalition. Algeria later made a more carefully prepared attempt, with confidential approaches to the main parties, and an avoidance of any attempt to propose or publish the terms of a settlement.

King Hussein urged that a broad approach was needed to the conflict:

> Any solution must address, if not simultaneously, at least sequenti-ally, the major underlying causes: the dispute between Iraq and Kuwait, the imbalance of wealth in the area, the unresolved confrontation between Israel, Palestine and the Arab states, and the perilous proliferation of weapons of mass destruction . . . Because these problems are inter-related, piecemeal solutions are not the answer.

The idea of a broad approach drew wide support. President Mitterrand incorporated it in his four points, which suggested that after a UN-supervised Iraqi withdrawal, direct negotiations between Middle Eastern countries and regional arms reductions could take place. The Soviet Union also pressed a broad approach through its proposal for a conference. These efforts failed because of US resistance to 'linkage', but linkage could have been avoided had the Security Council addressed other regional conflicts in parallel with, and not linked to, the crisis in the Gulf. Could unilateral steps of this kind have influenced the course of the conflict?

By the end of November, there were hints of a way out of the crisis. The USA restated its commitment to UN Resolution 242, thus acknowledging to some extent the value of a broad approach. The USA also agreed for the first time to the principle of a UN conference on the Middle East, though not until after Iraq had withdrawn from Kuwait. (Oddly enough, this exception recreated linkage in an unnecessary way.) Iraq agreed to release the hostages, and the USA proposed reciprocal talks. If these measures had been taken earlier, there might have been a different outcome.

However, the hopes were soon dashed. The US offer of talks came after a doubling of forces on both sides, and the passing of Resolution

678 which permitted member states to use 'all necessary means' to enforce Resolution 660 if Iraq did not comply by 15 January. Moreover, it soon became clear that the USA intended to use the talks only to reiterate its threat. Iraq at first accepted the talks, but then refused to participate in them until three days before the UN deadline. The talks were finally held in Geneva on 7 January, in an atmosphere so antagonistic that their breakdown caused no surprise. Both sides had contributed to their failure.

The last days before 15 January saw a further spurt of efforts by the Soviet Union, France and Pérez de Cuéllar. In his talks with Pérez de Cuéllar on 13 January, Saddam Hussein again indicated that he was prepared to accept a 'package deal'. Yet he confused these signals by repeatedly declaring that Kuwait was part of Iraq and that he would never withdraw. In any case, the time for developing a package deal had passed. Both sides were now preparing for war.

It seems clear that opportunities were lost to seek a settlement. This is explained, in part, by the parties' broader political objectives. On the Iraqi side, Saddam Hussein was intent on becoming a dominant power in the region. Ba'athist party policy emphasized the duty of Arabs to confront imperialism, and stressed the value of violence. Saddam's own personality combined extreme insecurity with a yearning for power and a strong streak of sadism and violence. Saddam saw himself in a tradition of Arab warriors and he clearly preferred a war, even one that he might lose, to capitulation.

On the US side, the underlying intention was to prevent a threat to its oil interests in the area. President Carter had pledged in 1980 that 'an attempt by any outside force to gain control of the Persian Gulf region will be regarded as an assault on the vital interests of the United States, and such an assault will be repelled by any means necessary, including military force'. Dick Cheney, the Secretary of Defense, repeated this pledge in testimony to the Senate Armed Forces Committee in 1990: it was 'settled US policy to ensure that no hostile power should dominate this vital area.' This policy had led the USA to support Iraq against Iran, and to collude in Iraq's build-up of a sophisticated military machine (Darwish and Alexander, 1991). It was now necessary to prevent Iraq from becoming the Prussia of the region. Iraq's aggression had to be stopped, and for this reason many US policy-makers and advisers preferred a preventive war now to another war later, by which time Iraq might have nuclear weapons. A war would allow the USA to 'de-fang' Saddam and remove his nuclear, chemical and biological weapons.

Once Iraq had invaded Kuwait, the UN Charter clearly required that its aggression be resisted and reversed. The Charter also makes it clear, however, that disputes are to be resolved by pacific means. Article 41 refers to the Security Council's power to 'decide what measures not involving the use of armed force are to be employed to give effect to its decisions'. If the coalition had given the objective of averting war a higher priority, it could have done more to seek to reverse Iraq's aggression by diplomatic means, even while insisting on Iraq's withdrawal from Kuwait. It could have (a) declared its intention to seek a political settlement without using force, (b) used intermediaries vigorously, (c) taken up the offer of direct talks made by Iraq on 21 August, (d) set up a procedure for addressing the border dispute in conjunction with Iraq's withdrawal, in keeping with Resolution 660,[1] and (e) endorsed the proposal for a Middle East peace conference, thus making progress on the 'broad approach', without relating these steps to Iraqi withdrawal.

On the Iraqi side, the government signally failed to seek a peaceful settlement or to avert a war. The invasion showed the Iraqi regime's contempt for the UN Charter and for the principle of peaceful settlement of disputes. Subsequently Iraq's threats and acts of violence subverted its peace offers, and its obdurate policy on withdrawal frustrated the efforts of third parties. Saddam's actions suggest that he courted the war.

Negotiating with Saddam was certainly not an easy task. Nevertheless, the failure to entertain negotiations may have closed the door on an acceptable diplomatic settlement. Had negotiations with Saddam failed, the next step would have been to maintain pressure on the Iraqi regime using sanctions, while appealing to a successor regime. For this purpose, all the steps identified above would have been worth taking.

Conclusions

This dispute illustrates the value of settling conflicts early. In considering its history, a number of questions arise.

1. During the period up to 2 August 1990, were the negotiations conducted in such a way as to be conducive to finding an agreed settlement? No. They appear to have been conducted in a bargaining manner, in which both sides aimed to concede as little as possible, and neither explored the real needs and interests of the other. As a result, mutually acceptable outcomes seem to have

been missed. Neither side attempted to take fully into account each other's real interests.

2. Was a sustained effort made to deal with the dispute? No. The parties allowed the dispute to lapse after each stand-off. The Kuwaitis appeared to breathe a sigh of relief when the attention of the Iraqi government turned elsewhere, instead of seeking a final agreement.

3. Was mediation effective and sustained? A third party could have helped the parties to identify their areas of mutual interests (the Arab League might have been the most appropriate forum). Was it on the agenda of the organization at times while the dispute was quiet? When the sides accepted mediation from the PLO, the effort was not sustained after the failure of the initial talks.

4. Did the UN keep the dispute on its agenda? No; the UN considered the conflict only when it became a crisis, with troops already involved.

Both sides, in fact, relied on power and might to settle the dispute: Iraq on its military superiority, Kuwait on its powerful political alliances. The result was that the dispute was never settled and it was finally left to be resolved through force. After the invasion, the US-led coalition and Iraq again relied on power and armed force to resolve the dispute.

NOTE

1. Besides condemning the Iraqi invasion of Kuwait and calling for immediate and unconditional withdrawal, Resolution 660 called upon Iraq and Kuwait 'to begin immediately intensive negotiations for the resolution of their differences.'

Part 4

Towards a New Dispute Settlement Regime

13 Conclusions

DISCUSSION OF FINDINGS

What factors has this study shown to be conducive to the peaceful resolution of conflicts?

Based on the 81 conflicts in the study, there is a clear association between the nature of a conflict and its prospects for peaceful settlement. Conflicts involving territorial issues or disputes over resources proved easier to resolve peacefully than those involving ethnic issues, minorities, ideology or struggles for control of government. There was also an association between whether disputes were international and whether they were peacefully resolved. A pure international dispute appeared to be more likely to be peacefully resolved than a civil or mixed dispute.

These findings suggest that the international dispute settlement system is better at coping with conflicts over 'interests' between states than with conflicts over values and relationships involving nonstate actors. This may be because, first, governments and diplomats are accustomed to negotiating and bargaining over tangible assets such as territory and resources, where deals can be reached directly between governments. They may be less good at dealing with issues where fundamental clashes of values are concerned; in such disputes parties are not willing to reach deals. There are approaches to conflict resolution which are particularly aimed at conflicts of values (for example, Burton, 1987), but these have been little used. Secondly, although there is an international dispute settlement system, with the UN and the regional organizations at its centre, this system was not designed to deal with non-international conflicts and is inadequately equipped to do so.

As regards the outcomes of the conflicts, this study does not give decisive support to the theory that peacefully resolved conflicts should have 'win–win' outcomes, which sustain the interests of all parties.

There were such outcomes among the peacefully resolved conflicts, but more common were outcomes which mainly sustained the interests of one side. Among territorial conflicts, little evidence was found that a 'win–win' outcome or a 'win–lose' outcome made a difference as regards whether a conflict was peaceful or violent. In a number of conflicts there was some form of compensation for the loser, but these were still a minority. More important, perhaps, than who won was the attitude the parties took to how they tried to win. Among the ethnic and minority conflicts, violence was likely when either side sought to impose a settlement on the other; when the parties were prepared to acknowledge each other's concerns, the prospects of a peaceful resolution were brighter. The outcomes were rarely 'win–wins' but neither were they 'outright wins–outright losses'. The crucial factor seemed to be that each party recognized the other's concerns.

With regard to the processes by which the conflicts were resolved, no single factor was found which influenced whether conflicts were peacefully resolved. However, it was found that the presence of at least one of a combination of factors was conducive to peaceful settlement. Of these, perhaps the most important was early third-party intervention. The study suggested that this was more common in conflicts resolved peacefully than in conflicts resolved after violence. Other factors were whether a declaration of intent was made to settle peacefully, whether the parties agreed on a procedure to settle the conflict, and whether the parties referred the conflict to a popular vote.

It has not been possible within the scope of this study to compare conflict processes in detail. The case of South Tyrol suggests that a conciliatory move or a sequence of co-operative moves at critical times in the conflict can make a crucial difference to whether the conflict is resolved peacefully. In the case of Cyprus, in contrast, coercive moves at an early stage led to violence. The case of Northern Epirus suggests that a process of making links and improving relations can create the momentum needed to reach a peaceful resolution, even if it does not directly touch on the issues in conflict. There is evidence in a number of cases that withdrawing from hostile positions and lifting coercive measures sets up a 'virtuous' circle of reciprocated steps towards settlement. These indications are suggestive but, since conflict processes were not systematically compared in a large number of peacefully and violently resolved conflicts, no firm conclusions were established.

No test was made of the theory that a more integrated community of societies would be conducive to peaceful resolution of conflicts. It is suggestive that European disputes were more likely to be resolved peacefully than those of Africa or the Middle East. Europe is a more integrated community, with more settled borders (Downing, 1980) and has more shared institutions. But of course this is not the only factor involved. Allowance must be made for the involvement of European powers in disputes which are classified as taking place in Africa or the Middle East. Moreover, the military concentrations built up in the course of the most important European conflict, that between NATO and the Warsaw Pact, remain. Nevertheless, the events brought the Cold War to an end, especially the development of the CSCE, suggests that integration is conducive to the settlement of disputes.

POLICY IMPLICATIONS

This section traces some of the implications for the practice of conflict resolution, assuming that the findings and suggestions of this study are correct. It deals first with particular conflicts, and then with the question of the dispute settlement regime as a whole.

First, two general points should be made. The first concerns the question of whether peaceful resolution of conflict is possible in all conflicts. There are many who believe that some types of conflict can never be resolved peacefully and therefore armed conflict is inevitable. There are others who believe that all conflicts could be resolved peacefully, given sufficient goodwill and skill. Because it is limited to a selection of conflicts, this study does not confirm or disprove either view. Its evidence is that the categories of conflict involving issues of territory, resources, independence, post-independence, jurisdiction and ethnicity all included peacefully resolved cases. The categories of conflict involving ideological and minority issues included cases which were peacefully or partially resolved. The categories of conflict involving secession, religion and struggles for control of government included no peacefully resolved cases.

The second point is that it is important that decision-makers should want to reach a peaceful settlement; often they do not. A higher priority may be to win, if necessary by force. Cases where one side seeks a peaceful settlement but the other is determined to be coercive are particularly difficult. It takes only one to initiate violence, but two to settle a conflict peacefully. On the other hand, it takes only one to open the door towards a peaceful settlement, and to be the first to step through it. The cases examined in this study suggest a number of procedures which, though not certain to produce a peaceful settlement, have been important in some of the peaceful settlements of the past. They are listed below.

Procedures for Particular Conflicts

1. It can help to separate issues and reach agreement on the less contentious, as a basis for establishing a momentum towards agreement. In particular, some territorial conflicts are resolved by separating them from resource issues, and some ethnic and minority conflicts by separating them from territorial issues.
2. A declaration of intent to settle peacefully can initiate a process that ends in a peaceful settlement, even if neither side is at first willing to shift its position.
3. It is often conducive to a peaceful settlement to agree on a procedure for settling, even if the parties are divided on substantive points. Examples of agreed procedures are the creation of a joint study group to examine the issue, an agreement to hold an election, or an agreement to use mediaton.
4. It may be conducive to a settlement to allow a conflict to proceed to a point where the parties are aware of the costs each is imposing on the other, because then a shared interest is created in resolving the conflict to avoid these costs.
5. Removing measures which impose costs can create a momentum for reciprocal co-operation.
6. Co-operative moves following a sequence of coercive steps can break a slide towards violence and signal a desire for settlement. In the right circumstances a unilateral gesture can open the way to exploring a settlement. Coercive moves following a sequence of co-operative steps may well be taken as a signal that violence is about to break out.
7. A sequence of moves to build links between parties without directly affecting the substance of the issues involved in the conflict can help to create a momentum towards a settlement. Whereas the cutting of such links is a sign of polarization, the making of them can begin a reverse process.
8. Parties cannot explore the possibility of a mutually acceptable outcome without adequate channels of communication, and the creation and maintenance of such channels is itself conducive to peaceful settlement, although it is not a sufficient condition of a settlement. In the absence of regular two-way communications between the parties, mediation is an important alternative. It is

important to set up a process through which parties can explore their differences and move towards a settlement. Listening to grievances is an important part of such communication.

9. Early third-party intervention is associated with peaceful resolution of conflicts.

10. Conflicts are more likely to be peacefully resolved if the parties respond to the situation they are in as a whole, and take account of others' interests as well as their own. It is always necessary to be open-minded about what these interests are.

Improving the Dispute Settlement Regime

A number of measures could be taken to improve the dispute settlement regime as a whole. First, there is a need to monitor the development of emergent conflicts at an early stage. This has been recognized at the UN (Kanninen, 1989), by mediators (Curle, 1986; Bailey, 1988a) and among the international peace research community. It is within the capabilities of the research community, although it is not without methodological difficulties (Rupesinghe, 1989).

Second, more effort needs to be made to provide some form of third-party mediation at an early stage. If conflicts are within states, the UN and the regional organizations are often reluctant to intervene, and non-governmental third parties may be the only organizations which can play a role. But the resources of non-governmental mediators are limited, and understandably armed conflicts are given a higher priority than situations which are only potentially violent. There is a strong case for more support for this form of intervention.

Mediation is not the only communications channel. The UN provides a valuable forum for the hearing of grievances between countries (Allsebrook, 1986), and has a recognized mechanism for offering good offices. Groups at the sub-national level need equivalent fora. Perhaps the remit of the UN and the regional organizations could be widened to permit more dealings with nongovernmental bodies. Another possibility would be to develop new forms of transnational assembly. Assemblies which represent peoples rather than governments are already developing in Europe.

There is a common international interest in improving procedures for peacefully settling disputes (Palme, 1982), but this interest is not yet very powerfully represented in the international system. The UN and the regional organizations embody it, but their effectiveness depends on the co-operation of the more powerful states. To the extent that these states compete to pursue narrowly conceived national interests and seek security through unilateral policies, the prospects for peaceful settlement of disputes will remain poor; on the other hand, the more the international community articulates common concerns and sets up common institutions, the better the prospects will become.

New patterns of communications, social development and economic organization are outgrowing the old system of sovereign states. As societies become more interdependent, it is evident that their decision-making systems must reflect this fact. The trend towards integration seems to be the way ahead. Organizations such as the EC and the CSCE have already created the basis for regional dispute settlement regimes. The co-operative arrangements for managing natural resources and the natural environment constitute a developing regime for managing conflicts of interest in global issues. As people in different societies recognize the common interest in co-operation and common security, it should become possible to reduce arms, agree dispute settling procedures, and strengthen common institutions in a self-reinforcing process. Ultimately the most important condition for an effective dispute settlement system is the recognition of a sense of community: in this case, a community of human interest amidst the unique and diverse interests of particular societies.

Part 5
Cases

1 Åland Islands 1808–1947

Area:	Europe
Parties:	Sweden
	Finland (Russia before 1917)
Third parties:	(Britain, League of Nations)
Issues:	Ethnic
	Territory
Coercion:	None
Hostilities:	None
Fatalities:	0
Resolution:	Resolved

See Chapter 6.

Sources: Isaakson (1985), Day (1987).

2 Albania–Yugoslavia (Kosovo) 1963–

Area:	Europe
Parties:	Albania, Albanians in Kosovo, Yugoslavia, Serbs
Third parties:	
Issues:	Ethnic
	Ideology
	Minority
	Religion
	Secession
Coercion:	Use of minor force
Hostilities:	None
Fatalities:	Not Known
Resolution:	Unresolved

Background: Kosovo is the most undeveloped part of Yugoslavia, and also the most densely populated. Eighty-five per cent of its population are ethnic Albanians; the rest are Serbs. There has been a protracted ethnic dispute between the Albanians and the Serbs. The Albanians complain that Yugoslavia has neglected the region, and that they are an oppressed minority in Yugoslavia. The Serbs complain that the Albanian majority in Kosovo have oppressed the Serbian minority.

There are also historical animosities between the two peoples, which go back to Albanian collaboration with the Fascists, and Serbian massacres of Albanians during the Second World War. After 1945, the Serbian leader Rankovic, who was Tito's head of security, pursued highly repressive policies towards the Albanian minority.

Development: In 1963, Kosovo became an autonomous province of Serbia, itself one of six federated republics making up Yugoslavia. There were student riots in 1968 in favour of greater self-government for the Albanians. In 1974, a new constitution gave Kosovo an assembly and equal status with other republics. Nevertheless there was further violent rioting in 1981, with Albanian nationalists demanding full republican status. The Yugoslav government clamped down after discovering arms in the hands of groups supporting what they called 'counter-revolutionary nationalism and irredentism'. The government dismissed a number of senior Albanian leaders from their posts in the provincial government. Meanwhile the Serbs in Kosovo were protesting about attacks on them by the provincial government, which they accused of attempting genocide. At least a third of the Serbs living in the area left the region. In the late 1980s, violence flared again as the Serbs in Kosovo organized demonstrations and self-defence committees.

Resolution: The ethnic conflict remains unresolved. However, inter-state relations between Yugoslavia and Albania improved after 1985, when Hoxha died. The two states have signed economic co-operation agreements, and have attempted to limit damage to their relations arising from the dispute.

Tito's attempts to resolve the problem by giving Kosovo autonomy in 1963, and giving it an assembly and greater powers in 1974, failed to defuse the ethnic tensions. To some extent they merely shifted the status of aggrieved minority from the Albanians to the Serbs in Kosovo. The relations between the ethnic groups were handled in the context of a centralised Communist government, which was more inclined to suppress ethnic dissent than to address it sensitively. Relations between Yugoslavia and Albania have not been good enough for interstate guarantees to come into operation in this case (as they did, for example, in South Tyrol).

Sources: Day (1987), *Financial Times* (14 October 1988).

3 Albania–Greece (Northern Epirus) 1945–85

Area: Europe
Parties: Albania
                 Greece
Third parties: Allied powers
Issues: Ethnic
                 Territory
Coercion: None
Hostilities: None
Fatalities: 0
Resolution: Resolved

Background: The peacefully resolved conflict between Greece and Albania over Northern Epirus is a case where a sequence of conciliatory moves created the momentum to settle a conflict. The dispute concerned the Greek claim to an area in southern Albania inhabited by ethnic Greeks who form 20 per cent of the Albanian population. The Greek claim was based on military occupation, first in 1914, then in 1940. The Albanian claim was based on the frontier demarcation of 1926 which had been agreed by the major European powers and Greece and Yugoslavia.

Development: At the end of the Second World War, Greece maintained its irredentist claim and considered itself technically in a state of war with Albania from 1940. All the Greek political parties except the Communists demanded that Northern Epirus be 'reunited with the motherland'.

Resolution: For some time the situation was deadlocked, but in 1958 both parties signalled an intention to settle the conflict peacefully. Greece reiterated its territorial claim but offered to settle it through normal diplomatic channels. Albania refuted the claim but expressed a desire for normal and good-neighbourly relations with Greece. There followed a process in which closer relations were established between the two states despite the continuing territorial disagreement. First in 1970 a trade agreement was signed, at nongovernmental level. Then in 1971 diplomatic relations were established. Further trade protocols followed and in 1978 a direct air link between the countries was established. In 1984 there were further agreements on transport, telecommunications, postal services and cultural and scientific exchanges. By 1985 the territorial dispute no longer seemed a serious issue. In January 1985, the border was reopened. In July 1985, the two countries signed a protocol agreeing a procedure for settling border disputes. Finally in August 1985, Greece formally annulled the state of war, effectively abandoning its territorial claim.

Source: Day (1987).

4 Albania–Soviet Union 1960–

Area:	Europe
Parties:	Albania
	Soviet Union
Third parties:	
Issues:	Ideology
	Territory
Coercion:	Non-military
Hostilities:	None
Fatalities:	0
Resolution:	Unresolved

Background: The Communist Party under Enver Hoxha came to power in Albania at the end of the Second World War, after a partisan war against Italian occupying forces. The Albanian party at first modelled itself on Yugoslav lines, but when the Yugoslavs split from the Soviet Union in 1948, Albania sided with the Soviet Union against reform.

Development: When the Soviet Union itself began deStalinization, Albania's Stalinist leaders condemned Soviet revisionism. When the Sino–Soviet split developed, Albania sided with China. The Soviet Union withdrew all forms of assistance to Albania, but did not attempt to impose its policies on Albania as on other East European states, presumably because of its strategic unimportance. Albania withdrew from the Warsaw Pact after the Czech invasion.

Source: Butterworth (1976), *Third World Guide* (1990).

5 Algeria–Morocco 1962–70

Area: Africa
Parties: Algeria
                        Morocco
Third parties: OAU, Arab League, Ethiopia, Mali
Issues: Ideology
                        Post-independence
                        Resources
                        Territory
Coercion: Use of major force
Hostilities: Major
Fatalities (log.10):   2.5
Resolution: Resolved

Background: Following independence, nationalists in the ruling Moroccan Istiqlal (Independence) party claimed a large area of the northwest Sahara, disputing the borders which had been established by the colonial power, France. The claim included Mauritania, the Western Sahara and an adjoining strip of territory in Algeria. The land disputed with Algeria was mainly desert, but included several settlements and local tribes. The area was believed to be rich in minerals and possibly oil and gas. The dispute became a focus for public hostility between Algeria and Morocco, and there were also ideological differences between their socialist and monarchical governments.

Development: Morocco signed an agreement with the Provisional Republican Government of Algeria, before Algeria became independent, to settle the border problem through a joint commission. However, following independence, Ben Bella was unwilling to give up any of the territory. Heavy fighting along the border broke out in 1963, resulting in a stalemate.

Resolution: After unsuccessful interventions by the Arab League and others, mediation by Haile Selassie of Ethiopia on behalf of the OAU secured a meeting between Hassan II and Ben Bella, who agreed on a cease-fire and an arbitration commission. In 1964 Algeria and Morocco agreed to troop withdrawals, and a demilitarized zone, with Malian and Ethiopian observers. Later prisoners were exchanged, the border was reopened and diplomatic relations were restored.

In 1966 Boumédienne overthrew Ben Bella and pursued a less conciliatory policy, nationalizing iron mines in the disputed area.

The arbitration committee was called and another crisis was avoided. Following the 1967 war with Israel, relations improved, and in 1969 the two countries signed a Treaty of Solidarity and Co-operation. In 1970 it was announced that the dispute was ended.

Outcome: Morocco failed to win the disputed area.

Subsequent developments: Relations worsened following Morocco's occupation of Western Sahara (1975). Algeria supported Polisario in the subsequent war.

Factors contributing to resolution:

1. Military stalemate.
2. OAU mediation.
3. Arbitration commission.
4. Common Arab identity (and common enemy in Israel).

Sources: Donelan and Grieve (1973), Butterworth (1976), *Third World Guide* (1990).

6   Algeria–Tunisia 1961–70

Area:	Africa
Parties:	Algeria
	Tunisia
Third parties:	
Issues:	Territory
Coercion:	None
Hostilities:	None
Fatalities:	0
Resolution:	Resolved

Background: While Algeria was a French colony, Tunisia claimed part of the colony's Saharan territory.

Development: Following independence, Tunisia negotiated directly with Algeria. Tunisia maintained its claim until 1970, but decided not to press it forcefully.

Resolution: Tunisia and Algeria agreed a series of border conventions in 1963, although Tunisia was still not willing to recognize the *de facto* boundary. Subsequent negotiations on economic co-operation were held to consider the economic exploitation of the region. A provisional border settlement was agreed for an area in which oil had been discovered. By 1970, Tunisia agreed to accept Algeria's post-independence borders.

Outcome: Tunisia accepted Algeria's sovereignty over the disputed area. Tunisia was compensated with economic co-operation in the region.

Factors contributing to resolution:

1. Good prior relations.
2. Low importance of territory.
3. Low public involvment.
4. Unwillingness to disrupt Arab and North African relations.

Source: Butterworth (1976).

7   Algerian independence 1945–62

Area:	Africa
Parties:	French government, French colonists
	Algerian nationalists
Third parties:	UN
Issues:	Independence
	Resources
	Territory
Coercion:	Use of major force
Hostilities:	Major
Fatalities (log.10):	5
Resolution:	Resolved

Background: In 1830 France invaded Algeria, previously part of the Ottoman Empire, and set up a colony, awarding land to French settlers. Resistance was sharp and recurrent, but the French troops crushed indigenous revolts. By 1945 there were a million French settlers and French interests in the colony were considerable; in the cities French whites were almost as numerous as Algerian Arabs. As Algeria was a 'department' of France, the settlers constituted a strong political lobby in France against decolonization. When the nationalist movement developed, a protracted conflict broke out between the French government and settlers, and Algerians fighting for independence.

Development: The nationalists demanded political reforms and a new constitution. The French government refused these demands, arrested nationalist leaders, and suppressed riots forcibly. The nationalists then set up the Front de Libération Nationale (FLN) and began guerrilla warfare, which was contained but not defeated by a large French army. There were clashes on the Algerian side between rival nationalists, and on the French side between supporters and opponents of reform.

Resolution: Conflict within France over Algerian policy precipitated a political crisis, which brought the Fourth Republic to an end and de Gaulle back to power. De Gaulle was able to stand up to the army and the colonial interests, and proceeded to take cautious steps towards granting independence. He announced that Algeria would be allowed self-determination, and in 1960 opened talks with the Algerian provisional government. These moves led to unsuccessful attempts by the French army in Algeria to overthrow or assassinate de Gaulle. However, opinion in France was turning against the colonists, and in 1961 a referendum in France and Algeria showed majority support for de Gaulle's proposal to hold a plebiscite on independence. Negotiations with the provisional government broke down over the issue of the sovereignty of the Algerian Sahara, but resumed in 1962 and led to a cease-fire agreement, a provisional executive, a referendum and the withdrawal of French forces over three years. France was to maintain its exploitation of the oilfields, and to continue to provide financial and technical aid. Despite a terrorist campaign against decolonization, the French population overwhelmingly endorsed independence in a referendum held in 1962. Algeria became independent in the same year. Most of the settlers, fearing reprisals from the Algerian government, left the country.

Outcome: Algeria became independent.

Subsequent developments: The radical nationalist leader Ben Bella was overthrown by Boumédienne in 1965. Boumédienne continued to collaborate with the French government and receive French aid, while nationalizing and industrializing the economy. In 1967 France removed its remaining bases.

Factors contributing to the settlement:

1. The military confrontation had reached a stalemate (neither the French army nor the FLN guerrillas could defeat each other).

2. Change of government in France (de Gaulle's accession to power, and his decision to seek a settlement).
3. Agreement on procedure for settling independence through a plebiscite.
4. Defeat of colonial and military interests through de Gaulle's authority and French frustration with the war.

Sources: Butterworth (1976), Calvocoressi (1987).

8 Angola 1956–

Area:	Africa
Parties:	MPLA, Cuba
	FLNA
	UNITA, South Africa, Portugal
Third parties:	OAU, UN, USA
Issues:	Control of government
	Ethnic
	Ideology
	Independence
	Post-independence
Other:	South Africa's forward security policy
Coercion:	Use of major force
Hostilities:	Major
Fatalities (log.10):	5.4
Resolution:	Unresolved

Background: A guerrilla war against Portuguese colonial rule began in 1961, and continued sporadically for 15 years. In 1974, the Portuguese decided to withdraw from their African colonies. Three liberation fronts had been involved in the fighting: the FLNA (supported by Zaire and China), the MPLA (with support in the cities and in the North) and UNITA (with support in the highlands, among working-class whites, and from South Africa). After the Portuguese announcement, negotiations between the liberation movements took place and a common front was formed in 1975. But this broke down, and fighting broke out the day after the new government was installed in office. A three-cornered civil war began, involving ethnic conflict and a proxy war between the superpowers. Cuba (with Soviet support) intervened on behalf of the MPLA. The Americans and South Africans supported UNITA.

Development: In 1976 a large Cuban and MPLA army with Soviet arms and command defeated the FLNA and forced South African forces to retreat. Jonas Savimbi's UNITA forces withdrew to the bush and, abandoned by the Americans, relied on South Africa and Rhodesia for support. With the MPLA government established in Luanda and UNITA well entrenched in the south, the war reached a stalemate. The MPLA could not dislodge the MPLA while it had support from South Africa, and UNITA could not take Luanda while the MPLA had Soviet support. In 1981, following Reagan's election as President, the USA resumed its support for UNITA, forcing the Soviet Union to increase its level of support for the MPLA. Fighting intensified in 1987–88, when South Africa sent a large force north to support UNITA against an MPLA attack. For a while UNITA almost swept the government and Cuban forces out of the south. Then Cuba sent reinforcements and recovered most of the lost ground when South African forces withdrew in 1988.

Resolution: By this time, US–Soviet tensions were easing rapidly, in the context of Gorbachev's foreign policy changes. During a summit meeting in Moscow, Reagan and Gorbachev agreed to seek a settlement of the Angolan issue on the basis of UN Security Council resolution 435. Gorbachev decided the Soviet Union could not afford to continue arms supplies to the MPLA at a cost of $1 billion/year. Following efforts by the US Assistant Secretary of State Chester Crocker, an agreement was negotiated whereby Cuban and South African troops would withdraw and a cease-fire would come into effect. The agreement provided a timetable for Cuban withdrawal from Angola and for the independence of Namibia. However, the MPLA government refused to negotiate an internal settlement with UNITA, and the civil war continued.

Outcome: Remains unresolved.

Subsequent developments: The war has had a destructive effect on Angola's economy, contributing to serious famine in the country.

Factors influencing the settlement:

1. Military stalemate.
2. New Soviet foreign policy, decision not to continue paying for war.

3. South Africa moving away from expensive 'forward' military policy.
4. US mediation by Chester Crocker.
5. Linkage to Namibian independence.

Sources: Butterworth (1976), Murray (1988), Brogan (1989).

9 Austria (status of) 1945–55

Area:	Europe
Parties:	USSR
	Austria, USA, UK, France
Third parties:	UN
Issues:	Jurisdiction
	Resources
	Territory
Coercion:	None
Hostilities:	None
Fatalities:	0
Resolution:	Resolved

Background: After the Second World War, Soviet forces occupied eastern Austria while Western forces occupied the rest of the country. An attempt to reach a settlement in 1947 broke down because of the Cold War.

Development: The Soviet government championed Yugoslav territorial claims against Austria and demanded control of Austrian resources as reparations against Germany. The Allies resisted this claim on the grounds that Austria was forced to assist Germany. In 1949, as a rift developed between the Soviet Union and Yugoslavia, a settlement seemed possible based on cash reparations, but the agreement broke down when it came to be implemented.

Resolution: In 1955 the Soviet Union reversed its policy and agreed to settle the dispute on condition that a union between Germany and Austria be prohibited.

Outcome: The Soviet Union was given Austrian oil and cash reparations. The Austrian State Treaty prohibited Austro–German political or economic union. The pre-1938 borders were restored and foreign troops withdrew. Austria pledged to remain neutral.

Subsequent developments: The settlement held. The Soviet Union later approved Austrian membership of the EC.

Factors in the settlement:

1. Elections held in 1945 gave the Communist Party in Austria a poor showing; a strike called by the Communist party failed in 1949.
2. The cash payments and a 10-year guarantee of oil compensated the Soviet Union.
3. The Soviet change of position was associated with Khrushchev's coming to power, and his policy of easing Soviet foreign relations.
4. Austria's declaration of neutrality satisfied Soviet security interests.

Sources: Donelan and Grieve (1973), Butterworth (1976).

10   Bahrain–Iran: Bahraini independence 1970–1

Area:	Middle East
Parties:	Iran
	UK
	Bahrainis
Third parties:	UN
Issues:	Independence
	Territory
Coercion:	None
Hostilities:	None
Fatalities:	0
Resolution:	Resolved

Background: Bahrain was under Arab rule until 1522, when it was occupied by the Portuguese. It fell under Persian control for most of the seventeenth and eighteenth centuries. From 1861 to 1971 it was a British protectorate. The administration was in the hands of local sheikhs, descended from the rulers of Qatar. The population of Bahrain is overwhelmingly Arab. There is a small minority of Iranian descent.

Development: The Persian government periodically reiterated its claim to Bahrain. In 1956 the Foreign Minister declared that Bahrian was an 'inseparable part of Persia' and the Persian Parliament declared that Bahrain was Persia's fourteenth province. The Shah in 1958 repeated his claim that Bahrain was 'an integral part of Persia'. He also claimed several other small islands in the Gulf. The rulers of Bahrain and the Arab League rejected these claims. When Britain decided to withdraw from East of Suez, the government favoured uniting Bahrain with the Trucial Sheikhdoms.

Resolution: In 1969, the Shah accepted that the inhabitants should be free to decide their own fate and, with British and Iranian agreement, a UN representative visited Bahrain to determine the wishes of the people. His report indicated that there was overwhelming support for an independent sovereign state of Bahrain. The UN Security Council endorsed this report, and the decision was approved by the Iranian Majlis in 1970. This appeared to settle the dispute, and in a subsequent visit by the Iranian Foreign Minister to Bahrain it was agreed that there were no issues in dispute between the two states.

Resolution: Bahrain became an independent state; neither the British nor the Iranian preferred outcomes were adopted.

Subsequent developments: In the 1970s, the growth of the oil industry attracted increasing immigration from Iran. After the Shah's overthrow, unofficial spokesmen for revolutionary Iran re-asserted the old claim, but it has not been actively maintained. Nevertheless, Bahrain remained concerned about Iranian irredentism. Bahrain joined the Gulf Co-operation Council (GCC) in 1981.

Factors contributing to the settlement:

1. The Shah may have decided to trade off his claim to Bahrain against the small islands of Abu Musa and the Tunbs; Iran secretly informed the UK at the time of the settlement over Bahrain that it maintained its claim to these islands, and it duly occupied them in 1971, two days before the United Arab Emirates became independent.
2. The parties agreed to seek UN assistance to resolve the conflict. The UN report that the Bahrainis wanted independence was legitimate and acceptable to all the parties.

Sources: Butterworth (1976), Day (1987).

11   Bahrain–Qatar 1971–

Area:	Middle East
Parties:	Bahrain
	Qatar
Third parties:	Saudi Arabia
Issues:	Territory
Coercion:	Display of force
Hostilities:	None
Fatalities:	0
Resolution:	Unresolved

Background: Bahrain and Qatar are in dispute over the sovereignty of the Hawar islands, which lie 1½ miles off Qatar, though they are contiguous at low tide. The islands are 18 miles from Bahrain. In 1938 the ruler of Bahrain laid claim to the islands, with a view to exploring for oil. Britain, in a relationship of protectorship to both countries, supported Bahrain's claim.

Development: The ruler of Qatar contested the legitimacy of the British decision. When the two states became independent, they agreed to submit these and other boundary differences to Saudi mediation. As a result, in 1978 both sides agreed not to alter the status quo, or to aim to strengthen their claims over the island, until they had achieved a negotiated settlement. However, in 1980 Bahrain announced that it had offered US oil companies drilling concessions in the Hawar Islands. Qatar responded indignantly by claiming the island as Qatari territory. The GCC, to which both states belonged, submitted the dispute again to Saudi mediation. Again the two states agreed to maintain the status quo pending negotiations. No agreement was reached, and in 1985 Bahrain began to construct military installations on the islands. Qatar responded by sending its own troops. The dispute remained unresolved by 1985.

Subsequent developments: Following further mediation by Saudi Arabia, Qatar agreed to remove its troops and Bahrain agreed to remove its installations, under GCC supervision. Both states accepted a Saudi suggestion that they establish a joint border commission, and, should that fail to settle the dispute, that they refer it to binding arbitration.

Source: Day (1987)

12 Belgian–Netherlands border 1957–9

Area: Europe
Parties: Belgium
                         Netherlands
Third parties: ICJ
Issues: Territory
Coercion: None
Hostilities: None
Fatalities (log.10):   0
Resolution: Resolved

Background: This dispute was over two plots of land, involving only 30 acres.

Development: The Netherlands claimed that they had been awarded to Belgium by mistake in the demarcation of 1943. Belgium asserted that they were rightfully Belgian.

Resolution: Both governments agreed to submit their claims to the ICJ, which found for Belgium.

Outcome: The two plots remained in Belgium.

Factors making for settlement:

1. The slight importance of the dispute.
2. Agreement on the procedure for settling the dispute.

Source: Butterworth (1976).

13 Berlin 1948–

Area: Europe
Parties: USSR, East Germany
                         USA, UK, France, West Germany
Third parties: UN
Issues: Great Power
                         Jurisdiction
Coercion: Use of major force
Hostilities: None
Fatalities: 0
Resolution: Interim or partial settlement

Background: The Second World War ended with Berlin under four-power occupation, but well inside the Russian controlled zone of Germany.

Development: In opposition to the Western Allies' plans for West Germany, the USSR began curtailing Western access to Berlin and imposed a blockade. This precipitated the Berlin crisis of 1949. The USA avoided a war and maintained supplies in Berlin through a prolonged airlift.

In 1958 Khrushchev demanded an end to four-power occupation, and transfer of the administration of the city to the GDR. The Western Allies refused to remove their troops until a final agreement on German unification had been reached. After an impasse, both sides agreed to settle their disputes by peaceful means, and opened negotiations.

Kennedy demanded continued Western access to its zone pending a multilateral settlement of German reunification issues, while Khrushchev insisted that the existing boundaries of the FRG were fixed, and that if the Soviet Union made a unilateral peace settlement with East Germany, the West would have to negotiate with the GDR. The flow of people leaving the East increased, and tensions between USA and USSR grew. Both sides carried out mobilizing or defence build-up actions. The GDR then built the Wall, closing access off, and effectively imposing a unilateral solution.

Resolution:

1. Talks in 1949 between the Soviet and US representatives to the UN led to a resolution of the crisis, whereby the blockade was lifted.
2. The 1958 crisis was resolved by an agreement to hold negotiations.
3. The 1961–2 crisis was ended by the GDR's decision unilaterally to build the Berlin Wall and thus make permanent the division of the city.

Subsequent developments: Western politicians continued to demand the removal of the Wall. The Wall has remained a powerful symbol of the East–West divide.

(For the fall of the Wall, see Chapter 6.)

14   Cameroons (British), independence 1955–63

Area:	Africa
Parties:	UK, Nigeria, Northern Cameroons
	Cameroun, Southern Cameroons
Third parties:	UN
Issues:	Independence
	Jurisdiction
Coercion:	None
Hostilities:	None
Fatalities:	0
Resolution:	Resolved

Background: The German colony of Kamerun lasted until 1916, when it was taken over by Britain and France under League, and later UN, Trusteeship. The British administered British Cameroons as part of Nigeria. When the Trusteeship came to an end, Britain intended to integrate the Cameroons with Nigeria, but many in the southern part of the British Cameroons wanted to integrate with the newly independent republic of Cameroun (formerly the French Cameroons).

Development: The pro-independence People's Union of Cameroon party (UPC) in the French Cameroons established itself in the southern British Cameroons and began a campaign for independence and unification with Cameroun. However, in 1957 the UPC was banned in the Southern Cameroons and its leaders deported. Nigeria offered the Southern Cameroons its own regional government as part of Nigeria. In 1958 a UN mission reported that the parties in the Southern Cameroons had agreed to hold a plebiscite to decide their future, but they split over whether the plebiscite should be held before or after the Cameroons were separated from Nigeria. The Northern Cameroons, which were administered as part of the northern region of Nigeria, wanted to become part of Nigeria.

Resolution: After discussions, the UN General Assembly decided to hold separate plebiscites in the south and north. The southern leaders disagreed on the questions to be put in the plebiscite, but eventually the General Assembly secured agreement between them. In 1959, the voters in the Northern Cameroons decided to postpone a vote rather than join Nigeria immediately. It was then decided that concurrent plebiscites would take place in 1961. The north voted to join Nigeria; the south voted to join Cameroun.

The Republic of Cameroun now objected that the result had been prejudiced by the UK administering the Northern Cameroons as part of the northern region, and took its case to the ICJ. However, the ICJ ruled that the decision of the UN General Assembly and the plebiscites was final.

Outcome: Northern Cameroons joined Nigeria, Southern Cameroons joined Cameroun.

Subsequent developments: There was some subsequent tension in the Republic of Cameroun between the formerly French and formerly British colonies.

Factors influencing the settlement:

1. UN as a third-party management agent, capable of negotiating between the parties, and holding high legitimacy with them.
2. Agreement on plebiscites as the method of resolution.

Sources: Butterworth (1976), Murray (1988).

15   Cameroun's independence 1948–61

Area:	Africa
Parties:	Camerouni nationalists
	France
Third parties:	UN
Issues:	Independence
Coercion:	Use of major force
Hostilities:	Major
Fatalities (log.10):	4.5
Resolution:	Resolved

Background: Unlike the British Cameroons, the independence of the French-administered Cameroons involved a violent struggle.

Development: The nationalist UPC began a campaign for independence in 1948. After eight years of legal protest and campaigning against colonial rule, in which it won massive support, the colonial government outlawed the party in 1956.

Resolution: The UPC then mounted a guerrilla campaign inside French Cameroun. France responded by offering autonomy and early independence to a government based on two conservative Islamic parties which merged to form the National Union of Cameroon (UNC). France notified the UN of its intention to offer independence to the colony (which was under UN Trusteeship from 1949 to 1960). The UPC objected that the UNC government was unrepresentative, and a UN mission was sent to the Cameroons to investigate. It found in favour of the French and UNC position, and recommended early independence. The UN rejected a UPC proposal for UN-supervised elections.

Outcome: Independence duly took place in 1960, with the UNC government in power.

Subsequent developments: The government increased its efforts to suppress the opposition, and took thousands of political prisoners. The UNC leader, Ahidjo, remained in power until 1982.

Sources: Butterworth (1976), *Third World Guide* (1990).

16   Cyprus 1954–

Area:	Europe
Parties:	Greece, Greek Cypriots
	Turkey, Turkish Cypriots
Third parties:	UN, NATO
Issues:	Ethnic
	Independence
	Jurisdiction
	Territory
Coercion:	Use of major force
Hostilities:	Major
Fatalities (log.10):	3.7
Resolution:	Unresolved

Background: 80 per cent of Cypriots are Greek, 20 per cent Turkish. The British faced a serious problem in granting independence as conflict between the Greeks, who favoured union with Greece, and the Turks, who favoured partition, seemed likely.

Development: The British sought to delay independence, but this led to a guerrilla campaign organised by EOKA, the Greek nationalist movement.

In 1959, Greek, Turkish and UK ministers reached an agreement in London, and a constitution was introduced giving Cyprus shared powers, with a Greek Cypriot President, Turkish vice-president, and a legislature 70 per cent Greek and 30 per cent Turkish.

Each party was permitted to keep security forces on the island. Disagreements over the implementation of these arrangements paralysed the government and the fighting which broke out between the Greek and Turkish Cypriots began to escalate. A UN peace-keeping force was brought in.

In 1964 Cyprus complained of a threatened Turkish invasion. The Greek Cypriots, then the Turkish, built fortifications. Tensions reduced in 1966 and talks between Greece and Turkey started, but were aborted when Turkish Cypriot leaders began to set up administrations for the Turkish-dominated areas.

In 1968–71, several efforts to reach a settlement were made, based on either continued independence with local autonomy for the Turkish minority, or union with Greece and territorial concessions for the Turkish minority. Makarios rejected both approaches. He began a campaign against EOKA-B and later ordered the removal of 600 officers from the Cypriot National Guard. This led to a coup (1974) in which he was overthrown.

Turkey responded to the threat to its interests by launching an invasion of Cyprus. Heavy fighting followed. The Greek junta, which had supported the coup, now fell. Turkey occupied the northern and eastern parts of the island. In peace talks, Denktash (the Turkish Cypriot leader) proposed partition, and Clerides (the new Greek Cypriot leader) proposed a large measure of internal autonomy to Turkish Cypriots within a federated structure. No agreement was reached and the Turkish forces achieved their military objectives and imposed a partition.

A Turkish Cypriot federated state was set up; the Turks stated that they favoured a 'bi-regional' federated state. Negotiations with the Greek Cypriots (now led again by Makarios) followed but foundered at first on Greek Cypriot insistence on a unitary state and the withdrawal of foreign troops. However, in 1975 Makarios and Denktash agreed on a set of guidelines for a bicommunal federal state, and the demilitarization of Cyprus. Negotiations, however, failed to reach agreement on the division of territory.

In 1981 the Turkish Cypriots announced an independent Turkish republic of North Cyprus. Only Turkey recognized this state (with some reluctance at first), and subsequent intercommunal talks made no progress, with hardening of attitudes on both sides, though some Greek support grew for a bicommunal federal solution.

Sources: Donelan and Grieve (1973), Butterworth (1976), Day (1988).

17   Cyrenaica 1949–51

Area:	Africa
Parties:	Italy, France
	Arab States
	US, UK, USSR
Third parties:	UN
Issues:	Independence
	Territory
Coercion:	None
Hostilities:	None
Fatalities:	0
Resolution:	Resolved

Background: Following the end of the Second World War, the UK took control of Cyrenaica, formerly an Italian territory. In 1949 the Great Powers agreed to Libya's independence, but the future of Cyrenaica remained to be settled. *

Development: The UK proposed that Cyrenaica should become self-governing but that its foreign policy and defence should remain under British control. Egypt and other Arab states favoured incorporating Cyrenaica into Libya. The UK began building a military base in Cyrenaica, with US backing. The USSR demanded its withdrawal.

Resolution: The UN recommended that Libya should set up a provisional government and the administering states should transfer their powers to it, supervised by the UN. In 1950 the Libyan National Assembly decided Libya should be a federal state, and proclaimed the Emir of Cyrenaica as King of Libya. The provisional government was set up and a constitution was ratified, making Cyrenaica a province of the United Kingdom of Libya.

Outcome: Cyrenaica was included in a federal Libyan kingdom, with the Emir of Cyrenaica becoming king. The Italian minority left the country.

Factors contributing to resolution:
1. The UN's proposal had legitimacy and was the basis of the solution.
2. The federal solution, with the Emir becoming king, won acceptance.

Sources: Butterworth (1976), Calvocoressi (1987).

18 Czechoslovakia 1968

Area:	Europe
Parties:	Czech reformers
	USSR, Warsaw Pact states, Czech hard-liners
Third parties:	UN, WTO
Issues:	Control of government
	Ideology
	Jurisdiction
Coercion:	Use of major force
Hostilities:	Minor
Fatalities (log.10):	2.7
Resolution:	Interim or partial settlement

Background: Background:
By 1968, Stalinist rule was discredited in Czechoslovakia, and economic reform was urgent. The replacement of Novotny by Alexander Dubček as First Secretary of the Party led to acceleration of reforms and the 'Prague Spring'. The government relaxed censorship and popular pressure for political reforms and democratization became intense.

Development: The East German and Polish governments felt threatened by Czech reforms, and the Soviet government was concerned to avoid liberalization going so far that it might threaten Communist power in Eastern Europe. Proposals by reformers to limit the power of the Communist Party and allow nonCommunist parties particularly alarmed them. For several months the Soviet Union and the Czech party negotiated and manoeuvred over the acceptable limits of reform, while Warsaw Pact troops exercised in Czechoslovakia. The conflict came to crisis point when the other Warsaw Pact member states demanded that the Czech party suppress 'anti-socialist' activities.

Dubček refused and Warsaw Pact forces invaded in August 1968. The Czech army did not resist, but there was vigorous popular non-violent resistance.

Resolution: The Soviet government was unable to form a new government that would collaborate. After negotiations with President Svoboda, the Soviet government was forced to reinstate Dubček, who remained in power until April 1969. The Czech party in turn was forced to abandon its programme of reforms. Eventually, the Soviets obtained a government more to their liking, under Husak.

Outcome: The Prague Spring was suppressed.

Subsequent developments: The invasion further damaged the legitimacy of Communist rule. Twenty-two years later, in 1989, the Communist government fell within a week in a bloodless popular revolution.

Sources: Calvocoressi (1987), Roberts (1969), Sharp (1973).

19   Denmark–UK fisheries 1961–4

Area:	Europe
Parties:	Denmark
	UK
Third parties:	European Fisheries Conference
Issues:	Fishing
Coercion:	Use of minor force
Hostilities:	None
Fatalities:	0
Resolution:	Resolved

Background: In 1961 Denmark decided to revise the then current Fisheries Agreement with Britain, in line with Iceland's new terms.

Development: A Danish vessel fired on a British trawler caught fishing in Faeroe Island waters.

Resolution: The UK and Denmark submitted the incident to an international commission of enquiry, which settled the incident. The two governments then held bilateral negotiations over fishing limits, but they broke down, and Denmark imposed a 12-mile limit. Britain convened the European Fisheries Conference. This endorsed a 6-mile limit, with certain foreign vessels permitted to fish in an outer 6-mile zone. Denmark accepted this arrangement for the waters around Denmark, but not for the Faeroes. The British fishing industry responded by restricting the landing of Faeroese trawlers in the UK. The Faeroese Parliament went ahead and imposed a 12-mile limit.

Outcome: The outcome was a compromise: Denmark, but not the Faeroes, modified its demands.

Factors affecting the settlement: The convening of the European Fisheries Conference represented an agreed procedure.

Source: Butterworth (1976).

20 East–West confrontation in Europe 1945–

Area:	Europe
Parties:	NATO
	WTO
Third parties:	
Issues:	Great Power
	Ideology
	Jurisdiction
Other:	Military security; Soviet role in E. Europe
Coercion:	Threat of force
Hostilities:	None
Fatalities:	0
Resolution:	Unresolved

Background: The end of the Second World War left Europe divided beween Western and Soviet forces. The wartime conferences at Yalta and Potsdam set out zones of occupation and led the way to the recognition of two spheres of influence.

Development: Relations between the former wartime allies quickly deteriorated over policy towards Germany, and the character of development in East and West Europe. The Soviet Union swept Eastern Europe into its control and began to set up Communist governments, to the objection of the USA and its allies. Meanwhile, the US government began to restore German industry and integrate the West German economy into the Western economy. These moves, as well as the ideological antagonism between the former allies, led to the Berlin crisis (see Case 13) and a dispute over German unification (Case 27). The US and its Western allies proceeded to set up NATO as a defensive alliance. The Soviet Union responded by establishing the Warsaw Pact. For the next 40 years the two alliances developed a massive military infrastructure, with its heaviest concentration in Europe, although the military confrontation became worldwide. Both sides developed nuclear weapons and the arms race added to other tensions. The main goal of US foreign policy became the containment of the Soviet Union and the defence of the 'free world' against Communist advances elsewhere. Soviet policy was equally dominated by fears of the USA. For years the military staffs of both alliances planned for war, but war was avoided, despite severe crises over Berlin, Cuba and the Middle East. Détente began to regulate the conflict in the 1970s and the Gorbachev reforms and further arms control agreements eased it further in the late 1980s. The Warsaw Pact put its forces on a defensive basis, easing military tensions. However, the military confrontation and nuclear stand-off continue, despite the resolution of the German problem (see Chapter 6).

21 East German uprising 1953

Area:	Europe
Parties:	East German workers
	East Germany, USSR
Third parties:	
Issues (other):	Work norms, wages, prices, authority
	of government
Coercion:	Use of minor force
Hostilities:	None
Fatalities (log.10):	1.1
Resolution:	Interim or partial settlement

Background: In 1952 the East German government, facing an economic crisis, imposed an increase in work norms for industrial workers. Shortages of food and political imprisonments added to popular discontent, and the workers went on strike.

Development: The workers demanded to meet representatives of the Party leadership, who refused. The strikers then extended their

demands from economic to political issues, and called for the resign-
ation of the government and free elections.

Resolution: The East German police failed to suppress the strikes, and
Soviet troops were used to restore control.

Outcome: The Politburo of the GDR was forced to rescind the
increase in work norms.

Source: Butterworth (1976).

22   Egypt–Israel 1948–79

Area:	Middle East
Parties:	Egypt
	Israel
Third parties:	USA, USSR, UN
Issues:	Territory
Other:	Palestinians
Coercion:	Use of major force
Hostilities:	Major
Fatalities (log.10):	4.8
Resolution:	Interim or partial settlement

Background: For the early history of the Arab–Israeli dispute, see
Case 39.

Development: Egypt joined with other Arab states in rejecting both the
establishment of Israel as a state, and the UN plan for the partition of
Palestine. When Israel declared its statehood in 1948, Egypt with other
Arab states invaded Israel. Their defeat and Egyptian determination to
avenge it set a pattern of warfare for the next 25 years. Although the
UN managed to arrange an armistice in 1948, Egypt continued to deny
Israel's right to exist. Egypt denied passage through the Suez Canal
and the Gulf of Aqaba to Israeli ships and supported Palestinian raids
into Israel. In response, Israel made heavy attacks on Gaza which
outraged Egypt. In the Suez War of 1956–7, Israel again inflicted
defeat on Egypt. In the following period up to the Six Day War of
1967 the conflict became aligned with superpower rivalry. Clashes
between PLO and Syrian forces led to increased tension in 1966 and
the outbreak of war in 1967. Israel imposed a stinging defeat on Egypt
and occupied the Sinai and the Gaza strip. Egypt's first concern now

became to recover the lost territory rather than to eliminate Israel, an objective which was becoming more unrealistic with the passage of time. In late 1967 the UN passed Resolution 242, which provided for 'a just and lasting peace in which every state in the area can live in security', and called for Israeli withdrawal from the occupied territories and the termination of the state of war. Egypt and Israel both accepted the resolution, but they differed on the interpretation of which territories Israel was to withdraw from. Nevertheless, this formula of 'land for peace' was to be the one on which the conflict was ultimately resolved. However, in 1967–73 tensions remained high, especially when Israel took over East Jerusalem and began the policy of settlements in the West Bank. Continuing PLO terrorism made Israel ill-disposed to take a conciliatory line. In 1970 Nasser died and Sadat became President of Egypt. Sadat proceeded to unify the Arabs, expel the Russians from Egypt, and then launched the fourth war with Israel on Yom Kippur in 1973. The war was again a defeat for the Arab armies, but this time their initial successes, and the high costs they imposed on Israel, turned the tide in the conflict.

Resolution: Although a defeat in military terms, the 1973 war was a stalemate in the political conflict. The Arabs had shown that they could be militarily effective, and Israel could not continue to sustain high losses. Moreover, the use of the oil weapon gave the Arabs considerable leverage with the superpowers. The USA now began a round of intensive diplomacy, which can be divided into three phases. The first was Kissinger's diplomacy of 1973–5, which led to disengagement agreements, under which Israel pulled back first to east of the Suez canal, and then east of the Mitla and Giddi passes. The USA became heavily involved, financially and technically, in providing the machinery to monitor and verify this agreement. The next stage was Sadat's remarkable unilateral gesture in 1973, when he said that he was willing to go even to Jerusalem to make progress towards peace. His speech led to direct negotiations with Israel and, despite the rise in tension caused by Israel's invasion of the Lebanon in 1978, the USA was able to convene negotiations at Camp David, in which President Carter acted as an intermediary. After tense discussions, which came near breakdown on several occasions, Begin, Sadat and Carter agreed to two framework agreements: one for a general Middle East settlement, the other for a bilateral peace between Israel and Egypt. The first provided for a 'self-governing authority' for the West Bank and the Gaza strip; the second provided for the return of Egyptian territories, and the demilitarization of the Sinai, with continuing US surveillance as a guarantee to Israel. Although the Arabs and Israel could not agree on the implementation of the first agreement, Israel and Egypt went ahead with signing the peace treaty in 1979.

Outcome: Egypt recovered the occupied territories and accepted Israel's right to exist.

Subsequent developments: The Arab world condemned Sadat for making a separate peace which did nothing for the Palestinians. An Egyptian assassin murdered him in 1981. His successor, Mubarak, turned his attention to restoring the Egyptian economy. Israel continued its policy of settlements, and remained in a state of war with Syria and the PLO.

Factors influencing the settlement:

1. Sadat's expulsion of the Russians left the US in the position of being the only power with influence with both sides. The USA was therefore able to act as a broker for a solution.
2. The end of the 1973 war had produced a situation of costly stalemate for both sides. Israel could not continue to suffer the attrition of further wars, Egypt could not afford the military burden.
3. The peacemaking process proceeded in two stages. The first was a process of separation of the two sides, with the USA playing a peacekeeping role. The second was the process of bringing the sides together, and peace-making. Sadat's visit to Jerusalem was the crucial gesture which marked the transition.
4. President Carter's personal role as a mediator at Camp David saved the talks from foundering.

Sources: Day (1987), Bailey (1990a).

23   Ethiopia–Eritrea 1946–

Area:	Africa
Parties:	Ethiopia
	Eritreans, Eritrean Liberation Front
Third parties:	UN

Issues:	Ethnic
	Independence
	Secession
Coercion:	Use of major force
Hostilities:	Major
Fatalities (log.10):	5.7
Resolution:	Unresolved

Background: Eritrea became an Italian colony in 1885. Although the Eritreans consisted of eight different ethnic groups and two religious groups (Copts and Moslems), a national identity developed in resistance to the Italians. Following Italy's defeat in 1941, Britain took over the administration of the colony, and in 1950 a UN Commission was asked to determine the wishes of the population. While Ethiopia and Sudan wished to absorb the territory, a majority of Eritreans favoured independence. The UN decided that Eritrea should be federated into Ethiopia. Elections were held in Eritrea for a regional assembly, which exercised autonomy until 1962.

Development: In 1962 Haile Selassie decided to incorporate Eritrea into Ethiopia, forcing Eritrean delegates at the assembly to renounce the federation. The government then suppressed local languages, attempted to impose an Ethiopian national identity, and required the use of Amharic in schools.

These measures led to an Eritrean revolt and the formation of the Eritrean Liberation Front. Student demonstrations against Ethiopia and terrorist incidents were followed by the declaration of a state of emergency in 1970 and the imposition of martial law.

There seemed to be an opportunity for a settlement when Haile Selassie was overthrown in 1974. Both sides expressed willingness to seek a settlement, but negotiations broke down, and Ethiopia intensified its military operations against Eritrea. Fighting has continued since then amid massive starvation, exacerbated by the war, the drought and the pressure of population on arid land.

Subsequent developments: Neither side is able completely to defeat the other. The Eritrean Liberation Front has set up an alternative state structure in its mountainous rural strongholds, while the Ethiopian government holds the ports and the towns.

Ethiopia remains unwilling to give up control of Eritrea, which gives access to the sea and to the ports through which the military government is supplied.

The Eritrean Liberation Front is seeking a referendum in Eritrea. At present Ethiopia is unwilling to offer more than regional autonomy. In 1989 ex-President Carter made an attempt to mediate in the dispute.

Sources: Butterworth (1976), *Third World Guide* (1990).

24   Ethiopia–Somalia: the Ogaden 1950–

Area:	Africa
Parties:	Somalia, Somalis in the Ogaden
	Ethiopia
Third parties:	UN, OAU
Issues:	Ethnic
	Secession
	Territory
Coercion:	Use of major force
Hostilities:	Major
Fatalities (log.10):	4.6
Resolution:	Unresolved

Background: Somali-speaking people live in Ethiopia and Kenya as well as Somalia, separated by colonial boundaries. Since winning independence in 1960, Somalia has pursued an irredentist policy, aiming to unite ethnic Somalis. In Ethiopia the Somali minority in the Ogaden sought to secede from Ethiopia.

Development: Both Somalia and Ethiopia claim the Ogaden. No agreement was reached before Somalia's independence, despite concern expressed by the UN that Ethiopia and Italy, the colonial power, should resolve the issue.

Somali secessionist claims led to guerrilla attacks in Ethiopia, border incidents and clashes between the Somali and Ethiopian armies. Despite OAU calls for a cease-fire, fighting continued until 1967 when, following a change of government, Somalia decided to disengage (in part because it could not sustain the costs of the conflict). However, Somalia maintained its claims and, failing to obtain any redress from the new military government in Ethiopia which took power in 1974, encouraged the guerrilla movement to escalate its activities. In 1977 the guerrillas made advances and Somalia again intervened with its own troops, but Russian support for the Ethiopian regime, together with Cuban intervention, led to Somalia's defeat. Over a million Somali refugees from the Ogaden fled to Somalia.

Border fighting broke out again in 1982. Somalia claimed Ethiopian units were invading Somalia. Ethiopia countered that the fighting was an internal offensive of the Somali Liberation Movement.

Sources: Butterworth (1976), Day (1987), Murray (1988), *Third World Guide* (1990).

25 Gabon–Congo 1960–2

Area:	Africa
Parties:	Gabon
	Congo
Third parties:	Douala conference
Issues:	Ethnic
	Resources
	Territory
Coercion:	Use of minor force
Hostilities:	Minor
Fatalities (log.10):	1.1
Resolution:	Resolved

Background: When Gabon and Congo became independent, a large area which had been part of Congo in the colonial period was included in Gabon. This area was rich in minerals, and ethnic divisions were created by the new borders.

Development: This led to strains between the two countries; both sides expelled each other's nationals, and on the occasion of a football match between the two countries there was minor fighting.

Resolution: The other French-speaking states in the area offered to mediate, and following some disagreements about the appropriate mediating body, a conference was held which improved relations between the two states.

Outcome: It was agreed that the expelled nationals should be compensated. The territorial issue was allowed to lapse.

Source: Butterworth (1976).

26 Gadaduma Wells 1955–70

Area:	Africa
Parties:	Ethiopia
	Kenya, UK
Third parties:	
Issues:	Resources
	Territory
Coercion:	None
Hostilities:	None
Fatalities:	0
Resolution:	Resolved

Background: Before Kenya's independence, no boundary had been demarcated with Ethiopia. Although a boundary commission had completed its work in 1955, Ethiopia refused to agree to its conclusions. At issue were the Gadaduma Wells, which were important to the local nomadic tribes.

Development: The UK refused to give up the wells, but the new Kenyan government was much more willing to make concessions.

Resolution: Shortly before independence, Kenya conceded the Gadaduma Wells to Ethiopia. In return Ethiopia ceded several smaller wells to Kenya. Both states signed a mutual defence treaty.

Outcome: The disputed territory was ceded to Ethiopia, with less important wells going to Kenya in compensation. This agreement was followed by further negotiations, ending in a formal border agreement signed in 1970.

Factors contributing to resolution:

1. Change of government (following decolonization).
2. Good relations between Ethiopia and the new Kenya government.
3. Shared enemy (Somalia).

Source: Butterworth (1976).

27   German unification 1945–72

Area:	Europe
Parties:	FRG, USA, UK, France
	GDR, USSR
Third parties:	UN
Issues:	Great Power
	Jurisdiction
	Territory
Coercion:	None
Hostilities:	None
Fatalities:	0
Resolution:	Interim or partial settlement

Background: The end of the war left Germany divided between Western and Soviet forces, with Berlin a divided city behind Soviet lines.

Development: The wartime allies had agreed on the division of Germany at the Yalta conference, and had recognized each other's spheres of interest. However, as the Soviet Union began to bring Eastern Europe into Communist control, and the West introduced a Western-style democracy and market system in West Germany, Cold War tensions began to mount. The four-power agreement on controlling Berlin broke down in the wake of disagreements about currency reforms. The Soviet government blockaded Berlin and the West mounted the Berlin airlift; this crisis was the first threat of a possible war.

The FRG and the government of the GDR were soon on bad terms. The FRG wished to reunify Germany on the basis of elections, while the GDR government aimed to build a separate socialist state. The Soviet government claimed that German borders had been fixed by the conference at Potsdam, whereas the FRG was not prepared to recognize them finally until a peace settlement had been signed. Until then, it was prepared to offer citizenship to all Germans. As economic conditions diverged, a further crisis developed as people began leaving the Eastern side; the GDR responded by building the Berlin Wall. In time the entire border came to be fenced and patrolled by ever-growing armies. Many scenarios for the third world war began with a feared Soviet seizure of West Berlin.

Resolution: See Chapter 6.

28 Ghana–Ivory Coast, Niger, Upper Volta, Togo 1965–6

Area:	Africa
Parties:	Ghana
	Ivory Coast, Niger, Upper Volta, Togo
Third parties:	OAU
Other:	Subversion
Coercion:	Use of minor force
Hostilities:	Minor
Fatalities (log.10):	1.1
Resolution:	Resolved

Background: After independence, Ghana's leader Nkrumah followed a policy of expansionism towards his neighbours, and was in dispute with Togo over the colonial borders, which had divided the Ewe people between the two countries.

Development: Nkrumah supported opposition movements in several of these neighbouring states and allowed them to operate from Ghana. At an OAU meeting held in Accra in 1965, Nkrumah promised to respect the sovereignty of his neighbours, but in fact he continued to support subversion there.

Resolution: Nkrumah was overthrown in 1966. The new government established better relations with the neighbouring states.

Outcome: Ghana stopped supporting subversive movements. The factor conducive to the settlement was the change of government in Ghana.

Source: Butterworth (1976).

29 Ghana–Upper Volta 1964–6

Area:	Africa
Parties:	Ghana
	Upper Volta
Third parties:	OAU
Issues:	Territory
Other:	Foreign policy differences, subversion
Coercion:	Use of minor force

Hostilities:	None
Fatalities:	0
Resolution:	Resolved

Background: The granting of independence to the British and French colonies in West Africa led to a flurry of boundary disputes between the new states. Ghana claimed the Sanwi region of the Ivory Coast, and this dispute became a focus for other political and diplomatic antagonisms between the two states.

Development: Ghana closed its border with Upper Volta in 1964 and asserted its claim by building a school in the disputed area. Upper Volta referred the issue to the OAU. After this Ghana said that it was prepared to withdraw from the territory and to negotiate with Upper Volta. In fact, however, the negotiations did not take place. Relations remained tense until Nkrumah was overthrown.

Resolution: The new Ghanaian government re-opened the border and set up a boundary committee with Upper Volta. This settled the dispute.

Outcome: Ghana abandoned its claims.

Factor contributing to resolution: The main factor which prompted the settlement was the change of government in Ghana.

Source: Butterworth (1976).

30 Gibraltar 1964–

Area:	Europe
Parties:	Spain
	UK
Third parties:	UN
Issues:	Jurisdiction
	Territory
Coercion:	None
Hostilities:	None
Fatalities:	0
Resolution:	Unresolved

Background: The Treaty of Utrecht (1713) gave Britain the right to occupy a military base on Gibraltar. A colony grew up around the

base area, with 30 000 Gibraltarians today. In 1954 Spain asserted its
sovereignty, claiming that the UK had expelled the original inhabitants
(the UK claimed they had left of their own accord) and that the colony
was in violation of the Utrecht treaty as well as of the UN's
decolonization principles.

Development: In 1963 Spain started pursuing the case at the UN,
where it won UN support: the Trusteeship Committee urged the two
sides to negotiate an agreement. Spain restricted movement over the
border; the UK refused to negotiate. In 1966 four rounds of talks were
held, but no progress was made. The UK offered to refer the issue to
the ICJ, but Spain refused. Spain introduced further border restrictions and talks were broken off. In 1967 the UK unilaterally held a
referendum, which showed massive support for the status quo among
the Gibraltarians. The UN General Assembly endorsed Spain's
position and called for further negotiations. In 1969 Spain closed the
land frontier and suspended the ferry service, and later cut phone links.
Consequently, 5000 Spanish workers lost their jobs in Gibraltar. A
number of Moroccans came in their place.

In 1969 a new Spanish Cabinet adopted a more conciliatory policy,
but renewed talks were unproductive, and the border restrictions
remained in force.

In 1977 Suarez's democratically elected government took over in
Spain (following Franco's death in 1975). David Owen held talks, and
detailed working groups were set up.

In 1979 the new Thatcher government threatened to block Spain's
entry into the EC if restrictions remained in force. The Lisbon
agreement of 1980 provided for the border to be re-opened, but
Spain did not in fact re-open the border, insisting that the rights of
Spanish workers be honoured first. In 1982 Spain supported Argen-
tine's claim to the Malvinas. Spain joined NATO in 1982. Spain
relaxed the border restrictions slightly in 1982.

Tensions arose in 1983 over visits to Gibraltar by British warships,
but in 1984 an agreement signed at Brussels, following 7 months of
unpublicized contacts, provided for the re-opening of the border and
talks between Spain and UK, in which for the first time the UK agreed
to talk about sovereignty with Spain. Spanish and Gibraltarian people
were to have equal rights under EC employment rules. Spain regarded
this as a success; Sir Joshua Hassan welcomed it, but with reservations
about the sovereignty talks; the opposition party in Gibraltar opposed
it.

Spain then joined the EC. The border was re-opened.

Since 1985–7 negotiations on sovereignty have made no real progress. Disagreement arose over the airport, which is sited on the isthmus, which Spain claims was never ceded to Britain.

Source: Butterworth (1976), Day (1987).

31   Greece–Turkey 1970–

Area:	Europe
Parties:	Greece
	Turkey
Third parties:	UN, ICJ
Issues:	Ethnic
	Minority
	Resources
	Territory
Coercion:	Use of minor force
Hostilities:	Minor
Fatalities:	Not Known
Resolution:	Unresolved

Background: The animosity between Greece and Turkey dates back to the days of the Ottoman Empire. Greece and Turkey had fought over Crete in 1897 and fought again in 1921–2.

After the treaty of Lausanne, a compulsory exchange of populations took place, and over a million Greeks living in Turkey were repatriated. The border now follows ethnic lines fairly closely. Nevertheless, minorities remain and each side accuses the other of mistreating them. The dispute over Cyprus has been a continuing source of bad relations and Turkey threatened Greece with war in 1967. Although the two states have now accepted the land border, their conflict has found a new focus in a dispute over territorial rights to the Continental Shelf.

Development: Following the discovery of oil on the continental shelf, the Turkish government claimed the rights to the Aegean seabed up to the median line between the two mainlands. Greece claimed the whole of the Aegean, on the grounds of its sovereignty over islands near the Turkish coast. The dispute became a crisis when a Turkish survey ship carried out a survey in disputed waters. NATO stepped in as a mediator and persuaded the two countries to refrain from escalating the dispute, and to begin bilateral negotiations. Negotiations took place in 1978–9, but failed to resolve the disagreement. In 1986 Greece established a contentious civil defence plan for the eastern Greek islands, and there have been further tensions and incidents. Greece has opposed Turkey's wish to join the EC.

Resolution: Neither NATO nor the CSCE have had any success in resolving the dispute. The parties have failed to agree to any mechanism for managing it. Other cases of similar disputes might suggest the possibility of separating the dispute over resources from the sovereignty question.

Sources: Downing (1980), Day (1987).

32 Hungary 1956

Area:	Europe
Parties:	Hungary (reformers)
	USSR, Hungarian hard-liners
Third parties:	UN
Issues:	Control of government
	Ideology
	Jurisdiction
Other:	Reforms
Coercion:	Use of major force
Hostilities:	Major
Fatalities (log.10):	4
Resolution:	Interim or partial settlement

Background: Large Soviet forces occupied Hungary following the end of the Second World War, and Communists seized power in 1947. After a period of alliance between Communists and social democrats, Stalinization followed, with forced industrialization, show trials and a police terror. When Khrushchev came to power, the Stalinist leader Rakosi was overthrown.

Development: A popular uprising ensued, bringing to power the Nagy government, which promised pluralism and the negotiated withdrawal of Soviet troops. The Nagy government proceeded to proclaim Hungary's neutrality and appealed for help. The Soviet government moved in troops and suppressed the Hungarian uprising in bloody street battles.

Outcome: A new government was installed under Kadar, which moved cautiously towards reforms after a period of repression. Thirty years later, Hungary took a lead in introducing economic reforms, and Communist power collapsed suddenly and bloodlessly in 1989.

Sources: Butterworth (1976), Calvocoressi (1987).

33 Hungary–Romania (N. Transylvania) 1945–

Area:	Europe
Parties:	Hungary
	Romania
Third parties:	Soviet Union
Issues:	Ethnic
	Ideology
	Minority
	Territory
Coercion:	Nonmilitary
Hostilities:	None
Fatalities:	0
Resolution:	Unresolved

Background: The ethnic dispute in Transylvania has a long history. Transylvania was populated by Hungarians, Romanians and Germans in the twelfth and thirteenth centuries. In the nineteenth century it was part of the Austro–Hungarian Empire, and ruled by an elite of Hungarian nobles, although Romanians were in the majority. Romania entered the First World War on the Allies' side in an attempt to secure Transylvania. Though Romania was defeated in the war, Transylvania was duly detached from Hungary and became part of Romania from 1920. In the Second World War Hungary, through its alliance with the Axis powers, recovered the northern part of Transylvania but, when the Axis forces were defeated in 1944, the Soviet Union forced Hungary to return Northern Transylvania to Romania. As a result there is a large Hungarian minority in Romania.

Development: Under President Ceauşescu, Romania attempted to eliminate separate ethnic identities under a national, Romanian,

Communist state. The Romanian government restricted the use of the Hungarian language in education, merged Hungarian universities into Romanian ones, suppressed Hungarian literature and changed Hungarian place-names to Romanian. There was job discrimination against Hungarians, and destruction of Hungarian villages to make way for agricultural modernization. This created strong continuing tensions between the two communities in Romania, and between Hungary and Romania. The Hungarian government frequently protests about Romanian maltreatment of Hungarians in Romania.

Subsequent developments: This is a rather classic case of ethnic conflict. The imposition of the ethnic identity of the national community on the minority intensified it, but it was already fuelled by the past animosity between the two nations and between social classes previously organized along ethnic lines. The revolution in Romania and the democratic transition in Hungary open new risks for the conflict to become violent, but also new opportunities for addressing the relationships between the two communities.

Sources: Day (1988), Brogan (1989), Bela Borsi-Kalman (1990).

34   Iceland–UK fisheries 1952–61

Area:	Europe
Parties:	UK
	Iceland
Third parties:	UN
Issues:	Fishing
Coercion:	Use of minor force
Hostilities:	None
Fatalities:	0
	Resolved

Background: In 1952, Iceland decided to extend the territorial limits of its coastal waters, first from three to four miles.

Development: The British government protested to Iceland and retaliated by halting imports of the Icelanders' fish.

Resolution: The parties agreed to submit the dispute to the Organization for European Economic Co-operation, which set up a committee of experts to review the issue. A temporary agreement was reached in

1956, whereby the parties agreed to leave the question of territorial limits until the UN General Assembly had considered it under the law of the sea. In the meantime, however, Iceland extended its territorial limits again, to 12 miles. British trawlers continued to fish in the disputed areas, and there were two incidents involving warships. Britain and Iceland convened bilateral talks, and Britain suspended fishing in the disputed areas while the talks were under way.

Outcome: In 1961 Britain dropped its objection to the 12-mile limit; in return, Iceland permitted British trawlers to operate within the limit for certain months of the year. This resolved the dispute until 1971, when the Cod War broke out.

Source: Butterworth (1976).

35 Iceland–UK: Cod War 1971–3

Area:	Europe
Parties:	Iceland
	UK, FRG, Denmark
Third parties:	ICJ, UN, NATO
Issues:	Fishing
Coercion:	Use of minor force
Hostilities:	Minor
Fatalities:	0
Resolution:	Lapsed

Background: The previous dispute between Iceland and the UK over fishing limits had ended in agreement to respect a 12-mile limit. In 1971 Iceland announced a further unilateral extension of its territorial waters to 50 miles.

Development: The UK began talks with Iceland, but no agreement was reached. Icelandic gunboats opened fire on British trawlers within the 50-mile limit. Britain responded by boycotting Icelandic ships and cargoes, and lodged a claim with the ICJ. Iceland denied that the Court had jurisdiction over the case, but agreed to bilateral talks with the UK. Meanwhile, Icelandic warships continued firing on British trawlers, and British warships responded by ramming them. Iceland threatened to cut off diplomatic relations and close an important NATO base.

Resolution: Britain and Iceland then agreed to work out an agreement, and under it British trawlers were permitted to continue to fish in the disputed waters for two years, with a limited catch. The ICJ ruled that the 12-mile limit still applied, but Iceland continued to maintain the 50-mile limit.

Outcome: The dispute remained unresolved, but Britain effectively abandoned its rights.

Sources: Butterworth (1976), Calvocoressi (1987).

36   Ifni 1964–9

Area:	Africa
Parties:	Morocco
	Spain
Third parties:	UN
Issues:	Independence
	Territory
Coercion:	None
Hostilities:	None
Fatalities:	0
Resolution:	Resolved

Background: Ifni is a small enclave on Morocco's coastline, which had been under Spanish occupation since 1860. Following independence, Morocco claimed both Ifni and the Spanish Sahara.

Development: The UN urged Spain to decolonize both territories. Spain and Morocco held unsucessful negotiations and tension between them rose.

Resolution: The UN called for the independence and self-determination of the territories, and for a referendum. While no agreement was reached for several years, Morocco maintained good relations with Spain and held negotiations about ways of implementing self-determination. In 1969 the two states signed a treaty which ceded Ifni to Morocco and provided for the evacuation of the Spanish forces.

Outcome: Spain agreed to cede Ifni to Morocco.

Factors contributing to the settlement:

1. Ifni was no longer of value to Spain.
2. The climate of opinion favoured decolonization.
3. UN calls for decolonization legitimated the transfer.
4. Spain may have wished to divert Morocco from its claims to Western Sahara.

Source: Butterworth (1976)

37 Iraq–Iran 1969–

Area:	Middle East
Parties:	Iran
	Iraq
Third parties:	UN
Issues:	Ethnic
	Ideology
	Minority
	Religion
	Territory
Other:	Regional balance of power
Coercion:	Use of major force
Hostilities:	Major
Fatalities (log.10):	5.6
Resolution:	Unresolved

Background: The conflict between Iraq and Iran involved a number of issues. There was a longstanding historical rivalry between Arabs and Persians. In the 1960s there was ideological conflict between revolutionary Iraq and the shahdom in Iran. Iraq opposed Iran's growing influence in the Gulf, and both sides supported Kurdish revolts in each other's territory. There were disputes over the Shatt al'Arab waterway, the land border, and Iran's territorial claims to Bahrain, Abu Musa and the Tunb islands. In 1937 a treaty had placed the boundary on the eastern side of the Shatt al'Arab. This meant that Iranian ships using it were bound to pay dues to Iraq.

Development: In 1969 Iran denounced the 1937 treaty and mobilized forces in the Shatt area. Iraq responded by expelling Iranians. Armed clashes took place in 1973 and 1974. Iraq was worsted in these engagements. In 1974, the UN secured a cease-fire and mutual withdrawal of forces. Bilateral negotiations followed, and a border commission was estabished. President Saddam Hussein agreed to redraw the boundary along the thalweg line in the middle of the river.

Subsequently, however, Saddam Hussein was determined to recover what he had lost, and in 1980 he took advantage of the revolution in Iran to launch war on Iran. It soon became clear that the Ayatollah's government would not accept an early cease-fire as Iraq had calculated, and a major war developed. The Iraqis fought defensively, and the Iranian tactic of human waves, together with ruthless Iraqi use of chemical weapons, led to enormous casualties. The war also led to missile attacks against cities and attempts by both sides to destroy each other's oil terminals and trade.

Resolution: An early Algerian attempt to mediate in the conflict ended when Iraq shot down the plane carrying the Algerian mediators. In 1982 Saddam Hussein offered to withdraw to the international frontier, but Ayatollah Khomeini insisted that Iran would continue fighting until Saddam was deposed and Iraq agreed to pay reparations. The war therefore dragged on. The Security Council was slow to take effective action to intervene, agreeing to Resolution 589 in 1987. This called for a cease-fire, a commission to determine war guilt, and sanctions against either side if it did not accept the resolution. Iraq accepted, but Iran rejected the resolution. However, as the Iranian position in the war deteriorated, the Ayatollah was forced to drink the 'poisoned cup' and accept Resolution 589. The war came to an end, but the two states could not agree to a peace treaty until in 1990, facing the international coalition in the Gulf crisis, Saddam Hussein agreed to all the Iranian terms for peace. It remains unclear whether this forced treaty will resolve the dispute.

Sources: Sir John Graham (unpublished talk, 1979), Urquhart (1989), Keesings, King (1987).

38 Iraq–Kuwait 1973–

Area:	Middle East
Parties:	Iraq
	Kuwait
Third parties:	Arab League, PLO

Issues: Resources
                    Territory
Coercion: Use of major force
Hostilities: Minor
Fatalities (log.10): 1.7
Resolution: Unresolved

See Chapter 12 for text and sources. The above data do not cover the Gulf War of 1991.

39 Israel–Palestinians 1920–

Area: Middle East
Parties: Israelis
                  Palestinian Arabs, Arab states
Third parties: UN
Issues: Ethnic
                  Independence
                  Minority
                  Religion
                  Territory
Coercion: Use of major force
Hostilities: Major
Fatalities (log.10): 4.0
Resolution: Unresolved

Background: The Jews had lived in the area of Israel until their dispersal by the Romans in 70AD and their final expulsion by Hadrian in 135AD.

By 1900, the population of Palestine was Arab, with a minority of Jews, mostly students and scholars. The Arabs were mostly poor, illiterate peasants living on uneconomic smallholdings.

Between 1900 and 1919, Arab nationalism developed rapidly, in reaction to the Ottoman Empire, then in decline. At the same time Zionism was gaining strength among Jewish communities in Europe, partly in reaction to anti-Semitism.

Development: In the peace settlements of 1920–3, Palestine became a Mandate of the League of Nations. The Jews were granted the 'national home' they had been pressing for. The Arabs opposed the mandates, as well as the continued occupation by Britain of Egypt and Sudan, and by France of Tunisia and Morocco, with strikes and violence. The Palestinian Arabs refused to co-operate with any measures which endorsed the Mandate or the Jewish National Home. They rejected legislative assemblies, partition, and other formulae, and feared and disliked – but could not stop – the build-up of Jewish immigration and land purchase. Meanwhile, the Zionists were dissatisfied because Britain had failed to assist the Jewish National Home or to control Arab violence. Both communities became increasingly hostile to each other, with outbreaks of violence in 1920, 1921, 1928, 1933 and 1936. Mutual fear grew and both sides armed.

Britain now swung round to a partition scheme (1936), but the Arabs would not accept it. The Arabs rebelled against the Mandate in 1937. The Zionists now became less restrained, and organized guerrilla fighting on both sides developed. Order was restored by 1939. Britain now abandoned partition and suggested strict regulation of Zionist immigration and land purchase, and an eventual integrated Palestinian government. This made the Zionists feel that Britain was hostile, and for Arabs it fell short of their objective: an Arab state. The onslaught on Jews by anti-Semitic forces in Europe increased Jewish support for Zionism and the desire to emigrate to Palestine.

During the Second World War Britain froze the situation, refusing immigration above the levels set in the White Paper. This made Jewish refugees from the Nazis desperate, and Zionist nationalism took on a new bitterness. The Zionists sought to evade British controls, and violence followed. Britain established a sea blockade.

The situation was deadlocked throughout 1945–6. The Arabs rejected any solution that did not give the Palestinians a unitary, democratic state; the Zionists rejected any solution which did not give them control of immigration and land transfers. In 1947 Britain gave up and referred the problem to the UN.

The UN General Assembly resolved to partition Palestine. The Zionists accepted this as the basis for statehood and created a provisional Jewish government (1948). This shocked the Arabs, who had not believed that Israel would be created. The Arabs massed armies, and hostilities in Palestine began. Zionists carried out atrocities against Arabs, and a large-scale Arab exodus began from Zionist-held areas. The state of Israel was proclaimed in 1948. Arab armies attacked and were defeated by the numerically smaller Israeli forces. Israel won an expanded state, including parts of Palestine which had been awarded to the Arabs in the 1947 Partition Plan.

In the following years, the UN failed to negotiate a settlement. The Arab countries and Israel hardened their positions. A firm foundation had been laid for a continuing conflict.

In 1956 Israel, with British and French support, attacked and defeated Egypt in the Suez War. The USA and Soviet Union forced Britain and France to withdraw their forces, but Israel was less easily dislodged. The Soviet Union now entered the conflict as an arms supplier for Egypt, Syria and Iraq. The USA, alarmed by Arab socialism and Nasser's pro-Soviet policy, heavily supported Israel.

Dissension developed between the socialist and traditional Arab countries, and between Egypt and Syria following the United Arab Republic break-up. There was growing guerrilla activity by the Palestinians against Israel. In 1964 the Palestinian National Council claimed Palestine, in the borders it had had during the British mandate, as their homeland, and declared that armed struggle was the only means to liberate it. They set up the PLO to carry out this armed struggle.

By 1967 Nasser managed to unite the socialist Arabs, who leaned towards support for the Palestinians. In 1967 Israel made an attack in Syria against guerrillas operating from there. Nasser responded by building up troops and closing the Straits of Tiran. Israel attacked and routed Syria and Egypt in the Six Day War. Israel now occupied the Sinai, Jerusalem and the West Bank. The war increased the number of Palestinians living under Israeli rule by four times.

In the aftermath of the war, the Arab states declared that they would continue not to recognize Israel, and would not negotiate with it or make peace with it while the 'rights of the Palestinian people in their homeland' were violated.

The UN passed Resolution 242 which called for a 'just and lasting peace', to be achieved by Israel withdrawing from the occupied territories, an end to the state of war and mutual recognition of states (an exchange of land for peace). Israel and the Arab states except Syria accepted the resolution, but the Palestinians rejected it because it did not refer to their own rights. In the following period, international diplomacy concentrated on the occupied territories, which Egypt, Syria and Jordan wanted to recover. Israel also began settling Israelis in the occupied territories, especially on the West Bank. In frustration the Palestinians responded with a campaign of terrorism against Israeli civilians and international airlines.

The 1973 war again ended in Egyptian and Syrian defeat, but the war was costly for Israel, which recognized that it could not keep fighting the Arabs at this level of intensity. These conditions, and Kissinger's diplomacy, laid the basis for an intense period of US peacemaking between Israel and Egypt, which culminated in the Camp David agreements and the 'separate' 1979 peace treaty between Egypt and Israel.

The Palestinians, however, were no further forward. Nevertheless, the 1973 war also marked a turning-point in Palestinian thinking. The PLO began to edge towards accepting Israel's right to exist. Informal talks began between the PLO and unofficial Israeli representatives. For the first time Palestinian representatives began to endorse the idea of a peaceful settlement to the conflict.

Israel denied the significance of these moves, and the USA refused to countenance negotiations with the PLO until the PLO accepted Security Council Resolution 242. In 1983, after the Israeli invasion of Lebanon had forced the PLO out of Lebanon, the Palestine National Council endorsed the principle of a confederation with Jordan and implicitly accepted the goal of a negotiated settlement. In 1985, it implicitly accepted UN Resolution 242, and explicitly stated that it would negotiate with Israel. These steps created a basis for negotiations, and it became clear that the Palestinians were prepared to accept a 'two-state' solution, with a Palestinian state on the West Bank and Gaza. The Israeli government remained adamant in its opposition to such a solution.

In 1987, the intifada (uprising) began. Palestinian people throughout the occupied territories showed their united opposition to Israeli rule. The PLO appealed directly to Israeli public opinion to seek a negotiated solution to the conflict, publicly acknowledging Israel's right to exist, and understanding 'the Jewish peoples' centuries of suffering'. In 1988, the PLO finally unambiguously accepted Resolution 242. However, Israel, which had been prepared to accept a Palestinian state in 1947, was now too distrustful of the Palestinians. The government brushed aside the Palestinians' overtures.

Factors affecting the failure to reach a settlement:

1. This has been, from the outset, a most intense conflict, in which both parties perceived the other as a threat to their own existence. The gradual occupation by Israelis of lands originally populated by Arabs, and the displacement of the Palestinians, has created a deep and longstanding Palestinian grievance, while the Israelis remain beleaguered, defensive and fearful of their Arab neigh-

bours. Both peoples had suffered deep traumas, which their leaders use to justify violent policies.

2. At the early stages of the conflict, the Zionists relied on their superior resources and power to impose themelves on the Palestinians and to buy up their land. This evoked Arab resistance and stored up the seeds of future violence.
3. At the time of the UN-proposed partition plan, the Palestinians could have had peace and a state if they had been prepared to negotiate.
4. Later, in the 1970s and 1980s, when the Palestinians were prepared to negotiate, the Israeli government was not.
5. Israel has hitherto always been able to rely on US support, or at least an absence of effective US opposition. The main reason for this has been the strength of the Jewish lobby in the USA and its support for Israel's policies.

Sources: Gilmour (1980), Rodinson (1982), Galtung (1989), Heraclides (1989), Segal (1989), Bailey (1990a).

40 Jordan–Palestinians 1970–1

Area:	Middle East
Parties:	Jordan
	PLO, Syria
Third Parties:	USA, USSR, Arab League
Issues:	Ethnic
	Jurisdiction
	Minority
Other:	Policy towards Israel and Palestine
Coercion:	Use of major force
Hostilities:	Major
Fatalities (log.10):	3.3
Resolution:	Interim or partial settlement

Background: Palestinians make up two-thirds of Jordan's population. The question of whether the occupied West Bank is Jordanian territory has a critical role in the Palestinian conflict. A number of Palestinian guerrilla groups established themselves in Jordan in the 1960s and flouted Jordanian laws.

Development: Occasional clashes between the Jordanian army and the Palestinian guerrillas took place, punctuated by agreements between King Hussein and Yasser Arafat. In 1970 tensions increased, and King Hussein used armoured troops to re-established control in Amman. Syria and Israel both mobilized; the superpowers intervened to prevent any widening of the conflict. Jordanian troops defeated Syrian forces who intervened and cleared the guerrillas from their Jordanian bases. The bulk of them withdrew to Lebanon.

Resolution: After the Yom Kippur War, King Hussein withdrew his claim to sovereignty over the West Bank and renewed relations with the PLO. The Palestinians in turn accepted that they could not act autonomously in Jordan. This led to a substantial reconciliation.

Source: Butterworth (1976).

41 Kurds–Turkey 1945–

Area:	Middle East
Parties:	Kurds
	Turkey
Third parties:	
Issues:	Ethnic
	Minority
Coercion:	Use of minor force
Hostilities:	Minor
Fatalities (log.10):	3.2
Resolution:	Unresolved

Background: The Kurds had been promised an independent Kurdistan following the collapse of the Ottoman Empire, but Kemal Atatürk thwarted these hopes, and Britain and France made lands inhabited by Kurds part of Iraq and Syria. The Kurds have a common culture and common national aspirations, but are a minority in Turkey, Iran, Iraq and Syria. All four states have attempted to suppress the Kurdish people's separate identity and oppose the Kurds' national aspirations. The repression has been the most brutal in Iraq, where Kurds have been resettled outside Kurdistan and Saddam Hussein's regime put down Kurdish resistance with great ferocity. The Shah of Iran also suppressed the use of the Kurdish language in Iran and acted against

Kurdish nationalist parties. Kurdish demands for autonomy led to violence in 1979 and the Iranian armed action against the Kurds. Syria has attempted to 'Arabize' its Kurdish minority.

Development: Turkey has also repressed its Kurdish minority and has prevented Kurdish from being taught in schools. The Kurds complain of job discrimination. The left-wing Kurdish Workers Party (PKK) launched a series of guerrilla attacks in Turkey from 1984.

Source: *Guardian* (9 June 1989).

42   Kuwait–Saudi Arabia 1957–65

Area:	Middle East
Parties:	Kuwait
	Saudi Arabia
Third parties:	
Issues:	Resources
	Territory
Coercion:	None
Hostilities:	None
Fatalities:	0
Resolution:	Resolved

Background: The city of Kuwait is surrounded by desert, and its borders were never set under colonial times. When they were, disputes over the borders arose. In the period after the collapse of the Ottoman Empire, Sheikh Salim of Kuwait and King Ibn Saud of Najd (later Saudi Arabia) were in dispute over this territory, and King Ibn Saud made several border raids into Kuwait, then a British protectorate. Sir Percy Cox met Ibn Saud in 1922 and drew new frontiers, which created a neutral territory on the coast between Kuwait and Najd. Kuwait and Najd were to have equal rights in this territory until they made a further agreement about it.

Development: Following the discovery of oil in the region, both sides signed treaties with oil companies permitting exploration in the neutral zone. Both also granted a Japanese oil company separate concessions to explore offshore. This led to administrative problems, and a new interest in the legal status of the area.

Resolution: In the late 1950s Kuwait and Saudi Arabia began to discuss the future of the region. In 1960 they agreed to set up a border commission to partition the neutral zone into equal shares. In 1965 it was agreed that each side would administer half of the zone, and a new international border was established half-way between. The governments agreed to share the oil resources, and they set up a joint committee to control the licensing of concessions in the area.

Some small offshore islands remain contested between the two.

Outcome: Partition and sharing or resources.

Source: Day (1987).

43 Liberia's boundaries 1958–61

Area:	Africa
Parties:	Liberia
	France, Guinea, Ivory Coast
Third parties:	
Issues:	Territory
Coercion:	None
Hostilities:	None
Fatalities:	0
Resolution:	Resolved

Background: Liberia had repeatedly claimed that parts of its territory had been incorporated by France and the UK into their adjacent colonies.

Development: In 1958 Liberia again pressed France to return areas in Guinea and the Ivory Coast. France, unwilling to break up its colonies on the point of granting them independence, again refused.

Resolution: Once Guinea and the Ivory Coast became independent, Liberia accepted the existing borders and renounced its territorial claims. In 1961 Liberia and Ivory Coast agreed to share their boundary rivers for commercial use.

Outcome: Liberia dropped its territorial claims. Liberia and Ivory Coast made an agreement on shared commercial use of the border rivers.

Factors contributing to resolution:

1. Liberia's own borders were vulnerable to secession and irredent-ism.
2. Decolonization.
3. Liberia endorsed the general African policy of maintaining independence boundaries.

Source: Butterworth (1976).

44 Malagasy independence 1947–60

Area:	Africa
Parties:	France
	Malagasy
Third parties:	
Issues:	Independence
Coercion:	Use of minor force
Hostilities:	Minor
Fatalities (log.10):	4.8
Resolution:	Resolved

Background: Madagascar became a French colony at the end of the nineteenth century, following a violent and costly war of occupation. The French imposed a system of plantations and cash crops which reduced the conditions of the peasants, although a local elite was used for administration. After the Second World War a nationalist move-ment developed to press for independence, with wide support from all Madagascar's ethnic groups.

Development: Nationalist deputies introduced an independence bill in the French Parliament, but instead France brought Madagascar under tighter control by making it a territory of France and setting up new provincial administrations and assemblies. The nationalists won the elections to these assemblies. Before they could take their seats, a spontaneous armed rising developed against the French. Malagasy rebels attacked French troops and took control of part of the island. The French government reinforced its garrison on the island and put the rebellion down harshly, with many Malagasy people losing their lives. France declared the nationalist party illegal and arrested its leaders.

Resolution: France could not for long deny the legitimacy of the independence movement. Progress towards it was complicated by internal divisions between the formerly dominant Hova people of the plateau and nationalists representing coastal groups. In the event a gradual transition to independence took place, with an amnesty to the rebels coming in 1954, and internal autonomy in 1956. In 1958 the Malagasy people voted for independence in a referendum, and in 1960 Malagasy became independent.

Factors in the failure to reach a peaceful settlement:

1. The French occupation and exploitation of the island had created nationalist opposition. After the war the French intention to re-establish firm colonial rule triggered the conflict.
2. The French government denied the Malagasy nationalists a legitimate means of seeking their aims through the French Parliament. This created a serious grievance and sparked violence, even though the nationalists claimed not to be involved in it.

Sources: Butterworth (1976), Calvocoressi (1987), *Third World Guide* (1990).

45   Malawi independence 1959–64

Area:	Africa
Parties:	Malawi (Nyasaland)
	Rhodesia, UK
Third parties:	
Issues:	Independence
	Secession
Coercion:	Use of minor force
Hostilities:	None
Fatalities (log.10):	1.7
Resolution:	Resolved

Background: Malawi, formerly Nyasaland, was a British colony, established by Cecil Rhodes's British South Africa Company. Rhodes wanted to set up an African empire, but the British government preferred to divide up his conquests, making Southern Rhodesia a self-governing colony, and Northern Rhodesia and Nysasaland protectorates. In the 1950s there was strong support in Southern

Rhodesia and in Britain for creating a central African federation. Malawian nationalists opposed it, for fear that they would fall under white domination.

Development: The idea of federation was discussed at several conferences, some attended by black leaders who always opposed it. Nevertheless Britain went ahead and created the federation in 1957. Malawi was included because it was economically dependent on Southern Rhodesia and South Africa, although the tribal leaders all opposed it. The new constitution provided safeguards for the black population but, on their first test, the UK government rejected an African appeal. These strains combined with rural unrest about restrictions imposed on farming methods, and agricultural prices which favoured the white farmers. Hastings Banda united opposition to British colonial rule under the banner of the secession of Nyasaland from the federation. Violence broke out on a small scale in 1959. The local British governors responded by sending troops from Rhodesia and arresting the nationalists.

Resolution: A British commission of inquiry criticized the use of the Rhodesian troops and judged that the federation was unworkable. A further constitutional conference on the affairs of the federation in 1960 ended in failure, while in Nyasaland the tide for independence was running strongly. Banda won an overwhelming victory in elections in 1961 and, in 1962, at a further constitutional conference, the British government agreed to allow Nyasaland to leave the federation and become independent.

Outcome: In 1964 the Federation was dissolved and Malawi became independent.

Subsequent developments: Banda became the first prime minister, and later made himself president for life.

Factors influencing the settlement: The British government was unwilling to force the federation on Nyasaland after elections had shown such unanimous opposition, and after a British commission had declared against it. The British government still had effective authority over the federation, yet to some extent it played a third-party role between the nationalists and the white settlers.

Sources: Butterworth (1976), Calvocoressi (1987), *Third World Guide* (1990).

46 Malawi–Tanzania 1964–

Area: Africa
Parties: Malawi
                          Tanzania
Third parties:
Issues: Ideology
                          Territory
                          (Dispute over sovereignty of Lake Nyasa)
Coercion: Threat of force
Hostilities: None
Fatalities (log.10):   0
Resolution: Lapsed

Background: Britain had defined the boundary between Malawi and Tanzania as running along the Tanzanian shore of Lake Nyasa, so the whole lake belonged to Malawi.

Development: Tanzania claimed that the boundary should run down the middle of the lake; Malawi responded by claiming not only the whole lake but parts of Tanzania, Zambia and Mozambique and by placing gunboats in the lake. Neither side took the dispute further and it was allowed to lapse.

Sources: Butterworth (1976), Brownlie (1979).

47 Mauritania–Mali 1960–3

Area: Africa
Parties: Mauritania
                          Mali
Third parties:
Issues: Ethnic
                          Resources
                          Territory
Coercion: Use of minor force
Hostilities: Minor
Fatalities (log.10):   1.7
Resolution: Resolved

Background: Mauritania and Mali disputed the ownership of the Hodh region. This had been part of Mali before 1944 when France, the colonial power, gave it to Mauritania. Before independence, the two autonomous governments negotiated peacefully over the dispute, without reaching a conclusion. After independence, Mali raised the issue again.

Development: The dispute grew more serious as a number of violent incidents took place between different ethnic groups living near the disputed territory, and Malians made a number of guerrilla raids into Mauritania. At the same time, Morocco was claiming the whole of Mauritania.

Resolution: In order to strengthen its hand against Morocco, the Mauritanian government agreed to talks with Mali in 1963, and conceded the territory that Mali was demanding.

Outcome: Mali recovered the disputed territory; Mali also stopped supporting Morocco against Mauritania.

Subsequent developments: Subsequently relations between the two states improved.

Source: Butterworth (1976).

48 Mauritania–Morocco 1958–70

Area:	Africa
Parties:	Mauritania
	Morocco
Third parties:	Senegal, Tunisia and the Ivory Coast,
	Algeria
Issues:	Jurisdiction
	Post-independence
	Resources
	Territory
Coercion:	None
Hostilities:	None
Fatalities:	0
Resolution:	Resolved

Background: Morocco emerged from French colonial rule strongly nationalist and anti-colonialist. Both the King and the nationalist Istiqlal party supported irredentist claims to a 'greater Morocco', based on the historical conquests of the seventeenth century Moroccan sultans. Morocco claimed the whole of Mauritania, as well as Spanish Sahara and Ifni.

Development: In 1960 France agreed in principle to Mauritania's request for independence. Morocco pressed its claim to Mauritania at the Arab League and elsewhere. Following the official granting of independence in 1960, tensions between Morocco and Mauritania became acute. Eleven former French colonies, including Algeria, supported Mauritania. Egypt, Mali, Guinea and at first the Soviet Union supported Morocco. Later the Soviet Union dropped its veto on Mauritanian membership of the UN (in return for the USA dropping its veto on Mongolia) and support for the Moroccan cause dwindled. In 1961, the Arab League dropped the Moroccan case, and in 1963 the OAU admitted Mauritania.

Resolution: King Hassan II, who succeeded his father in 1961, seemed willing to drop the claim, but popular opposition made him change his mind. Radio propaganda between the two states continued for some years until in 1969, following Algerian mediation, Hassan announced a change of policy. In 1970 Hassan met the President of Mauritania and signed a friendship treaty which formally ended the conflict.

Outcome: Morocco dropped its claim.

Factors contributing to resolution:
1. Crumbling of support for Morocco's claim, and Mauritania's success in getting international recognition.
2. Change in Moroccan government.
3. Morocco had been in a State of Emergency from 1965 to 1970, with strong opposition to the monarchical government; this may have made Hassan unwilling to abandon the claim earlier.

Subsequent developments: Mauritania and Morocco jointly attempted to occupy Western Sahara in 1980.

Sources: Butterworth (1976), Calvocoressi (1987), *Third World Guide* (1990).

49   Minquiers Islands 1951–3

Area:	Europe
Parties:	France
	UK
Third parties:	ICJ
Issues:	Fishing
	Territory
Coercion:	None
Hostilities:	None
Fatalities:	0
Resolution:	Resolved

Background: The two small islands of Minquiers and Erechos lie between Jersey and the French coast. England took them from Normandy in the fourteenth century.

Development: Neither side regarded the territory in dispute as of importance, but the need to delimit fishing rights in the English Channel required a resolution.

Resolution: Both France and Britain agreed to take the question of ownership to the ICJ. They also reached an agreement on fishing rights, which they agreed would hold regardless of the ICJ decision. The ICJ ruled that the islands belonged to Britain.

Factors affecting the settlement:

1. Separation of the issue of fishing rights from the territorial claims.
2. Settlement of the fishing issue by negotiation.
3. Settlement of the territorial issue by referral to the ICJ.
4. Insignficance to both sides of the territory.

Source: Butterworth (1976).

50   Morocco's independence 1943–56

Area:	Africa
Parties:	Moroccan nationalists, Mohammed V,
	France, French colonists
Third parties:	UN
Issues:	Independence

Coercion: Use of major force
Hostilities: Minor
Fatalities (log.10): 3.5
Resolution: Resolved

Background: Morocco had been under the rule of its own Sultans until 1912, when France and Spain established colonial rule.

Development: French forces established control over most of the country after a major military campaign to subdue Moroccan resistance. French colonists settled and the French set up a colonial administration, allowing the Sultan to remain as a figurehead. Moroccan nationalism developed in the 1930s and 1940s, with the Istiqlal party (founded 1943) playing the major role. Its demands for reform and independence were supported by the Sultan, Mohammed V, but resisted by the French *colons*, who had an influential say over the colonial administration. The *colons* blocked reform and managed to keep Moroccans out of decision-making, and this led to riots in 1952. The French colonial forces suppressed these riots, causing heavy loss of life and making many arrests. The following year the colonial government deposed Mohammed V.

This led to a state of violent tension, with nationalists and colonist organizations both engaged in terrorism. Nationalist forces began preparing for war in Spanish-controlled enclaves of Morocco.

Resolution: A full-scale war, as in Algeria, did not develop because the French government decided it could not afford to fight the nationalists in both Morocco and Algeria. Instead the French government began to make a series of concessions. Mohammed V negotiated the restoration of his throne and complete internal autonomy; once back in Morocco he joined the nationalists in demanding complete independence. The Moroccans proceeded to set up their own government and, in further negotiations, the French government accepted immediate independence.

Outcome: Morocco became independent in 1956. The nationalist forces were absorbed into the Moroccan army.

Subsequent developments: Mohammed V's son, Hassan, became King in 1961. He broke with the elements of the nationalists who favoured social reform, and instead pursued an expansionist policy, aiming to annex the Western Sahara and Mauritania. By the later 1970s the war in the Sahara was taking up almost half of the government budget, and leading to new internal conflicts.

Factors influencing the settlement:

1. The main factor was the French strategic decision to avoid war in Morocco, and the readiness of the nationalists to launch a war unless the French withdrew.
2. Under these circumstances, negotiations with the Sultan led to the settlement (the existence of the Sultan as a figure with whom both the French government and the nationalists had had previous dealings eased the transition to independence).

Sources: Butterworth (1976), Calvocoressi (1987).

51 Mozambique's independence 1962–74

Area:	Africa
Parties:	Frelimo
	Portugal
Third parties:	UN
Issues:	Independence
Coercion:	Use of major force
Hostilities:	Major
Fatalities (log.10):	4.5
Resolution:	Resolved

Background: Portuguese colonial rule was particularly harsh. The colonial government and private entrepreneurs used forced labour, often in conditions not much better than slavery. The Portuguese government also encouraged large-scale immigration into Mozambique of Portuguese settlers. These policies aroused resistance, and in 1962 the nationalist groups united to form FRELIMO (Frente Libertação de Moçambique).

Development: FRELIMO began its armed struggle in 1964. A savage war developed. FRELIMO gained control of northern Mozambique with help from Tanzania and Zambia, but could not dislodge the Portuguese army from the south. Neither could the Portuguese defeat FRELIMO. The war continued for the next 10 years, becoming increasingly unpopular with Portugal's conscript soldiers.

Resolution: In 1974, leaders of the Portuguese armed forces concluded that Portugal could not continue to sustain its colonial wars, and they overthrew the Salazar government.

Outcome: Mozambique became independent in 1975, and most of the Portuguese colonists left the country.

Subsequent developments: Mozambique was in a terrible economic condition after the departure of the Portuguese skilled workers and entrepreneurs. FRELIMO proceeded to apply a Marxist development model, nationalizing and collectivizing agriculture. These changes led to a drastic drop in production. Rhodesia and South Africa sponsored opponents of the FRELIMO government who set up the guerrilla movement Renamo. This led to civil war in Mozambique (see Case 52).

Sources: Brogan (1989), *Third World Guide* (1990).

52 Mozambique Civil War 1981–

Area:	Africa
Parties:	Mozambique government
	MNR guerrillas, South Africa
Third parties:	
Issues:	Control of government
	Ideology
	Post-independence
Coercion:	Use of major force
Hostilities:	Major
Fatalities (log.10):	5.6
Resolution:	Unresolved

Background: After FRELIMO came to power in Mozambique, Portuguese settlers and disaffected FRELIMO guerrillas set up the Mozambique National Resistance Organization (Renamo) and began a campaign against the Mozambique government with help first from Rhodesia and later from South Africa.

Development: Mozambique offered bases in its territory to the ANC. This led South Africa to increase support for Renamo. The Mozambique government received large-scale military aid from the Soviet Union. Renamo's tactics have been to avoid direct military battles and instead to attack schools, villages, health centres, crops, railways and power lines. The war, combined with drought, has brought famine and economic collapse.

Sources: Brogan (1989), Third World Guide (1990).

53 Namibia 1946–

Area:	Africa
Parties:	UNITA, South Africa
	SWAPO, Cuba
Third parties:	UN, ICJ
Issues:	Control of government
	Ethnic
	Ideology
	Independence
	Jurisdiction
	Territory
Coercion:	Use of major force
Hostilities:	Major
Fatalities (log.10):	4
Resolution:	Unresolved.

Background: After the First World War, the League of Nations made the former German colony of South-West Africa a League mandate, under South African administration. In 1947 the UN withdrew the mandate, but South Africa refused to give up control of this profitable territory, rich in diamonds and minerals. South Africa defied all subsequent resolutions and rulings by the UN and the ICJ concerning the mandate.

Development: The liberation movement SWAPO (South-West Africa People's Organization) began a guerrilla war for independence in the 1960s, which continued for 40 years. The war intensified after Portugal left Angola, although South African forces frequently drove back SWAPO from Namibia deep into Angola. UN efforts to demand Namibian independence made no progress because of the lack of effective sanctions on the South African government. In 1974 the UN demanded independence for Namibia by 1975. South Africa responded by setting up homelands and a whites-only parliamentary assembly. These moves were unacceptable to the UN.

Resolution: On the initiative of Andrew Young, President Carter's Foreign Secretary, five Western nations formed a Western Contact Group to carry out negotiations with South Africa and SWAPO in 1977. Both sides agreed to participate in these talks, while continuing to prosecute the war. The Western Contact Group made a set of proposals for Namibian independence based on UN resolutions. These called for UN-supervised elections, the drafting of a constitution and a transition to independence. After a year of mainly bilateral talks between the Western Contact Group and each of the two parties, and of talks with the front-line states, who supported the initiative, agreement was reached on the basis of UN Resolution 435 in 1978. However, the South African government would not agree to implement details of the plan while Cuban troops remained in Angola. With the election of the Reagan Administration, the US government supported this position, though the front-line states, SWAPO and the other four members of the Western Contact Group were opposed to linking the two conflicts. As the war in Angola flared, the policy of linkage unexpectedly led to a settlement in Namibia. This followed intensive mediation by the US Assistant Secretary of State, Chester Crocker, and an intensification of fighting in the war that was costly to South Africa, Cuba and its Soviet patron. The detente between the superpowers and their agreement to co-operate in settling regional conflicts also facilitated a settlement, since each superpower had significant leverage over one of the parties.

Outcome: The agreement provided for a cease-fire, a timetable for the withdrawal of Cuban troops, and arrangements for elections.

Subsequent developments: Given the deep distrust on both sides, there was a real danger that the agreement would unravel as it was put into practice. Indeed, fighting broke out again after the cease-fire. Nevertheless, elections were held, and SWAPO won a majority. Walvis Bay, Namibia's main port, remained in South African hands.

Factors favouring the settlement:

1. The war had reached stalemate, and was costly to South Africa, Angola, Cuba and the Soviet Union. The fighting was beginning to cost South Africa more than the mineral resources of Namibia were worth.
2. The USA and the Soviet Union were prepared to co-operate in ending the war: the Soviet Union could 'deliver' Cuba, the USA could 'deliver' UNITA.

3. The US Assistant Secretary of State, Chester Crocker, mediated successfully and persistently between Angola, Cuba and South Africa. The Cubans, Angolans and South Africans acknowledged that his mediation was indispensable to a settlement, and compromises he proposed (for example, over the timetable for Cuban withdrawal) led to agreement (Berridge, 1989).
4. Linkage between Namibian independence and Cuban withdrawal offered South Africa a 'deal' it was prepared to accept.

Sources: Spiegel (1985), Berridge (1989; 1991), Brogan (1989).

54 Niger–Dahomey 1963–5

Area:	Africa
Parties:	Niger
	Dahomey
Third parties:	Union Africaine et Malgache (UAM),
	Conseil de l'Entente (CDE)
Issues:	Territory
Coercion:	Use of minor force
Hostilities:	None
Fatalities:	0
Resolution:	Resolved

Background: Niger and Dahomey each claimed jurisdiction over Lete Island in the Niger river. The island was of little value, being flooded for half the year and used for pasture the other half.

Development: Disagreements had begun in colonial times, and there had been violence between local groups disputing the island in the 1960s. After independence, the two states negotiated about the island, but the talks broke down in 1963 and the dispute began to broaden. Diori, President of Niger, suspected Dahomey of aiding opposition within Niger. Niger expelled Dahomey nationals in 1963, and occupied Lete. Dahomey sent troops to defend Lete, closed the frontier and seized Niger's merchandise.

Resolution: Negotiations resumed but without success. However, at a conference of the UAM, Diori announced that Niger would be willing to pay compensation for Dahomey's refugees. Dahomey continued to aid guerrillas in Niger, and tensions rose again; further negotiations broke down. In 1965, however, following mediation by the CDE, a bilateral settlement was reached.

Nationals of both states were to be allowed to use the island pending a final border demarcation; compensation to expelled Dahomeyans was agreed, and in 1965 the parties announced that the dispute was resolved.

Outcome: Nationals of both sides could use the island; expelled Dahomeyans were compensated.

Factors contributing to resolution:

1. Withdrawal of threats and attacks; offer of compensation for expelled nationals.
2. Mediation by UAM and CDE.
3. Internal political change in Dahomey favoured conciliation.

55 Nigerian Civil War 1967–70

Area:	Africa
Parties:	Nigeria
	Biafra
Third parties:	OAU, Commonwealth, Pope, Quakers, others
Issues:	Ethnic
	Secession
Coercion:	Use of major force
Hostilities:	Major
Fatalities (log.10):	6.3
Resolution:	Resolved

Background: Nigeria was created out of the merger of the British protectorates of Northern and Southern Nigeria in 1914. It was a huge and diverse country, containing many different ethnic groups and cultures, all put under one administration by British colonialism. In 1960 Nigeria became independent with a federal constitution based on three regions. These were dominated by the Yoruba in the West, the Ibos in the East and the Hausa and Fulani in the Northern region. The Islamicized Fulani were in conflict with the Hausa, and all the regions had significant minority groups. The Ibos, who were better educated and more entrepreneurial, held the best jobs and spread throughout the country. Their status was resented by other groups, especially northerners. The 1960 constitution tended to magnify the power of these major groups, and following independence a struggle for power took place between them.

Development: At first a coalition of northern and eastern parties dominated the government, followed by a coalition of North and West. This led to political instability and near anarchy by 1965. A military coup took place in 1966, led by Ibo officers, resulting in killings of northern politicians and soldiers and the establishment of a military government under Ibo leadership. Six months later the northerners organized a counter-coup, in which the Ibo commander-in-chief and other Ibos were killed. Massacres of Ibos in the northern region took place in 1967. The Ibos withdrew to the eastern region and demanded a degree of autonomy to maintain their safety. The federal government insisted on maintaining the integrity of the country and on the protection of minority groups in the East. In May 1967, the easterners proclaimed Biafra's independence. A fierce war followed, with the Federal Military Government determined to prevent secession. Civilian suffering was immense, with large-scale starvation inside Biafra. Despite many mediation efforts, no settlement was reached and in 1970 Biafra was forced to capitulate.

Resolution: The Federal Government practised a conciliatory policy in victory, and Ibo fears of genocidal massacres did not materialize. The country was divided into 12 states and later, following the return of civilian rule in 1979, into 19. The new constitution, by reducing the power of the larger ethnic groupings, and transferring more functions to regional states, appeared to be effective in dispersing and managing the ethnic conflict.

Outcome: The secession was defeated. In 1979 civilian government returned and a new federal constitution was adopted which reduced ethnic conflict.

Subsequent developments: The oil boom brought great wealth to Nigeria, and also great corruption; divisions between rich and poor grew, and agriculture remained weak A further military coup took place in 1983.

Factors contributing to resolution:

1. Military defeat of Biafra.
2. Conciliatory policy of Gowon.
3. Return of civilian government.
4. New federal constitution, dispersing ethnic conflict from politics at the centre, and giving state governments more power.

Sources: Curle (1971), Mitchell (1981), Horowitz (1985).

56   Northern Ireland 1968–

Area:	Europe
Parties:	Loyalists, UK
	Nationalists, Ireland
Third parties:	
Issues:	Jurisdiction
	Minority
	Religion
Coercion:	Use of major force
Hostilities:	Minor
Fatalities (log.10):	3.4
Resolution:	Unresolved

Background: The partition of Ireland in 1921–2 created a Protestant majority in Ulster, and a substantial Catholic minority. The Irish Free State did not accept partition as a permanent solution and hoped for the eventual unification of Ireland. However, the government established a Catholic state which left little room for accommodation with the Protestants. In Ulster the Protestant majority was determined to resist unification and wanted to retain the Union with Britain. The Nationalist minority refused to have anything to do with the new state, which therefore came to represent only the majority community. Most employers were Protestant, and employment became divided on sectarian grounds. Schools remained divided, too. The government prevented the use of Irish street names and in other ways refused to allow the Catholics to express an Irish identity. Unemployment among Catholics was double the Protestant level, and Catholics felt excluded and alienated from the state. Combined with the longstanding historical animosities between the two communities, this situation fuelled the 'troubles' in the north that began in 1968.

Development: The period of overt conflict dates from the demands of the civil rights movements for equal economic and political rights for Catholics in Northern Ireland. The Unionist government failed to respond in other than sectarian terms. When civil rights marches were met by counter-marches by Ian Paisley and the extreme loyalists, the government and police fell back on banning the marches. Sectarian confrontations continued and Britain sent troops to the province in 1969. This led to a new campaign of terrorist violence by the Provisional IRA. In 1971 the government (at Unionist insistence) introduced internment without trial. This led to a sharp increase in violence and united the Catholic community against the Stormont regime. After 'Bloody Sunday', when paratroopers fired shots into a crowd of demonstrators in 1972, the British government decided to impose direct rule, and suspended the Stormont Parliament. Although this was intended to be a temporary expedient, the British army has continued to maintain a large presence in the province. With political relations between the Catholic and Protestant communities apparently deadlocked, the IRA and Protestant terrorist groups have continued their campaign of violence.

Efforts to resolve the conflict: William Whitelaw held talks with the major parties in 1973 and won support for the proposal of a power-sharing executive. The Sunningdale agreement (1973) declared that there could be no change in the status of Northern Ireland unless a majority accepted it and provided for the establishment of a Council of Ireland and an all-Ireland police authority. However, a Protestant backlash led to a strike which brought down the power-sharing executive, and brought electoral victory to the Paisleyites. The British government continued to seek a basis for a power-sharing administration, without success. The Northern Ireland Convention of 1974 failed to reach agreement. Further talks failed in 1979/80. In 1982, the British government re-established the Northern Ireland assembly, but the Social Democratic and Labour Party boycotted it because the Unionists would not share power.

In 1985 the British and Irish governments signed the Hillsborough agreement which created a framework for progress at the intergovernmental level (see Chapter 10). However, the Unionists opposed the agreement and forced elections in Ulster to demonstrate their disapproval, and the momentum of the agreement did not lead to changes in the political structure in the North.

Sources: Royle and Hadden (1985), Day (1987), Bailey (1988).

57   Norway–UK fishing 1949–51

Area:	Europe
Parties:	UK
	Norway
Third parties:	ICJ
Issues:	Fishing
Coercion:	None
Hostilities:	None
Fatalities:	0
Resolution:	Resolved

Background: A dispute had developed between Norway and the UK in 1935 over the limits of Norwegian territorial waters.

Development: Norway attempted to prevent foreign boats from fishing in waters off the northern coast which it claimed as its territory. This led to a clash with British fishing interests.

Resolution: In 1947, the UK decided to take the issue to the ICJ.

Outcome: The ICJ ruled in favour of Norway. Britain accepted the ruling and British boats stopped fishing in the contested areas.

Factors affecting the settlement: Both sides accepted the validity of the ICJ as a means of settlement.

Source: Butterworth (1976).

58   Oman–Dhofar rebels 1963–

Area:	Middle East
Parties:	Oman, UK, Iran, Jordan
	PFLO, South Yemen
Third parties:	Arab League, Kuwait, United Arab Emirates
Issues:	Control of government
	Ideology
Coercion:	Use of major force
Hostilities:	Major
Fatalities (log.10):	2.5
Resolution:	Unresolved

Background: Oman is a poor country, and from the 1930s it was ruled by an extremely conservative Sultan who opposed all modernization. A left-wing nationalist insurgency developed in the Dhofar area, with support from Yemen.

Development: The Popular Front for the Liberation of Oman began fighting against the Sultan in Dhofar (eastern Oman) in 1963 and controlled most of Dhofar by the 1970s. From 1970 a new Sultan took over and modernized the country. With the support of Britain, Iran and Jordan, he pushed the insurgents back to a small mountainous area. The Arab League sent a conciliation team to attempt to mediate between the Sultan and the rebels, but it had no success.

Sources: Butterworth (1976), *Third World Guide* (1990).

59   Oman–Imam's rebels 1954–71

Area:	Middle East
Parties:	Oman (Sultan), UK
	Imam's rebels, Saudia Arabia, Egypt
Third parties:	UN, Arab League
Issues:	Control of government
	Independence
	Secession
Other:	Imam of Oman for independence from Muscat
	and Oman
Coercion:	Use of major force
Hostilities:	Major
Fatalities (log.10):	2.5
Resolution:	Lapsed

Background: There has traditionally been conflict in Oman between the inland peoples and the coastal rulers. In the early twentieth century the inland people elected their own imam in opposition to the Sultan of Muscat.

Development: A nationalist movement developed in opposition to the extremely conservative rule of the Sultan. The imam sided with this movement and opposed the Sultan's decision to grant control of the country's oil deposits to the Shell oil company. He was supported by Saudi Arabia, but the Sultan occupied his capital and drove him out.

He returned in 1957 and again proclaimed his imamate. In 1959 the Sultan, with British support, suppressed the rebellion.

Sources: Butterworth (1976), *Third World Guide* (1990).

60 Poland 1956

Area:	Europe
Parties:	Poland
	USSR
Third parties:	
Issues:	Ideology
	Jurisdiction
Other:	Polish development; Soviet control
Coercion:	Threat of force
Hostilities:	None
Fatalities (log.10):	1.1
Resolution:	Resolved

Background: In 1956, workers in the Polish city of Poznan rioted against Stalinist rule. The Polish army quelled the riots, but the uprising split the Polish Communist Party into factions for and against reform.

Development: The hard-line (Natolin) faction attempted to seize power, but were thwarted by factory workers and large segments of the army. The Soviet government demanded that the Polish government negotiate with the workers. It refused to do so. Khrushchev then arrived uninvited. Simultaneously Soviet tanks began to move towards Warsaw.

Resolution: Negotiations between the Polish and Soviet Politburos then led to a settlement.

Outcome: Gomulka, who was associated with the reformers, became First Secretary of the Polish Party. Relations between Poland and the Soviet Union were strengthened, and Soviet tanks returned to their bases.

Subsequent developments: By mid-1957, Gromulka re-asserted party discipline and ousted the reformers. His rule ended in 1970, following fresh riots over food prices in Gdansk. There was then a further period of weak reforms under Gierek, followed by further repression.

Eventually with the rise of Solidarity, the popular pressure for reforms became irresistible.

Factors influencing the settlement: A full Soviet occupation of Poland was avoided through negotiations (not without intimidation) between the two Politburos. The underlying tensions between the workers and the government remained unresolved.

Source: Butterworth (1976).

61   Romania–Soviet Union 1964–76

Area:	Europe
Parties:	Soviet Union
	Romania
Third parties:	
Issues:	Ideology
	Jurisdiction
	Minority
	Territory
Coercion:	None
Hostilities:	None
Fatalities:	0
Resolution:	Interim or partial settlement

Background: The eastern part of Moldavia, now a Soviet Socialist Republic, has a majority of Romanians. Since 1812 Russia has had sovereignty over Bessarabia, which was previously controlled by Turkey. The rest of Moldavia became independent Romania in 1878. In 1918, Romania acquired Bessarabia from Russia, but the Soviet Union did not recognize the transfer, and recovered the territory in 1940. Romania allied with Germany in the war against the Soviet Union and recaptured Bessarabia, but was again forced to relinquish it to the Soviet Union following the Soviet victory. Soviet-backed Romanian Communists took power, and Romania joined the Warsaw Pact.

Development: From 1956, Romania began to distance itself from the Soviet Union ideologically, notably in 1964 when it published Marx's *Notes on the Romanians*, in which Marx condemned the Tsar's annexation of Bessarabia in 1812. Romania became more nationalistic and following the election of Ceauşescu as First Secretary in 1965, Romania proposed greater economic independence for itself, and the dissolution of NATO and the Warsaw Pact. Romania denounced the Soviet invasion of Czechoslovakia.

Resolution: The Soviet Union tolerated Romania's ideological differences, and fears of a possible invasion did not materialize. In 1976, Ceauşescu asserted that Romania had 'no territorial or other problems with the Soviet Union', while Brezhnev said that there were 'no important unsolved problems between our countries'. New constitutions in the Soviet republics, introduced in 1978, extended the rights of national minorities.

Outcome: During the period of Ceauşescu's rule, the issue lapsed.

Subsequent developments: However, following the Gorbachev reforms, Moldavians in the Soviet Union once again campaigned for secession from the Soviet Union, indicating that the ethnic element of the conflict was still very much alive.

Source: Day (1987).

62 Saar 1950–7

Area:	Europe
Parties:	France
	Germany
Third parties:	Council of Europe
Issues:	Ethnic
	Territory
Coercion:	None
Hostilities:	None
Fatalities:	0
Resolution:	Resolved

Background: At the end of both the First and Second World Wars, France sought control of the rich coal and iron resources of this German-speaking territory. France had previously claimed the Saar after the First World War, but Britain and the USA had wished to prevent such a blatant flouting of the principle of self-determination. In 1919 the League of Nations had taken control of the Saar for 15 years, pending a plebiscite. French troops were stationed there until

1927, under League control. When the time for the plebiscite became due, Hitler was in power in Germany, and at first it seemed possible that he would retake the Saar by force. However, it was clear to all parties that the plebiscite would be overwhelmingly in favour of Germany. In these circumstances it was allowed to go ahead under the control of an international League force. The plebiscite was free and fair and the Saar passed into German control.

Development: France again tried to annex the Saar after the Second World War, but again the Allies prevented this. However, France took control of the coal and steel production in lieu of reparations, while the Saar became an autonomous territory, outside Germany, and for a while a separate member of the Council of Europe. In the early 1950s, a political movement demanding reunification with Germany developed in the Saar. France tried to suppress this movement, and Germany formally objected to the Council of Europe in 1952. This led to bilateral negotiations between France and Germany in 1954.

Resolution: The dispute was greatly eased by the development of the European Coal and Steel Community, which became the integrating factor in the Franco–German reconciliation. 'The Franco–German problem must become a European problem,' said Monnet, the architect of the proposal. Coal and steel were 'the key to economic power and the raw materials for forging weapons of war'. Furthermore, 'to pool them across frontiers would reduce their malign presence and turn them instead into a guarantee of peace.' Chancellor Adenauer strongly backed the plan for the iron and steel union, which subsequently grew into the basis for the EC. In these circumstances the bilateral negotiations led to an agreement that a referendum would determine the status of the Saar in 1955.

Outcome: The referendum gave a majority to candidates favouring reunion with Germany and the Saar was incorporated into the FRG in January 1957.

Subsequent developments: The Saar was integrated into the West German economy.

Factors influencing the settlement:

1. The settlement of the Saar was part of the broader post-war settlement between France and Germany. Unlike the 1919 settlement, that of 1957 helped to strengthen the bonds between France and West Germany. Undoubtedly the main factor was the

improved relations created by the integrative solution of the European Coal and Steel Community, which removed the reason to compete over coal and iron resources.

2. The dispute was settled by a gradual process, starting with bilateral negotiatons, leading to an agreed procedure (the referendum), and ending in a new treaty. The referendum provided a legitimate procedure that both parties regarded as binding for deciding the outcome.

Sources: Freymond (1960), Butterworth (1976), James (1990).

63 Saudi Arabia–Oman, Abu Dhabi 1949–75

Area:	Middle East
Parties:	Saudi Arabia
	Oman, Abu Dhabi, UK, local tribes
Third parties:	UN, Arab League, USA
Issues:	Resources
	Territory
Coercion:	Use of minor force
Hostilities:	None
Fatalities:	0
Resolution:	Resolved

Background: This dispute arose over Buraimi, an oasis 85 miles from Abu Dhabi and 400 miles from the nearest Saudi settlement. When oil was discovered there, a dispute arose over the owndership of the area. Saudi Arabia claimed the region, as did the sheikh of Abu Dhabi. Britain supported the sheikh and rejected Saudi claims.

Development: After some dispute negotiations began. In the negotiations Saudi Arabia expanded its territorial claims. The two sides agreed to set up a border commission which should establish the loyalties of the tribes living in the disputed area. In a further conference Saudi Arabia failed to obtain the territory, and in 1952 Saudi Arabia sent political representatives, and a tiny detachment of guards, to occupy the oasis. The sheikh of Abu Dhabi requested aid from Oman, which prepared a force of 9000 troops. Britain demanded that the Saudis withdraw, but the Saudis strengthened their positions.

Resolution: On the intervention of the USA, both sides agreed to take no further military action and to resume negotiations. However, the negotiations led to no agreement, and in 1953 Britain threatened to take military action. The Omani forces blockaded the Saudis in Buraimi. The parties then returned to the negotiating table and agreed to submit the dispute to arbitration. Arbitration proceedings began in 1955, but broke down amid accusations of bias among the arbiters. Britain then advised Oman and Abu Dhabi to use force, and they duly took over the oasis and ejected the Saudi police detachment there. The Soviet Union offered to support Saudi Arabia with troops. Negotiations between Britain and Saudi Arabia began but broke down after the Suez crisis. In 1959 the Secretary-General of the UN, Dag Hammarskjöld, mediated between the two sides in New York, and a UN envoy visited the area to talk to local sheikhs. Hammarskjöld failed to win an agreed settlement, but no further efforts were made to use force. In 1963 Britain and Saudi Arabia resumed diplomatic relations. They agreed to discuss the Buraimi issue with the good offices of the Secretary-General, although no agreement was reached until Britain's decision to withdraw from East of Suez. When the Trucial States, which had been British protectorates, became independent as the United Arab Emirates, Saudi Arabia agreed to resolve its territorial disputes. Saudi Arabia agreed to drop its claim in exchange for two small areas of Abu Dhabi.

Outcome: The conflict was settled by one party abandoning its claim in return for compensation.

Factors influencing the settlement: The intervention of the USA, and later the UN Secretary-General, averted armed conflict. In particular, Dag Hammarskjöld's mediation appears to have defused the tensions. Subsequently the major change in the situation brought about by the withdrawal of a powerful party (Britain) allowed the situation to be peacefully settled.

Source: Butterworth (1976).

64   South Africa 1946–

Area:	Africa
Parties:	South African government, whites
	Blacks, ANC, other black opposition parties
	'Front-line' black African states
Third parties:	UN

Issues: Class
                        Control of government
                        Ethnic
                        Ideology
                        Minority
                        Territory
Other: Apartheid
Coercion: Use of major force
Hostilities: Major
Fatalities (log.10):   3.6
Resolution: Unresolved

Background: South Africa has experienced severe conflict between the white minority, which comprises 15 per cent of the population, and the black majority, which is 70 per cent. The total population is 32 million and there are 5 million whites, 23 million blacks, 1 million Indians and 3 million 'coloured' people.

Before the Europeans arrived, Bantu societies populated South Africa, including Zulus, Xhosa, Ndebele, Swazi and Tswana. European colonization began in 1652 when the Dutch established a colony at the Cape. In 1806 Britain seized control of the colony. In the resulting conflict between British colonists and the Dutch settlers (Boers), the Boers set out on the 'Great Trek' and created two inland republics, the Orange Free State and Transvaal. They continued to use slavery after the British had abolished it. Both the British and the Boers suppressed resistance from the indigenous societies. The discovery of gold and diamonds and the development of industry in South Africa exacerbated tensions between the British colonies and the Boers, leading to the Boer Wars of 1880–1 and 1899–1902. The British defeated the Boers and unified South Africa. Parties representing the British settlers and pro-British Afrikaners were in government until 1948, when the National Party, representing conservative Afrikaners, came to power.

Development: The National Party introduced the policy of apartheid, creating 'homelands' for the blacks and carrying out mass transfers of people. They also introduced a battery of draconian laws and arrested or killed the leaders of black opposition movements. Black opposition was co-ordinated by the ANC, which sought peaceful change by nonviolent means, using strikes and boycotts. In 1959 the PAC split off from the ANC to advocate an armed struggle. The African leaders continued to organize a nonviolent campaign even after the Sharpeville massacre in 1960, when police fired on a crowd of blacks who were protesting against the pass laws. However, one wing of the ANC began to sabotage government buildings, avoiding civilian casualties. In 1963 the government arrested many of the black leaders, including Nelson Mandela and Walter Sisulu, and imprisoned them for life. The government banned opposition parties and groups as soon as they appeared, and the security forces ruthlessly suppressed political opposition.

Sharpeville prompted the development of an international campaign for sanctions against South Africa, but these were blocked by the USA and Britain. South Africa was rapidly expanding its economy and its gold, coal and other assets were playing an important role in international trade. Further repression, however, including the massacre of schoolchildren in Soweto in 1976, led to the revolt of the townships and the introduction of the State of Emergency, and the white minority in South Africa became increasingly beleaguered, violent and isolated. ANC attacks and the successes of left-wing movements in the neighbouring states led South Africa into an aggressive foreign policy aimed at destabilizing the 'front-line' black states. Ultimately, like the domestic repression, this policy rebounded on the South African government.

For the recent moves towards a settlement (and sources), see Chapter 2, box 1 pp. 28–31.

65 South Tyrol 1960–71

Area:	Europe
Parties:	Italy
	Austria
Third parties:	UN
Issues:	Ethnic
	Minority
	Territory
Coercion:	None
Hostilities:	None
Fatalities:	0
Resolution:	Interim or partial settlement

See chapter 6

Sources: Alcock (1970), Donelan and Grieve (1973), Day (1987), Pickvance (1988).

66   Sudanese Civil War 1956–

Area:	Africa
Parties:	Sudanese government and northern parties
	Sudanese rebels and southern parties
Third parties:	UN, Ethiopia, World Council of Churches
Issues:	Ethnic
	Post-independence
	Religion
	Resources
	Secession
Coercion:	Use of major force
Hostilities:	Major
Fatalities (log.10):	5.7
Resolution:	Unresolved

Background: Sudan is a product of colonialism. It contains within its borders more than 50 ethnic groups speaking over 100 languages. It is divided into a mainly Islamic Arabic population in the north and non-Islamic, non-Arabic ethnic groups, including Dinka, Nuer, Shilluk and others, in the south. The south is poorer and even less developed than the north. Following independence, northerners dominated the government. From 1958 to 1964 Sudan was under military rule.

Development: Southerners felt increasingly threatened by government policies which nationalized schools, made the use of Arabic in them compulsory, banned Christian missionaries and neglected the development of the south. Excluded from power and harrassed by the military government, the opposition turned to violent methods. From 1963 to 1965 the Anya Nya guerrilla movement fought government troops in the south, at great cost to the precarious existence of civilians. In 1965 northern and southern leaders held talks in Khartoum to seek a settlement, but no common ground was found between southern demands for a federal constitution and Northern rejection of separatism. Fighting continued until 1972, with Egypt and the USSR supporting the government and Ethiopia, Uganda and the Central African Republic providing bases for the guerrillas.

   The costs of the war and the poor state of the economy led President al-Nemery to offer the south autonomy in 1971 and to open communications with Anya Nya, through the mediation of the World Council of Churches and Haile Selassie. Formal negotiations began in

1972 and an agreement was reached to end the conflict, on the basis of a cease-fire, gradual implementation of regional autonomy, and incorporation of the guerrillas into the Sudanese Army.

However, al-Nemery failed to implement the autonomy agreement and, in response to political pressures in the North, introduced drastic new Islamic laws and penalties. Together with an unconstitutional alteration to the provincial structure of the south, this further inflamed opinion, and with mounting debt, public services failing, and growing starvation, complicated by the influx of refugees, war intensified again in 1983. By 1984 the rebel army was in control of most of the south, besieging government troops in the loyal garrisons. The fighting and blockade led to massive starvation and an exodus of refugees.

The war has forced more than three million people in southern Sudan to leave their homes and hundreds of thousands have starved to death. In 1988, following the acceptance of UN relief supplies, the government parties and the rebels came to a new agreement providing for a cease-fire, a constitutional conference, and a freeze on the implementation of Islamic laws.

Sources: Doob (1970), Butterworth (1976), Murray (1988), Brogan (1989), *New African* (June 1989).

67　Sudanese independence 1946–56

Area:	Africa
Parties:	Egypt
	UK
	Sudanese nationalist parties
Third parties:	UN
Issues:	Ethnic
	Independence
	Jurisdiction
Coercion:	Use of minor force
Hostilities:	Minor
Fatalities (log.10):	2.5
Resolution:	Resolved

Background: Sudan had been governed by Egypt's autonomous Otto-man ruler between 1820 and 1881 and by an Anglo Egyptian condominium from 1899 to 1955, though it was then under effective

British control. At the end of the war Egypt hoped to recover Sudan, while the Sudanese nationalist movement wanted independence.

Development: A new treaty between Britain and Egypt was due to be negotiated in 1946. Britain insisted that the Sudanese should determine their own future after a period of autonomy under continued British control. Egypt demanded the unification of the Nile valley peoples. In 1944 Britain set up an Advisory Council in Sudan to assist the Governor-General and to represent Sudanese nationalist parties; this Council excluded southerners. In 1947 Egypt accepted the principle of self-determination, within a framework of Egyptian–Sudanese unity, but the anti-Egyptian nationalist party protested violently against Egypt's proposals. In negotiations with Britain over a future constitution, Egypt refused to countenance independence and the talks were deadlocked. Egypt appealed to the UN, but the Security Council failed to reach agreement and deferred the issue.

Britain proceeded to take unilateral steps towards granting independence. In response Egypt unilaterally abrogated the Condominium treaty and declared King Farouk to be king of both Egypt and Sudan. Farouk was overthrown in 1952 and the new Egyptian government, under General Neguib, decided to reach a settlement with Britain.

Resolution: Following negotiations between Britain and Egypt, in which Egypt secured better terms for Sudan, an agreement was signed in 1953, providing for a three-year transition to independence and elections to decide whether Sudan should join Egypt or be independent. General Neguib (himself half-Sudanese) gained the support of the main Sudanese parties for the agreement. Elections were held in 1953 and the pro-Egyptian Union Nationalist Party formed a government. Subsequently this government dropped its support of union with Egypt and instead moved towards independence and rapid 'Sudanization' of the government and armed forces. This policy created tensions with Egypt and between southern and northern Sudanese, leading to the mutiny of an army corps in southern Sudan. Egypt demanded that British and Egyptian troops should be sent in to put down the mutiny, but Britain refused to get further involved, and the British Governor-General resigned. The Sudanese government put down the mutiny with considerable brutality.

Outcome: In 1956 Sudan proceeded to declare its independence. The new state was recognized by both Egypt and Britain.

Factors contributing to resolution:

1. The change of government in Egypt.
2. The temporarily improved relations between Egypt and Sudanese nationalist parties.
3. Egyptian willingness to accept a referendum, and to negotiate on Sudan without linking the issue to the Suez Canal question.
4. Agreement on a transition plan with elections for Sudanese to determine their own status.
5. The preoccupation of the Egyptian government with the Suez war of 1948–9.

Subsequent developments: The domination by northerners of the new government, together with the existing ethnic, cultural, religious and economic divisions between north and south, led to protracted conflict within Sudan, and eventually to civil war.

Sources: Butterworth (1976), Calvocoressi (1987).

68   Syria–Lebanon 1949

Area:	Middle East
Parties:	Syria
	Lebanon
Third parties:	Egypt, Saudi Arabia
Issues:	Jurisdiction
Other:	Syrian attacks in Lebanon
Coercion:	Use of minor force
Hostilities:	Minor
Fatalities (log.10):	1.1
Resolution:	Resolved

Background: This dispute arose from an attack by Syrian troops on opposition Syrian exiles in Lebanon. The Lebanese government held four Syrian soldiers who had killed a number of Lebanese civilians; the Syrian government wanted the soldiers handed back to be tried under its own jurisdiction.

Development: Syria blocked shipments of food into Lebanon to support its demand. The Lebanese government asked Egypt to mediate, which it began to do, but Syrian troops again made incursions over the border.

Resolution: Syria and Lebanon then agreed to accept Egyptian and Saudi arbitration in the dispute.

Outcome: The Egyptians and Saudis found in favour of the Syrian claim for Syrian jurisdiction. Lebanon returned the soldiers. Syria withdrew its troops.

Subsequent developments: Syria continued to make threats and troop movements for a further two years, but Egypt intervened to prevent a serious escalation. The Syrian government was then overthrown in a coup, and the source of the dispute was removed.

Factors influencing the settlement:

1. Lebanon responded to Syria's food blockade by asking for mediation instead of by using a coercive response.
2. Saudi and Egyptian arbitration removed the immediate source of the dispute.
3. The change of government in Syria removed the underlying issue.

Source: Butterworth (1976).

69 Syria–Turkey (Hatay) 1945–

Area:	Middle East
Parties:	Syria
	Turkey
Third parties:	
Issues:	Ethnic
	Jurisdiction
	Minority
	Territory
Coercion:	Use of minor force
Hostilities:	Minor
Fatalities (log.10):	1.1
Resolution:	Lapsed

Background: The Syrian province of Hatay was the former Ottoman Sanjak of Alexandretta, lying on the Mediterranean coast adjacent to

Turkey. It has a substantial Turkish population as well as a Syrian one. When the Ottoman Empire broke up, France incorporated the Sanjak into Syria. Turkey recognized this in the Treaty of Lausanne (1923) but, when Syria became independent (1946), Turkey sought to recover the province.

Development: Turkey raised the issue with the League of Nations in 1936, after French and Syrian representatives began negotiations for Syrian independence. The League sent a commission of enquiry to Hatay, which proposed that Syria would be responsible for the foreign affairs of the province, while the Sanjak would be responsible for its own internal government. The province would be demilitarized, Turkish and Syrian would both be official languages and the rights of all the ethnic groups would be guaranteed. France accepted these provisions and put them into effect, but they were opposed by the Syrian and Armenian minorities. Violence broke out between the ethnic communities in 1937 and martial law was introduced by the French. In 1938 there was further intercommunal fighting, and Turkey moved troops to the border. In 1938 France and Turkey agreed that the Turks should have a majority of the seats in the local government, and that Turkish officers could play a part in garrisoning the province. Against Syrian protests, in 1938 the Turkish forces were allowed in. In 1939 France agreed to cede the province to Turkey, as a quid pro quo for Turkey keeping out of the war with Germany. A new agreement allowed the non-Turkish minorities to leave the province if they wished, and Turkey took control of the province. Further Syrian protests and demonstrations took place. After the war, relations between Syria and Turkey were bad, and Syria accused Turkey of massing troops on the border and planning to overthrow the Syrian government in 1937. Turkey objected to Syria allowing Kurds free passage through its territory, and there were also disputes over water issues.

Resolution: In 1985, the two governments made moves to improve their relations, and signed a series of agreements covering border security and bilateral co-operation. Although Syria has not actively pursued its claim, it has not abandoned it.

Outcome: The province remains in Turkish control.

Source: Day (1987).

70   Trieste 1945–75

Area:	Europe
Parties:	Italy, USA, UK, France
	Yugoslavia, USSR
Third parties:	UN
Issues:	Ethnic
	Great Power
	Jurisdiction
	Territory
Coercion:	Display of force
Hostilities:	None
Fatalities:	0
Resolution:	Resolved.

See Chapter 6.

71   Tunisian independence 1922–56

Area:	Africa
Parties:	Tunisian nationalists
	France
Third parties:	UN
Issues:	Independence
Coercion:	Use of minor force
Hostilities:	Minor
Fatalities (log.10):	3.5
Resolution:	Resolved

Background: Tunisia had been under French control since the 1880s, although the bey remained the nominal ruler. In 1888 a nationalist movement developed, demanding reform and the restoration of the bey's powers.

Development: The nationalists set up the Destour political party and in 1922 the bey came out in support of the nationalists by threatening to abdicate. France responded by repressing the nationalists. In the 1930s Bourgiba built up the party as an organized opposition to French rule. He was arrested in 1939 but after the war he was released, and continued a nonviolent campaign for independence. French policy fluctuated between an inclination to accept independence, and support for the French settlers who wanted to maintain the status quo. However, unlike in the case of Algeria, a civil war was avoided.

In 1950 the French government promised to grant autonomy in stages and negotiations began, but failed. The French government again cracked down on the nationalists, arresting Bourgiba and other leaders. The nationalists set up a trade union and other organizations, but these were suppressed. Guerrilla fighting now began. The UN General Assembly called on France to negotiate with the nationalists.

Resolution: A change of government in France then brought a more pro-independence president. France abandoned the policy of repression and started negotiations with the nationalists. In 1955 the parties reached an agreement on internal self-government, and in 1956 Tunisia became independent. The terms of the agreement allowed France to retain troops and a military base in Tunisia, and Bourgiba accepted this in order to avoid a war. Other nationalists wanted to pursue an armed struggle to force France to leave completely.

Outcome: Tunisia thus won its independence.

Subsequent developments: A conflict developed among the nationalists. Bourgiba became President and enjoyed a long period of rule.

Factors influencing the settlement:

1. The change of government in France.
2. The nationalists had pursued a long and relatively moderate campaign with popular support; had France continued repression a war would have been likely.

Sources: Butterworth (1976), Calvocoressi (1987), *Third World Guide* (1990).

72   Tunisia–France (Sakiet and Bizerte) 1958–63

Area:	Africa
Parties:	Tunisia
	France
Third parties:	UN, US, UK

Issues: Jurisdiction
Other: French bases and border incursions
Coercion: Use of major force
Hostilities: Major
Fatalities (log.10):   3
Resolution: Resolved

Background: After Tunisia became independent from France, the two
states remained in dispute over the military base which France retained
at Bizerte, and the use of Tunisian territory by Algerian nationalists
fighting France for the independence of Algeria.

Development: French counter-insurgency raids violated Tunisian sovereignty and led to the bombardment of Sakiet, a Tunisian town. In
retaliation Tunisia besieged the French military bases. The UN
Secretary-General persuaded Tunisia to allow supplies to the bases
while negotiations proceeded under the auspices of a British and
American Good Offices committee. There was deadlock for some
months but eventually, after the French had taken measures to seal the
Tunisian/Algerian border, the parties agreed (through the mediation of
the Anglo–American committee) to an interim resolution of the
dispute. France withdrew all its forces except those based at Bizerte;
Tunisia agreed to tolerate the presence of this base until a later
negotiated evacuation. In the following years, France continued to
procrastinate over withdrawing from Bizerte. In 1961 a crisis arose
when France began to extend its runway there. Tunisia broke off
diplomatic relations and re-established a blockade of the base. This led
to fighting in the town of Bizerte. The UN Secretary-General visited
Bizerte but the French refused to negotiate with him. After further
procrastination and UN calls on both sides to negotiate a French
withdrawal, the two sides agreed to disengage their forces.

Outcome: Several months later, diplomatic relations were restored and
France agreed to evacuate the base.

Factors influencing the settlement: The Algerian war had ended.
France ungraciously came to accept that it could no longer maintain
a long-term military presence in North Africa.

Sources: Butterworth (1976), Calvocoressi (1987).

73 Tutsi–Hutu 1958–

Area:	Africa
Parties:	Tutsi, Burundi
	Hutu, Rwanda
Third parties:	OAU, UN, Zaire
Issues:	Class
	Control of government
	Ethnic
	Minority
	Post-independence
Other:	Massacres, refugees, border incursions
Coercion:	Use of major force
Hostilities:	Major
Fatalities (log.10):	5.3
Resolution:	Interim or partial settlement

Background: Burundi and Rwanda are among the poorest countries in Africa. Each state has a minority of about 15 per cent Tutsi people and a majority of about 85 per cent Hutu. The Tutsis overran the Hutu in the fifteenth century and established a semi-slave/semi-feudal rule. In the nineteenth century Burundi and Rwanda became a German colony. The colony passed to Belgium under League of Nations mandate after the First World War. Belgium continued the German practice of ruling through the dominant Tutsi minority, but separated Burundi from Rwanda and ruled it from the Congo.

Development: Influenced by European ideas and the coming of independence, the Hutu attempted to overthrow Tutsi rule when independence was granted. In Rwanda, a popular uprising led to the flight of the Tutsi monarch, and a coup brought a Hutu government to power. In Burundi, however, the Tutsis held on to power, despite UN-supervised elections in both countries. After independence a popular pogrom of Tutsis began in Rwanda, which led to a large-scale flight of Tutsis to Burundi. In Burundi, Tutsi exiles from Rwanda organized frequent invasions and terrorist incursions, aimed at restoring the Tutsi monarchy. A Hutu uprising in Burundi in 1972 led to a massive Tutsi pogrom against the Hutus.

Resolution: The OAU and Zaire made several attempts to mediate between the two countries. In 1966 and again in 1967 the two countries made agreements to disarm exiles and set up a commission to allow the return of refugees. These agreements were not implemented and tensions between the states remained high. In 1973, however, after a change of government in Rwanda and further mediation by Zaire, the interstate element in the conflict abated. The ethnic tensions remained high.

Subsequent developments: Ethnic persecution continued in Burundi. A new government in 1987 offered to introduce equal rights for the Hutus; this triggered a further outbreak of ethnic violence. Amid mutual fears, the Hutu attacked Tutsis in northern Burundi. The Burundi army, which is Tutsi, took reprisals and massacred about 20 000 Hutu.

Sources: Butterworth (1976), Murray (1988), Brogan (1989), *Third World Guide* (1990).

74   Uganda 1971–

Area:	Africa
Parties:	Uganda, Amin
	Tanzania, Asians
	Buganda, Acholi, Moslem and other ethnic groups
Third parties:	Kenya, Somalia, Ethiopia, OAU
Issues:	Control of government
	Ethnic
Coercion:	Use of major force
Hostilities:	Major
Fatalities (log.10):	5.6
Resolution:	Unresolved

Background: Uganda contains a mixture of ethnic groups which became one polity when Britain established its colony in 1894. When Britain withdrew and Uganda became independent, a terrible period of dictatorship and ethnic conflict ensued.

Development: Britain transferred power to the Kabaka (leader) of Buganda, the representative of the most important pre-colonial kingdom, and Milton Obote, who became prime minister. Obote ousted the Kabaka and took increased powers, reducing federal checks in the constituion. In turn Idi Amin ousted Obote. Amin proceeded to carry out an ethnic purge, first of the army and then of the rest of the country.

Facing economic collapse, Amin invaded Tanzania. In the subsequent war Tanzanian forces defeated Ugandan troops and occupied Kampala. Obote returned to power but a civil war followed. A guerrilla army under Musaveni (based in the south and west) fought against the Ugandan army, which itself split along ethnic lines. Musaveni managed to establish a broadly-based government in 1986, and his army suppressed or absorbed most of the opposition forces. Nevertheless guerrillas continued to operate, and the Iteso people, Uganda's second main ethnic group in the north-east, suffered depradations in government attempts to re-establish security in the north-east.

Sources: International Alert (1987), Brogan (1989), Furley (1990), *Third World Guide* (1990).

75   Wadi Halfa 1958–9

Area:	Africa
Parties:	Egypt
	Sudan
Third parties:	UN, Arab League, Ethiopia
Issues:	Resources
	Territory
Coercion:	None
Hostilities:	None
Fatalities:	0
Resolution:	Resolved

Background: The dispute arose because the construction of the Aswan Dam would flood agricultural land in Northern Sudan.

Development: Instead of seeking Sudan's consent to the flooding, Egypt challenged the border demarcation and claimed Wadi Halfa, the area that would be flooded by the dam. Egypt moved frontier police into the disputed territory and prepared to conduct a plebiscite. Egypt also offered to exchange Wadi Halfa for territory elsewhere. Sudan refused. An attempt to settle the dispute through arbitration failed. Bilateral talks broke down and armed conflict seemed possible.

Resolution: Haile Selassie of Ethiopia urged the parties to postpone action until the Sudanese elections had been held. Egypt agreed, removed patrols from the area, and dropped its planned plebiscite. Relations between the two countries improved following a coup in Sudan. In 1959 negotiations were resumed and an agreement was reached, fixing a level of compensation for the Sudanese farmers and giving Sudan a substantial increase in water extraction rights. Egypt also offered Sudan cash compensation and technical assistance in draining marshes in southern Sudan.

Outcome: The territorial issue remained unresolved (though quiescent), but the dispute over the dam was resolved by agreement, with compensation for Sudan's losses.

Factors contributing to resolution:

1. Change of government in Sudan.
2. Ethiopian mediation.
3. The separation of the issue of water from territory.

Source: Butterworth (1976).

76   Western Sahara 1964–

Area:	Africa
Parties:	Polisario, Algeria
	Morocco, Mauritania
	Spain
Third parties:	UN
Issues:	Ideology
	Independence
	Jurisdiction
	Post-independence
	Resources
	Territory
Coercion:	Use of major force
Hostilities:	Major
Fatalities (log.10):	4
Resolution:	Unresolved

Background: Spanish Sahara (later, Western Sahara or Saharwi) was formed in 1958 through the merger of two former Spanish colonies on the West coast of Africa, Rio de Oro and Saguia el Hamra. Until recently it was populated by nomadic peoples, though the majority now live in towns. The population is about a million. It has huge phosphate deposits and rich fisheries in its coastal waters.

Development: Because of the phosphate wealth, Spain was unwilling to give the colony up. The UN passed resolutions calling for self-determination, but Spain delayed granting independence. Morocco also maintained a territorial claim to Western Sahara, and Mauritania had a claim on Rio de Oro. In 1969, Morocco, Mauritania and Algeria combined to press for the territory's decolonization. In 1973 Polisario, an internal liberation front, launched an armed struggle for independence. In 1974 Spain accepted the principle of self-determination and offered Western Sahara internal autonomy. Morocco and Mauritania denounced this plan as a 'puppet state'. Morocco referred the question of the Western Sahara to the ICJ and, while it was still deliberating, launched the 'Green March', (a peaceful invasion of Western Sahara by 350 000 Moroccans led by the King). In 1975 Spain agreed to transfer Western Sahara to Morocco and Mauritania, who then partitioned it. Algeria and the Saharwi liberation groups opposed this settlement, and Polisario began to fight against Morocco and Mauritania, with Algerian support. Mauritania was forced to withdraw in 1978, but heavy fighting continued between Morocco (which had French and US arms) and Polisario. Although the ICJ denied Morocco's claim to sovereignty in 1975, and 71 countries have recognized Saharwi, Morocco holds most of the country with 100 000 troops and has poured money and aid into the capital, La'Youn.

In 1988 the UN Secretary-General sought to break the deadlock by proposing a referendum and a cease-fire. Algeria (now under the presidency of Bendjedid) resumed diplomatic relations with Morocco and talks between Morocco and Polisario took place in Jeddah. Saudi Arabia, which has given Morocco aid in the past, is pressing Morocco to settle.

Sources: Calvocoressi (1987), *Financial Times* (12 August 1988), *Christian Science Monitor* (20 April 1989), *Third World Guide* (1990).

77   Yemen (South)–Yemen (North) 1969–79

Area: Middle East
Parties: Yemen South (PDYR)
                 Yemen North (YAR), Front for the Liberation of
                 South Yemen (FLOSY), Saudi Arabia
Third parties: Arab League
Issues: Control of government
                 Ideology
Coercion: Use of major force
Hostilities: Major
Fatalities: Not Known
Resolution: Resolved

Background: After independence, South Yemen was governed by increasingly radical left-wing regimes. Tensions grew with Saudi Arabia, and internal opponents of the regime joined with the exiled leaders of FLOSY to set up bases in North Yemen.

Development: Border clashes led to fighting between the two Yemeni states, with serious fighting in 1973 and 1979.

Resolution: The Arab League sent mediators in 1973 and obtained a cease-fire; in subsequent direct negotiations the North and South Yemenis agreed to withdraw their troops and unify the country. Turbulent political developments in both the Yemens led to a further armed conflict between them in 1979 but eventually, after a civil war in South Yemen in 1986, unification took place.

Sources: Butterworth (1976), Brogan (1989), *Third World Guide* (1990).

7   Yemeni Civil War 1962–70

Area: Middle East
Parties: Yemeni Republicans, Egypt
                 Yemeni Royalists, Saudi Arabia, N. Yemeni tribes
Third parties: UN, Arab League, Saudi Arabia
Issues: Control of government
Coercion: Use of major force
Hostilities: Major

Fatalities (log.10):   5
Resolution: Resolved

Background: Until 1962 Yemen was ruled autocratically by a highly traditional imam, a secular and religious leader, who opposed all modernization. From the 1940s an opposition developed, favouring social revolution, modernization and a republican government.

Development: The Republicans took power in a coup in 1962, with Egyptian support. The imam fled to Saudi Arabia and formed a government in exile. With the help of Saudi money and North Yemeni tribes, the imam attempted to restore his government. In the ensuing war, Egypt sent 50 000 troops to help the Republicans, but the war was indecisive. The UN sent negotiators to talk with the Saudi and Republican governments, and in 1963 the parties agreed to a UN Disengagement Agreement, under which Egyptian forces would leave, Saudi Arabia would stop helping the Imam, and UN observers would patrol a demilitarized zone in northern Yemen. However, neither Egypt nor Saudi Arabia carried out the terms of this agreement, and fighting continued. Nevertheless, the possible extension of the conflict to a war between Egypt and Saudi Arabia was averted. In 1964, Egypt and Saudi Arabia held direct negotiations following Algerian mediation, and agreed to a cease-fire. The talks found no formula for agreement between the Republicans and the monarchists and fighting continued. The same pattern was repeated in 1965.

Resolution: Defeat in the Six Day war forced Egypt to arrange to withdraw its troops. A further conference was held in Khartoum, and Saudi Arabia and Egypt again agreed to withdraw support for the parties in Yemen. After Egypt's withdrawal, the Royalists made another attempt to retake the Yemen, but the Republicans defeated them with Soviet military help. Both the Royalists and the Republicans had changes of leadership, which brought forward leaders who were prepared to entertain a reconciliation. The Saudis, alarmed by the more radical developments in South Yemen, now became willing to back the new moderate leadership. Under Saudi sponsorship, talks took place between the moderate Republicans and the new Royalist leaders.

Outcome: These led to an agreement to set up a Republican government including some of the Royalist leaders.

Factors influencing the settlement:

1. UN intervention produced the contours of an agreement for Saudi and Egyptian withdrawal, which was eventually put into practice, though not before several years of indecisive and costly warfare.
2. The royalists and republicans found an integrative solution for their differences by finally agreeing to participate in a common government.

Sources: Donelan and Grieve (1973), Butterworth (1976), *Third World Guide* (1990).

79 Yemen: conflict over Aden and independence 1948–67

Area:	Middle East
Parties:	UK
	Yemen, South Yemen
Third parties:	UN
Issues:	Independence
	Territory
Coercion:	Use of major force
Hostilities:	Major
Fatalities (log.10):	2.6
Resolution:	Resolved

Background: Britain had occupied Aden in 1839, as a strategic port controlling the entrance to the Red Sea for ships *en route* to India. After losing India in 1947, British policy was to retain control of Aden but reduce its commitments in the surrounding area. This policy, and Britain's support for semi-independent tribes in the area, brought Britain into conflict with Yemen, which was then a conservative and backward monarchy.

Development: Britain attempted to set up a united protectorate of sheikhdoms in South Yemen. Yemen opposed this plan and a number of border incidents ensued, with Britain attacking Yemeni military posts, and Yemenis making raids into the British controlled area. There were also rebellions against British rule in the protectorate area. Yemen laid claim to the entire protectorate, and there was growing nationalist opposition. In 1962 the conflict was influenced by the outbreak of civil war in Yemen; from then on the dispute became a struggle between Britain and South Yemeni groups. In 1963 the National Front for the Liberation of South Yemen began an armed campaign for independence; Britain used air strikes against their bases.

Resolution: The UN called for Britain to withdraw and for the Secretary-General to use his good offices, but this was without effect. Local support for Britain disintegrated and in 1965 Britain was obliged to impose direct rule. The following year Britain decided to withdraw, and to pull back from its other commitments east of Suez. In South Yemen the situation was now complicated by a three-way struggle for power after Britain's withdrawal, between the National Front for the Liberation of South Yemen, the rival FLOSY and the government of the Federation of sheikdoms and Aden that Britain had set up. Britain withdrew in chaotic conditions, out of which the National Front for the Liberation of South Yemen emerged as the maker of a new government.

Outcome: South Yemen won its independence and became a socialist republic.

Sources: Butterworth (1976), Brogan (1989), *Third World Guide* (1990).

80 Zairean independence (the Congo) 1960–5

Area:	Africa
Parties:	Zaire, rival nationalist groups
	Katangan secessionists
	Belgium, UN
Third parties:	UN, OAU
Issues:	Control of government
	Ethnic
	Post-independence
	Resources
	Secession
Coercion:	Use of major force
Hostilities:	Major
Fatalities (log.10):	5
Resolution:	Resolved

Background: The borders of Zaire were established in 1885 by the Treaty of Berlin, at a time when the European powers were carving up Africa amongst themselves. The Congo, which was given to King Leopold II of Belgium, was populated by a variety of ethnic groups, speaking Bantu, Sudanese and Nilotic languages, and organized into many small political units, as well as a few larger trading kingdoms (such as Kuba, Lunda and Luba). Leopold exploited his colony ruthlessly, using enslavement and forced labour to extract its resources. From 1908 to 1960 the Belgian government administered the colony, granting concessions for minerals and cash crops to commercial companies. In 1955 a nationalist movement developed and riots broke out against Belgian rule in 1959. Belgium was relatively late to offer independence and, when it came in 1960, it came suddenly; Belgium agreed to leave the country within six months. The nationalist parties represented different ethnic groups, and disagreed about the form the government should take. Lumumba's 'Mouvement National Congolais' favoured a centralized national state, while Kasavubu's 'Akabo' preferred a federal system. Tshombe's 'Conakat' favoured autonomy for Katanga, which was richer than other provinces on account of its mineral wealth.

Development: Independence was proclaimed in 1960. Lumumba became Prime Minister and Kasavubu President. Immediately the army mutinied and Belgian troops intervened. Tshombe declared Katanga's secession and asked for Belgian help. Lumumba appealed to the UN, and the Security Council agreed to send UN troops. Tshombe declared that UN troops would not be permitted in Katanga. The UN force fell out with Lumumba and there followed a power struggle, in which Kasavubu attempted to dismiss Lumumba, Lumumba attempted to overthrow Kasavubu; the army commander, Mobutu, attempted to take power; and Tshombe held out in Katanga. The UN was also split, with the Soviet Union and the Western powers backing rival Congolese governments in Leopoldville and Stanleyville. Eventually a united Congolese government was formed and, with help from UN forces, began to engage in heavy fighting in Katanga.

Resolution: The UN Acting Secretary-General sought to settle the conflict on the basis of a cease-fire, a federal constitution, and a transitional period in which Katanga was to get a half-share in the revenue from the mines. The Congolese and Katangan governments agreed to the plan but failed to implement it. UN forces proceeded to occupy Katanga and in 1963 Tshombe acknowledged that the secession attempt had failed. UN forces were then withdrawn in 1964. Tshombe subsequently became Prime Minister of the Congolese government, only to be dismissed by President Kasavubu. Mobutu then seized power, and this time held it. He proceeded to defeat the remaining rebels, nationalize the mines and reduce the number of provinces.

Outcome: The secession of Katanga was defeated.

Factors contributing to resolution:

1. UN support for the Congo government, and the agreement of rival Congolese governments in Leopoldville and Stanleyville to unite, led to the secession's downfall.
2. Even in Katanga the secession had never been fully successful because of ethnic rivalries within the region.
3. After Mobutu took power, he established a dictatorship and made effective the rule of the central government.

Subsequent developments: In 1977 and 1978 Katangan exiles and others favouring the secession of Katanga (now Shaba province) invaded from Angola, but they were defeated by the central government with French and Belgian help.

Sources: Donelan and Grieve (1973), Butterworth (1976), Horowitz (1985), Murray (1988).

81 Zimbabwe: independence and majority rule 1963–80

Area:	Africa
Parties:	UK
	Rhodesian government, whites
	ZANU, ZAPU
Third parties:	UN
Issues:	Control of government
	Ethnic
	Ideology
	Independence
	Minority
	Post-independence

Coercion:	Use of major force
Hostilities:	Major
Fatalities (log.10):	4.1
Resolution:	Resolved

Background: Southern Rhodesia emerged as a white-dominated British colony from the break-up of the old Federation of Rhodesia and Nyasaland. Nationalist leaders had taken power in Zambia (formerly northern Rhodesia) and Malawi (formerly Nyasaland). In southern Rhodesia the white minority retained power, but Britain refused to grant the colony independence without clear provisions for a transfer to majority rule. The white minority government, in opposition to majority rule, unilaterally declared independence in 1965.

Development: This led to a long conflict between Britain and the minority government. Britain and the UN imposed economic sanctions on Rhodesia in an effort to force the white minority to accept Britain's terms; but South Africa and the Portuguese colony of Mozambique were, for years, massive loopholes in the sanctions. Negotiations between Britain and the Rhodesian government made no progress, and the British Prime Minister, Harold Wilson, and the Rhodesian Prime Minister, Ian Smith, failed to find a basis for agreement. Britain remained committed to majority rule and the white minority was determined to avoid giving up power for a very long time.

The following years saw the beginning of a guerrilla war with several nationalist armies and a steady increase in the isolation of Rhodesia. At the same time numerous attempts were made to negotiate an end to the conflict. In the end a negotiated settlement was reached, though not before the armed struggle and the economic and political isolation had put great pressure on Ian Smith's government. The decisive events were the loss by Portugal of its colonies in Africa, and South Africa's decision to stop helping Rhodesia.

For a long time the negotiators wrestled with the disputed issues: the principle of majority rule, the holding of elections, the design of a new constitution and the degree to which it would protect the white minority's interests, security arrangements in the transitional period, and the duration of the return to British rule before independence.

Resolution: Under US and South African pressure, Ian Smith accepted the principle of majority rule. He constructed an 'internal settlement' with Muzorewa, Sithole and other 'moderate' black leaders. However, he could not persuade the guerrilla leaders to come into government, and neither could he persuade the US and British governments that his internal settlement was acceptable. Eventually Smith came to accept that he would need to agree to an internationally recognized settlement.

Outcome: The settlement, worked out at the Lancaster House talks in 1979, provided for a brief return to British rule, followed by free elections. There were sufficient guarantees for the whites to provide them with a safeguarded place in Parliament, and their economic position was safe for a while. Elections were duly held and power passed into the hands of Robert Mugabe.

Subsequent developments: There was subsequent violence between the guerrilla forces, and after a time Mugabe set up a one-party state and introduced legislation to remove the whites' constitutional privileges. This happened gradually, however, and did not cause further fighting.

Factors influencing the settlement:

1. Prolonged mediation by the USA and Britain between the white minority government, the black leaders and the leaders of the surrounding black states eventually produced a formula which was mutually acceptable.
2. The white government came to realize that its position was hopeless as the armed conflict and sanctions became increasingly costly, after it had lost South African support.
3. The armed conflict had reached a stalemate.

Sources: Low (1985), Calvocoressi (1987).

Bibliography

Alcock, A. E. (1970), *The History of the South Tyrol Question* (London: Michael Joseph).

Alker, H. R. Jr and C. Christensen (1972), 'From causal modelling to artificial intelligence: the evaluation of a UN peace-making simulation', in J. Laponce and P. Smoker, *Experimentation and Simulation in Political Science*, (Toronto: University of Toronto Press).

Alker, H. R. Jr and Frank L. Sherman (1982), 'Collective security seeking practices since 1945', in D. Frei, (ed.), *Managing International Crises* (Beverly Hills, California: Sage).

Allsebrook, M. (1986), *Prototypes of Peacemaking: The First Forty Years of the United Nations* (UK: Longman).

Annals of the American Academy of Political and Social Science (1970), 'How wars end'.

Axelrod, R. (1984), *The Evolution of Co-operation* (New York: Basic Books).

Azar, E. (1972), 'Making and measuring the international event as a unit of analysis', *Sage Professional Papers in International Studies*, 1.

Azar, E. and J. W. Burton (eds) (1986), *International Conflict Resolution: Theory and Practice* (Brighton: Wheatsheaf).

Bailey, S. D. (1971), *Peaceful Settlement of Disputes: Ideas and Proposals for Research*, UNITAR Study PS No. 1 (New York: UNITAR).

Bailey, S. D. (1982), *How Wars End: The United Nations and the Termination of Armed Conflict 1946–64* (2 vols) (Oxford: Clarendon Press).

Bailey, S. D. (1985), 'Non-official mediation in disputes: reflection on Quaker experience', *International Affairs*, 2, pp. 205–22.

Bailey, S. D. (ed.) (1988a), *Human Rights and Responsibilities in Britain and Northern Ireland* (London: Macmillan).

Bailey, S. D. (1988b), Personal communication.

Bailey, S. D. (1989), Personal interview.

Bailey, S. D. (1990a), *Four Arab-Israeli Wars and the Peace Process* (London: Macmillan).

Bailey, S. D. (1990b), 'A case study in Quaker mediation', *Friends Quarterly*, vol. 26, no. 2 (April), pp. 88-95.

Bebler, A. (1987), 'Conflicts between socialist states', *Journal of Peace Research*, 24, 1.

Beer, F. A. (1981), *Peace against War* (Oxford: W.H .Freeman).

Bentwich, N. and A. Martin (1951), *A Commentary on the Charter of the United Nations* (London).

Bercovitch, J. (1986), 'International mediation: a study of the incidence, strategies and conditions of successful outcomes', *Co-operation and Conflict*, XXI, pp. 155–68.

Bercovitch, J. (1987), *Social Conflicts and Third Parties – Strategies of Conflict Resolution* (Boulder, Colorado: Westview).

Bercovitch, J., J. T. Anagnoson and D. L. Wille (1991), 'Some conceptual issues and empirical trends in the study of successful mediation in international relations', *Journal of Peace Research*, 28, 1, pp. 7–17.

Berridge, G. R. (1989), 'Diplomacy and the Angola/Namibia accords', *International Affairs*, 65, 3, pp. 463–79.

Berridge, G. R. (1991), *Return to the UN* (London: Macmillan).

Bluth, C. (1987), 'The British resort to force in the Falklands/Malvinas conflict 1982', *Journal of Peace Research*, 24, 1.

Borsi-Kalman, Bela (1990), 'La minorite hongroise de la Transylvanie', Paper to the 25th International Peace Research Association Conference, Groningen, Holland.

Boulding, K. E. (1978), *Stable Peace* (Austin: University of Texas Press).

Boyle, K. and T. Hadden (1985), *Ireland: A Positive Proposal* (Harmondsworth: Penguin).

Bracken, P. (1983), *The Command and Control of Nuclear Forces* (New Haven, Connecticut and London: Yale University Press).

Braudel, F. (1979), *The Perspective of the World* (London: Fontana).

Brecher, M., J. Wilkenfeld and S. Moser (1988), *Crises in the Twentieth Century* (2 vols) (Oxford and New York: Pergamon).

Brogan, P. (1989), *World Conflicts: Why and Where They Are Happening* (London: Bloomsbury).

Brownlie, I. (1979), *African Boundaries, A Legal and Diplomatic Encyclopaedia*. (London and Los Angeles).

Brundtland, G. (1987), *Our Common Future*, World Commission on Environment and Development (Oxford: Oxford University Press).

Burton, J. (1969), *Conflict and Communication* (London: Macmillan).

Burton, J. (1982), *Dear Survivors* (London: Frances Pinter).

Burton, J. (1984), *Global Conflict: The Domestic Sources of International Crises* (Brighton: Wheatsheaf).

Burton, J. (1987), *Resolving Deep-rooted Conflict: A Handbook*, (Lanham, Maryland: University Press of America).

Butterworth, R. L. (1976), *Managing Interstate Conflict, 1945–74. Data with Synopses* (Pittsburgh, Pennsylvania: University of Pittsburgh).

Butterworth, R. L. (1978), 'Do conflict managers matter?', *International Studies Quarterly*, XXII, June, pp. 195–214.

Calvocoressi, P. (1987), *World Politics since 1945* (London: Longman).

Caportiti, F. (1979), *Study on the Rights of Persons Belonging to Ethnic, Religious and Linguistic Minorities* (New York: UN).

Carr, E. H. (1939), *The Twenty Years' Crisis 1919-1939* (London: Macmillan).

Commonwealth Group of Eminent Persons (1986), *Mission to South Africa* (Harmondsworth: Penguin).

Crocker, C. (1990), 'Conflict resolution in the Third World: the role of the superpowers'. Paper given at a conference on 'Conflict Resolution in the Post-Cold War Third World', US Institute of Peace, 1550 M Street NW, Suite 700, Washington DC.

Curle, A. (1971), *Making Peace* (London: Tavistock).

Curle, A. (1986), *In the Middle: Non-Official Mediation in Violent Situations* (New York: Berg).

Curle, A. (1989), Personal interview.

Darwish, A. and G. Alexander (1991), *Unholy Babylon: The Secret History of Saddam's War* (London: Gollancz).

David Davies Memorial Institute of International Studies (1966), *Report of Study Group on the Peaceful Settlement of International Disputes* (London: Europa).

David Davies Memorial Institute of International Studies (1972), *International Disputes: The Legal Aspects* (London: Europa).

Day, A.J. (ed.) (1987), *Border and Territorial Disputes* (London: Longman).

De Reuck, A. (1984), 'The logic of conflict: its origin, development and resolution' in M. Banks (ed.) (1984), *Conflict in World Society* (Brighton: Harvester).

De Reuck, A. (1989a), Talk on Conflict Resolution to the Conflict Research Society (London: Institute of Education).

De Reuck, A. (1989b), Interview.

Deutsch, M. (1973), *The Resolution of Conflict: Constructive and Destructive Processes* (New Haven, Connecticut and London: Yale University Press).

Deutsch, M. (1987), 'A theoretical perspective on conflict and conflict resolution', in Sandole and Sandole-Staroste (1987).

Doob, L.W. (ed.) (1970) *Resolving conflict in Africa: The Fermeda Workshop* (New Haven, Connecticut and London: Yale University Press).

Donelan, M.D. and M.J. Grieve (1973), *International Disputes, Case Studies* (London: Europa).

Downing, D. (1980), *An Atlas of Territorial and Border Disputes* (London: New English Library).

Falkenmark, M. (1986), 'Fresh Waters as a Factor in Strategic Policy and Action', in A. Westing, (ed.), *Global Resources and International Conflict* (Oxford: Oxford University Press).

Falkenmark, M. (1990), 'Global water issues confronting humanity', *Journal of Peace Research*, 27, 2, pp. 177–90.

Fisher, R. and W. Ury (1983), *Getting to Yes* (Harmondsworth: Penguin).

Freymond, J. (1960), *The Saar Conflict* (London: Stevens).

Furley, O. (1990), 'Uganda: A Second-phase Bid for Legitimacy under International Scrutiny', Paper to the 25th International Peace Research Association Conference, Groningen, Holland.

Galtung, J. (1965), 'Institutionalised conflict resolution: a theoretical paradigm', *Journal of Peace Research*, 4, pp. 348–97. Reprinted in J. Galtung, *Essays in Peace Research*, 3.

Galtung, J. (1984), *There Are Alternatives! Four Roads to Peace and Security* (Nottingham: Spokesman).

Galtung, J. (1989), *Solving Conflicts: A Peace Research Perspective* (Honolulu: University of Hawaii Press).

Gardner, K. (1989), Personal interview.

Gilmour, D. (1980), *Dispossessed: The Ordeal of the Palestinians* (London: Sphere).

Gochman, C. S. and Z. Maoz (1984), 'Militarised interstate disputes 1916–1975', *Journal of Conflict Resolution*, 10, 3, pp.585–615.

Gorbachev, M. (1986), *Speech to Indian Parliamentarians*, 27 November 1986.

Goose, S.D. (1987), 'Armed conflicts in 1986 and the Iran–Iraq war', in *Yearbook of World Armaments and Disarmament* (Stockholm: SIPRI).

Greenhouse, C. (1987), 'Cultural perspectives on war', in R. Vayrynen (ed.), *The Quest for Peace* (London: Sage).

Gulliver, P.A. (1987), *Disputes and Negotiations* (New York: Academic Press).

Haas, E. B., R. L. Butterworth and J. S. Nye (1972), *Conflict Management by International Organizations* (Morristown, New Jersey: General Learning Press).

Haas, E. B. (1983), 'Regime decay, conflict management and international organizations, 1945–81', *International Organization*, 37, 2, pp. 189–256.

Haas, M. (unknown), 'Dimensions of international conflict resolution', *World Peace through the United Nations*, (Seoul: Kyung Hee University Press), pp. 65–111.

Hamwee, J. (1989), Personal interview.

Hardin, G. (1968), 'The tragedy of the commons', *Science*, No. 162, pp. 1243–8.

Heraclides, A. (1989), 'Conflict resolution, ethnonationalism and the Middle East impasse', *Journal of Peace Research*, 26, 2, pp. 197–212.

Holsti, K. J. (1966), 'Resolving international conflict: a taxonomy of behaviour and some figures on procedure', *Journal of Conflict Resolution*, 10, 3.

Horowitz, D. L. (1985), *Ethnic Groups in Conflict* (Berkeley and London: University of California Press).

Howard, M. (1976), *War in European History* (Oxford: Oxford University Press).

Howard, M. (1981), *War and the Liberal Conscience* (Oxford: Oxford University Press).

Howard, M. (1983), *The Causes of Wars* (London: Unwin).

Hughes, R. (1962), *Films of Peace and War* (New York: Grove Press).

Hveem, H. (1986), 'Minerals as a factor in strategic policy and action', in A. Westing, (ed.), *Global Resources and International Conflict* (Oxford: Oxford University Press).

International Alert (1987), *Uganda: Seminar on Internal Conflict*, (London: International Alert).

International Institute for Strategic Studies (1990), *Strategic Survey 1989–90* (London: Brassey's).

Isaakson, M. (1985), 'The demilitarisation of the Åland Islands', in Peace Society of Åland, *The Åland Islands: Autonomous Demilitarised Region* (Mariehamn, Åland: Ålands Fredsförening).

Jackson, E. (1983), *Middle East Mission* (New York and London: W. W. Norton).

James, A. (1990), *Peacekeeping in International Politics* (London: Macmillan).

Kanninen, T. (1989), 'Frameworks for monitoring of emergent or ongoing conflicts'. Paper given at the International Studies Association Conference, London.

Kende, I. (1986), 'Local wars since 1945' in E. Laszlo and J. Y. Yoo (eds), *World Encyclopaedia of Peace* (New York: Pergamon), pp. 545–9.

King, R. (1987), 'The Iran-Iraq war: the political implications', *Adelphi Papers*, 219 (London: International Institute of Strategic Studies).

Low, S. (1985), 'The Zimbabwe settlement, 1976–79' in Touval and Zartman (1985).

Luard, E. (1986), *War in International Society* (London: I.B. Tauris).

Luard, E. (1988), *Conflict and Peace in the Modern International System*, 2nd edn. (London: Macmillan).

Matsunaga, S. (Chairman) (1981), *To Establish the United States Institute of Peace*, Report of the Commission on Proposals for the National Academy of Peace and Conflict Resolution to the President and Congress (Washington, DC: US Government Printing Office).

Maull, H. W. (1984), *Raw Materials, Energy and Western Security*, International Institute for Strategic Studies, 22 (London: Macmillan).

Miall, H. (1975) 'Social differentiation and conflict' (University of Lancaster: PhD thesis).

Miall, H. (1988), *Non-Governmental Third Party Intervention in Conflicts: A Review of Four Approaches* (Oxford Research Group).

Mitchell, C. R. (1981), *The Structure of International Conflict* (London: Macmillan).

Mitchell, C. R. and K. Webb (1988), *New Approaches to International Mediation* (New York and London: Greenwood).

Mitchell, C. R. (1989), Personal interview.

Murray, J. (ed.) (1988), *Cultural Atlas of Africa* (Oxford: Phaidon).

Naess, A. (1958), 'A systematisation of Gandhian ethics of conflict resolution', *Journal of Conflict Resolution*, 11, 2, pp. 140–55.

Nhat Hanh, T. (1976), *The Miracle of Mindfulness* (Boston, Massachusetts: Beacon).

Nicholson, M. (1971), *Conflict Analysis* (London: English Universities Press).

Northedge, F. S. and M. D. Donelan (1971), *International Disputes: The Political Aspects* (London: Europa).

Osgood, C. E. (1962), *An Alternative to War or Surrender* (Urbana: University of Illinois Press).

Palme, O. (Chairman) (1982), *Common Security* (London: Pan).

Patchen, M. (1988), *Resolving Disputes Between Nations: Coercion or Conciliation?* (Durham and London: Duke University Press).

Pecota, V. (1972), *The Quiet Approach. A Study of the Good Offices of the UN Secretary General in the Cause of Peace*, UNITAR PS No. 6 (New York: UNITAR).

Peterson, S. B. and J. M. Teal (1986), 'Ocean fisheries as a factor in strategic policy and action', in H. Westing, (ed.), *Global Resources and International Conflict* (Oxford: Oxford University Press).

Pickvance, T. J. (1988), 'Third-party mediation in national minority disputes: some lessons from the South Tyrol problem', in Mitchell C.R. and Webb, K. (eds.), *New Approaches to International Mediation* (New York and London: Greenwood).

Pruitt, D. G. and J. Z. Rubin (1986), *Social Conflict: Escalation, Stalemate and Settlement* (New York: Random House).

Rapoport, A. (1971), 'Various conceptions of peace research', Presidential Address at the Ann Arbor Conference of the Peace Research Society, *Peace Research Society (International) Papers*, XIX, pp. 91–106.

Rapoport, A. (1974), *Conflict in Man-Made Environment* (Harmondsworth: Penguin).

Rapoport, A. (1989), *The Origins of Violence: Approaches to the Study of Conflict* (New York: Paragon House).

Rapoport, A. and A. Chammah (1965), *Prisoner's Dilemma* (Ann Arbor: University of Michigan Press).

Richardson, L. F. (1952), 'Is it possible to prove any general statements about historical fact?', *British Journal of Sociology*, 3, pp. 77–84.

Richardson, L. F. (1960), *Statistics of Deadly Quarrels* (Pittsburgh, Pennsylvania: Boxwood Press).

Roberts, A. (1969), *Czechoslovakia 1968* (London: Chatto & Windus).

Rodinson, M. (1982), *Israel and the Arabs* (London: Pelican).

Rogers, C. (1984), 'The alternative to nuclear planetary suicide', *The Counselling Psychologist*, 12, 2.

Rupesinghe, K. (1989), 'Early warnings: some conceptual problems', *Bulletin of Peace Proposals*, 20, 2, pp. 183–191.

Salinger, P. and E. Laurent (1991), *Secret Dossier: The Hidden Agenda Behind the Gulf War* (London: Penguin).

Sandole, D. and I. Sandole-Staroste (eds) (1987), *Conflict Management and Problem Solving: Interpersonal to International Applications* (London: Frances Pinter).

Segal, J. M. (1989), *Creating the Palestinian State: A Strategy for Peace* (Chicago, Illinois: Lawrence Hill).

Sharp, G. (1973), *The Politics of Nonviolent Action* (Boston, Massachusetts: Porter Sargent).

Sherman, F. L. (1987), 'The United Nations and the road to nowhere' (Dept of Political Science, University of Pennsylvania: PhD dissertation).

Singer, J. D. (1988), 'The Behavioral Correlates of War Data Set', described in Russel J. Leng and J. David Singer (1988) 'Militarized Interstate Crises: The BCOW Typology and its Applications', *International Studies Quarterly*, 32, pp. 155–73.

Singer, J. D. and M. Small (1972), *The Wages of War, 1816–1965: A Statistical Handbook* (New York: John Wiley and Sons).

Singer, J. D. and M. Small (1984), *The Wages of War, 1816–1980*, (Ann Arbor, Michigan: Inter-University Consortium for Political and Social Research).

SIPRI (1969), *World Armaments and Disarmament: SIPRI Yearbook 1969* (Stockholm: Stockholm International Peace Research Institute).

Sivard, R. L. (1987), *World Military and Social Expenditures* (Washington, DC: World Priorities).

Skjelsbaek, K. (1991), 'The UN Secretary-General and the mediation of international disputes', *Journal of Peace Research*, 28, 1, pp. 99–115.

Small, M. and J. D. Singer (1982), *Resort to Arms: International and Civil Wars 1816–1980*, (Beverly Hills, California: Sage).

Smoker, P. (1969), 'A time series analysis of Sino–Indian relations', *Journal of Conflict Resolution*, XIII, 2, pp. 172–91.

Spiegel, M. A. (1985), 'The Namibia negotiations and the problem of neutrality', in Touval and Zartman (1985).

Taylor, A. J. P. (1985), *How Wars End* (London: Hamish Hamilton).

Third World Guide (1990), (Montivideo: Third World Editors).

Thorsson, I. *et al.* (1982), *Relationship Between Disarmament and Development*, Disarmament Study Review no. 5 (New York: UN Department of Political and Security Council Affairs), quoted in Brundtland (1987), *Our Common Future.*

Tjonneland, E. J. (1990), 'Negotiating apartheid away? Race, ethnicity and class in the politics of transition and constitution making in South Africa.' Paper presented at 25th International Peace Research Association conference, Groningen, 3–7 July.

Touval, S. and I. W. Zartman (eds) (1985), *International Mediation in Theory and Practice* (Boulder, Colorado: Westview).

Townsend, J. (1988), Interview.

UN (1990), *Report of the Secretary General on the Work of the Organization* (New York: UN).

UN Association, (1989), *Working with Africa Appeal* (London: UN Association).

UN General Assembly (1991), *Draft handbook on peaceful settlement of disputes between states.* Special Committee on the Charter of the UN and strengthening the role of the organization (New York: UN).

Urquhart, B. (1989), 'The United Nations system and the future', *International Affairs*, 65, 2, pp. 226–31.

Ury, W., J. Brett and S. Goldberg (1988), *Getting Disputes Resolved* (San Francisco and London: Jossey-Bass).

Valenta, J. (1989), *Gorbachev's New Thinking and Third World Conflicts* (New York: Transaction).

Van der Merwe, H. W. (1989), *Pursuing Justice and Peace in South Africa* (London and New York: Routledge & Kegan Paul).

Van der Merwe, H. W. (1990), 'Mediating for a post-apartheid South Africa'. Paper presented at the 25th International Peace Research Association conference, Groningen.

Venn, F. (1986), *Oil Diplomacy in the Twentieth Century* (London: Macmillan).

Walesa, L. (1987), *A Path of Hope* (London: Pan).

Wehr, P. (1979), *Conflict Regulation* (Boulder, Colorado: Westview).

Wright, Q. (1942), *A Study of War* (University of Chicago Press).

Yarrow, C. H. M. (1978), *Quaker Experiences in International Conciliation* (New Haven, Connecticut, and London: Yale University Press).

Young, O. R. (1967), *The Intermediaries: Third Parties in International Crises* (Princeton University Press).

Young, O. R. (1989), *International Co-Operation: Building Regimes for Natural Resources and the Environment* (Ithaca, New York: Cornell University Press).

Zacher, M. W. (1979), *International Conflict and Collective Security 1946–77* (New York: Praeger).

Index

Northern Epirus, *see* Albania–Greece conflict
Northern Ireland, 8, 91, 99, 101, 113, 148–9, 151–2, 153–4, 260–1
Norway–UK fishing conflict, 112, 262
Nye, J., 109

OPEC, 162, 174
Ogaden, *see* Ethiopia–Somalia conflict
Oil conflicts 155–8, 160, 162–3
Ojukwu, Colonel Odumegwu, 78
Oman, 70
Oman–Dhofar rebels, 113, 262–3
Oman–Imam's rebels, 263–4
Organization of African Unity (OAU), 6,7, 23
Organization of American States (OAS), 7, 23
Organizational conflicts, 69, 84–6

'Package deals', 71–2
Pakistan, 76, 131
Palme Commission, 13, 104
Paris Peace Conference, 98
Partition, 135–6
Peace of Moscow, 93
Peaceful settlements, 46–7, 110–11
    declarations for, 6
    factors conducive to, 61–2, 110–11, 188–9
    and international norms, 25
    and UN Charter, 5
Peacekeeping, 8, 42, 96
Peacemaking, 42, 68–9, 86–7
Peloponnesian war, 51
Penn, William, 76
PLO, 177–8
Poland, 3–4, 105
Poland (1956), 112, 264–5
Polarization, 42, 59, 62, 141, 188
    helpful to settlement, 59
Prisoner's dilemma, 60
Problem-solving workshops, 68, 74–6
Procedures, 110, 136–7, 139, 186, 188–9

Prunskiene, Kazimiera, 168

Quakers, 29, 66
    and mediation, 76–8

Rapoport, Anatol, 39
Rationality, 65
Reagan, Ronald, 12, 103
Realism, 34–5
Reciprocation 21, 60, 62, 106, 176, 188
Reconciliation, 42
Regimes, 161–3, 189–90
Regional conflicts, 12–13
Relaxation of tensions, 59
Resource conflicts, 58, 118, 123, 138, 155–63, 185
Rhodesia, 9, 28
Richardson, Lewis F., 38, 119
Rodman, Peter, 176
Rogers, Carl, 66
Romania–Soviet Union conflict, 112, 133, 139, 149–50, 265–6
Rwanda, 143
Ryzhkov, Nikolai, 168

Saar, 8, 112, 133, 139, 140, 142, 266–8
Sadat, Anwar, 59
Sajudis, 19–20, 165–8
Saudi Arabia, 70
Saudi Arabia–Oman, Abu Dhabi conflict, 112, 133, 139, 140, 160, 268–9
Saunders, Hal, 21, 176
Secession, 118, 123
'Second-track' diplomacy, 68
Settlements, costs and benefits, 63–5
Sherman, F., 110, 127–30
Shevardnadze, Eduard, 166–7
Singer, David, 38
Single-text procedure, 73, 79
Sino–Indian conflict, 12, 131
Sino–Soviet conflict, 12, 131
Sivard, R., 119
Slabbert, Fredrik van Zyl, 29
Small, Melvin, 38
Smith, Ian, 71
Solidarity, 3–4, 14, 61